Rules, Politics, and the International Criminal Court

In this new work, Dutton examines the International Criminal Court (ICC) and whether and how its enforcement mechanism influences state membership and the court's ability to realize treaty goals, examining questions such as:

- Why did states decide to create the ICC and design the institution with this uniquely strong enforcement mechanism?
- Will the ICC's enforcement mechanism be sufficient to hold states accountable to their commitment so that the ICC can realize its goal of ending impunity for genocide, crimes against humanity, and war crimes?
- Will states view the ICC's enforcement mechanism as a credible threat and refuse to join unless they already have good domestic human rights practices and institutions that are independent and capable of prosecuting human rights abuses?
- If states that most need to improve their domestic legal practices as relates to protecting against human rights abuses do not join the court, is there any hope that the threat of punishment by the ICC can play a role in bettering states' human rights practices and deterring individuals from committing mass atrocities?

This work provides a significant contribution to the field, and will be of great interest to students and scholars of international law, international relations, international organizations and human rights.

Yvonne Dutton is currently an Associate Professor at Indiana University Robert H. McKinney School of Law where she teaches International Criminal Law, Criminal Law, Federal Criminal Law, and Evidence.

Routledge Global Institutions Series

Edited by Thomas G. Weiss
The CUNY Graduate Center, New York, USA
and Rorden Wilkinson
University of Manchester, UK

About the series

The Global Institutions Series has two "streams." Those with blue covers offer comprehensive, accessible, and informative guides to the history, structure, and activities of key international organizations, and introductions to topics of key importance in contemporary global governance. Recognized experts use a similar structure to address the general purpose and rationale for specific organizations along with historical developments, membership, structure, decision-making procedures, key functions, and an annotated bibliography and guide to electronic sources. Those with red covers consist of research monographs and edited collections that advance knowledge about one aspect of global governance; they reflect a wide variety of intellectual orientations, theoretical persuasions, and methodological approaches. Together the two streams provide a coherent and complementary portrait of the problems, prospects, and possibilities confronting global institutions today.
Related titles in the series include:

International Law, International Relations, and Global Governance (2012)
by Charlotte Ku

The UN Human Rights Council (2011)
by Bertrand G. Ramcharan

International Judicial Institutions (2009)
by Richard J. Goldstone and Adam M. Smith

The United Nations and Human Rights (2nd edition, 2009)
by Julie A. Mertus

The UN General Assembly (2005)
by M.J. Peterson

Rules, Politics, and the International Criminal Court

Committing to the Court

Yvonne Dutton

LONDON AND NEW YORK

First published 2013
by Routledge
2 Park Square, Milton Park, Abingdon, Oxfordshire OX14 4RN

Simultaneously published in the USA and Canada
by Routledge
711 Third Avenue, New York, NY 10017

First issued in paperback 2016

Routledge is an imprint of the Taylor & Francis Group, an informa business

British Library Cataloguing in Publication Data
A catalogue record for this book is available from the British Library

Library of Congress Cataloging in Publication Data
Dutton, Yvonne.
Rules, politics, and the international criminal court : committing to the court / Yvonne Dutton.
pages cm. – (Global institutions)
Summary: "In this new work, Dutton examines the ICC and whether and how its enforcement mechanism influences state membership and the court's ability to realize treaty goals"– Provided by publisher.
Includes bibliographical references and index.
1. International Criminal Court. 2. International criminal courts. I. Title.
KZ7312.D88 2013
345'.01–dc23
2012044269

ISBN 13: 978-1-138-28956-7 (pbk)
ISBN 13: 978-0-415-65810-2 (hbk)

Typeset in Times New Roman
by Taylor & Francis Books

Contents

Illustrations

Figure

Tables

Foreword

Yvonne Dutton's book *Rules, Politics, and the International Criminal Court: Committing to the court* is the eleventh in a growing number of research volumes in our "global institutions" series examining crucial global problems as well as policies and solutions for them. These volumes serve as lengthier and more specialized treatments of given topics than is possible in the general series. As such, they are essential components in advancing the overarching aim of the series to render more visible the often complex and poorly understood world of "global governance."

In addition to these longer research volumes, the series strives to provide readers with user-friendly and short (usually 50,000 words) but definitive guides to the most visible aspects and institutions of what we know as "global governance" as well as authoritative accounts of the issues and debates in which they are embroiled. We now have over 75 books that act as key reference points to the most significant global organizations and the evolution of the issues that they confront. Our intention has always been to provide one-stop guides for all readers—students (both undergraduate and postgraduate), interested negotiators, diplomats, practitioners from nongovernmental and intergovernmental organizations, and interested parties alike—seeking information about most prominent institutional aspects of global governance.

The International Criminal Court (ICC), the world's first permanent tribunal to prosecute individuals for mass atrocity crimes, has been in operation for over a decade. In fact, the expansion of international judicial pursuit has been a key development of the post-Cold War era. While much research in that time has focused on the impact of the ICC on international criminal law and how it has influenced state decision making, little has been written on the reasons that states decide to join or sit on the sidelines. Dutton explores this issue in the light of the perceived weakness of international tribunals—they have no state power to enforce their decisions and so are commonly thought of as being paper tigers. Dutton instead asks: What makes the ICC more powerful than previous international criminal tribunals? Why have some states with poor human rights records nevertheless agreed to join? Why did the United States decide not to join if the ICC is as weak as many commentators believe?

This insightful book is written by a scholar with both a legal and political science background—a combination too infrequently found in international legal research. Ideally, this and other volumes in the research stream will be used as complementary readings in courses in which other specific titles in this series are pertinent—a selection of which can be found in the "About the Series" section at the front of this book. Our aim is to provide enough room for specialized topics of importance to be dealt with exhaustively but also to complement them with shorter, authoritative treatments. At the same time, maintaining the quality of the series is foremost in our minds.

As always, we look forward to comments from our readers.

Thomas G. Weiss
The CUNY Graduate Center, New York, USA
Rorden Wilkinson
University of Manchester, UK
November 2012

Acknowledgments

This project has benefited immensely from the advice, guidance, and support of others. Moonhawk Kim deserves special recognition for being a devoted mentor: he has read countless drafts and always provides patient and constructive feedback. I am also especially grateful to Vanessa Baird, Steve Chan, and Joe Jupille for providing guidance and helpful comments from the very inception of this project. I thank Michael Struett, who I met early in my graduate school career, for so willingly sharing with me his expertise on the International Criminal Court. I have also received helpful suggestions and advice from many other scholars during the course of this project. Of those many people, I must extend particular thanks to Eamon Aloyo and Nicholas Georgakopoulos.

Several institutions have also generously supported the research for this project at various stages of its development.I thank One Earth Future Foundation, The University of San Diego School of Law, and Indiana University Robert H. McKinney School of Law for the assistance they have provided me.

Finally, I am grateful to Thomas G. Weiss and Rorden Wilkinson for their extremely useful and constructive comments on earlier drafts of the book and for their interest in including this work in Routledge's Global Institutions Series. At Routledge, for making this process seem effortless, I thank Martin Burke, Nicola Parkin, and Megan Graieg. Alison Neale deserves kudos for her careful editing.

Abbreviations

ASPA	American Service-Members' Protection Act of 2002
CAT	Convention Against Torture and Other Cruel, Inhuman or Degrading Treatment or Punishment
CCAIL	Code of Crimes Against International Law (Germany)
CEDAW	Convention on the Elimination of All Forms of Discrimination Against Women
CERD	International Convention on the Elimination of All Forms of Racial Discrimination
CICC	Coalition for the International Criminal Court
CRC	Convention on the Rights of the Child
EU	European Union
GDP	gross domestic product
IACtHR	Inter-American Court of Human Rights
IAHRC	Inter-American Human Rights Commission
ICC	International Criminal Court
ICCPR	International Covenant on Civil and Political Rights
ICESCR	International Covenant on Economic, Social and Cultural Rights
ICTR	International Criminal Tribunal for Rwanda
ICTY	International Criminal Tribunal for the former Yugoslavia
ILC	International Law Commission
INCSR	International Narcotics Control Strategy Reports
KANU	Kenyan African National Union
NARC	National Rainbow Coalition of Kenya
NGO	Nongovernmental organization
ODA	official development assistance and aid
OECD	Organisation for Economic Co-operation and Development

P-5	the five permanent members of the United Nations Security Council
RPF	Rwandese Patriotic Front
UDHR	Universal Declaration of Human Rights
UN	United Nations

Introduction

Since World War II, the world community has increasingly turned to international institutions as a way to monitor and improve states' human rights practices.[1] The international human rights regime now boasts six primary treaties to which the great majority of states belong. Indeed, the number of states ratifying these treaties ranges between 147 and 193.[2] Does the fact of near universal commitment mean that states embrace treaty norms and want to improve their domestic practices, or are states committing for other reasons entirely and with no intention of adhering to treaty terms? After all, these treaties are typically designed with weak enforcement mechanisms: they often only require the state to self-report its behavior to a committee that is authorized only to comment on, not to punish or impose sanctions for, bad and noncompliant behavior. Therefore, states can make their ratification decisions without fearing they will suffer significant sovereignty losses should they fail to comply with treaty terms.

The treaty creating the International Criminal Court (ICC) in 2002, however, has a much stronger enforcement mechanism than is usually associated with international human rights treaties. States have delegated to the court and its independent prosecutor the authority and resources to investigate, arrest, prosecute, and punish a state's nationals for mass atrocities should the state be unwilling or unable to do so. States that ratify the ICC treaty, therefore, agree that they will prosecute any of their citizens who commit mass atrocities, or otherwise surrender their citizens to the ICC for prosecution.

The powers of the ICC are not only unusually strong as compared to other international human rights treaties. The ICC also has powers that set it apart from various other international ad hoc criminal tribunals. Those ad hoc courts likewise can prosecute individuals who commit crimes of international concern. However, the ICC is a permanent court and states agree in advance to surrender to it some of their rights to manage their domestic affairs as relates to punishing human rights abuses. Ad hoc tribunals, by contrast, are only created to address certain atrocities after they occur and are most often imposed on weak states by strong and powerful states. By the terms of the ICC treaty, strong states that ratify also agree that the court and its independent prosecutor can try the state's citizens should they commit mass atrocities if the state fails to prosecute them domestically. The United States, for example, has refused to join the ICC precisely because the ICC has an independent court and prosecutor that could seek to prosecute Americans—especially American military personnel—who may commit crimes that are seemingly within the court's jurisdiction.

Of course, the very fact that the ICC is an international institution seeking to bind sovereign and independent states to comply with international law means that even with an unusually strong enforcement mechanism, the ICC may not always be able to enforce compliance. The ICC is not a domestic court operating within a single state with state resources, such as a domestic police force, to back and implement its decisions. The ICC must rely on states to make arrests. This means that some suspects may escape arrest by visiting only "friendly" states or by remaining in their home state where the international community cannot reach them.

When considered in the international context, though, the ICC's powers to enforce treaty terms are great. An ICC arrest warrant limits a suspect's ability to act and travel since it can be acted upon by any state. In addition, states risk repercussions from the international community should they willingly and obviously fail to act on the warrant. Furthermore, although the fact of the arrest warrant may actually provoke some suspects to engage in additional abuses or repressive behavior in order to fight against the ICC's authority, in many ways this only demonstrates the strength of the ICC's enforcement mechanism. Indeed, states have arrested suspects wanted by the ICC,[3] and some other suspects have surrendered themselves to face charges.[4] That the ICC has not been able to execute on every arrest warrant does not mean that its enforcement mechanism is weak or that the court is powerless to compel compliance. Even in the domestic context, some suspects escape arrest because they move locations, change names, or go into hiding.

When suspects are arrested, the ICC also has the ability to try them and punish them if they are found guilty. This is a power well beyond that possessed by any of the committees overseeing compliance of the international human rights treaties. It is a power possessed by the ad hoc criminal tribunals. However, arguably, states should view the ICC's powers as stronger than those possessed by the ad hoc tribunals since only the ICC is permanent. That permanence alone is a threat since states could rationally believe that if a new mass atrocity occurred, states would not necessarily spend the time, effort, or money to create a new tribunal. The ICC's permanence is also a threat since it means that even the citizens of rich and powerful states may potentially be prosecuted. To date, the ad hoc tribunals have only been created by the United Nations (UN) Security Council to prosecute the citizens of weaker states.

Why did states decide to create the ICC and design this new and permanent institution with an enforcement mechanism that is so uniquely strong in the context of the international human rights regime? Will the ICC's enforcement mechanism be sufficient to hold states accountable to their commitment so that the ICC can realize its goal of ending impunity for genocide, crimes against humanity, and war crimes? What states comprise the court's membership? Are states with bad domestic human rights practices joining the court or do they view the ICC's enforcement mechanism as a credible threat and refuse to join to avoid being punished for bad and noncompliant behavior? If many states that most need to improve their domestic legal practices as relates to protecting against human rights abuses do not join the court, can the ICC's punishment mechanism actually play a role in bettering states' human rights practices? These are some of the questions this book explores by examining the ICC and whether and how its enforcement mechanism influences state membership and the court's ability to realize treaty goals.

The credible threat argument and its implications

The literature is replete with reasons why states may be motivated to join international human rights treaties. States with good human rights practices may join to bind themselves or others to treaty norms—because they believe in those norms, and also because the ultimate outcome may be a more peaceful world where states do not have to engage in costly interventions to help "solve" other states' mass atrocities. States with bad human rights practices may sincerely join to "tie their hands" and credibly commit to being "better" in the future.[5] On the other hand, those "bad" states may ratify for reasons unrelated to the treaty's goals, for example, because they are pressured to do so by more powerful states or nongovernmental organizations (NGOs),[6] or because they wish to obtain extra-treaty benefits such as aid or trade which might be tied to how legitimate the state appears to be.[7] This book, however, proceeds from the premise that although all states may have many reasons to want to join the ICC treaty, states should view the ICC's ability to investigate, arrest, and prosecute a state's leaders or citizens as a credible threat and be wary of committing unless their domestic human rights practices are already relatively good so that commitment will not lead to a significant sovereignty loss—in particular, a trial of the state's citizens in The Hague.

The prior literature has not explored or empirically tested a commitment theory that focuses on the role treaty enforcement mechanisms might play in discouraging states to ratify. This book shows why the other theories that predict states with bad domestic human rights practices will nevertheless join international human rights treaties are problematic. Theories about credible commitment are problematic precisely because the ICC treaty has means to punish bad and noncompliant behavior. Domestic laws and behavior do not generally change overnight, and even if some leaders want themselves and their citizenry to be "better" in the future, those same leaders may not want to risk an ICC prosecution should the status quo continue. Theories about the influence of external pressures are problematic for the same reason: even if "bad" states can obtain some extra-treaty benefits from ratifying, those benefits are likely outweighed by the risk of prosecution. In short, the ICC's enforcement mechanism is stronger than the mechanisms states usually include in international human rights treaties to hold states accountable to their commitment. That stronger enforcement mechanism should not generally discourage states with good human rights practices from joining the court, but it should discourage states with bad human rights practices from joining.

If the credible threat theory is correct, the necessary outcome is that the ICC treaty's institutional design may have the negative effect of discouraging "bad" states from joining. This does not necessarily mean, though, that the court's membership will include no states with bad human rights practices (in fact, some such states have joined the court). Nor does it mean that the ICC has no hope of actually positively influencing state behavior and realizing treaty goals. First, a "bad" state is not permanently constrained to be bad, and states can sometimes fluctuate in whether and how strongly they protect against human rights abuses. Those states may experience certain "windows of opportunity"—such as a change in leadership or a point where external or internal calls for commitment can no longer be ignored—where the benefits of joining may seem to outweigh the risks associated with noncompliance. These transient windows of opportunity can cause some states with poor practices to join the ICC. Should these states commit, the ICC can then exert some positive effect because it has authority and resources to punish bad and noncompliant behavior should the state not improve its practices.

Layout of the book

Quantitative data and case study empirical evidence support the book's thesis. It explores how the ICC's institutional design influences membership and, accordingly, the likelihood that the ICC can ultimately play a role in improving human rights practices and ensuring that those who commit serious crimes of international concern are prosecuted. One particular focus of the analyses is whether states—especially states with poor human rights practices—view the court's enforcement mechanism as a credible threat and refuse to commit as a result. The quantitative tests of ICC ratification help to explain the broad trends of state behavior. To identify and isolate the precise reasons why certain types of states join or refuse to join the ICC, the book includes case studies of eight different states that vary in their level of human rights practices and also how powerful they are in the world community.

Chapter 1 discusses the creation of the ICC and traces the evolution of the ICC treaty's institutional design as relates to the ability of the institution to enforce treaty terms. To provide context for understanding the ICC and its enforcement mechanism, the chapter surveys other enforcement mechanisms used in international human rights treaties to monitor states' domestic human rights practices. It also looks at the role played by international ad hoc criminal tribunals in holding individuals accountable for human rights abuses.

To set up the quantitative analysis of state commitment to the ICC, Chapter 2 briefly explores various theories about why states join international human rights treaties and explains the credible threat theory in that context. The chapter then statistically examines state decisions to ratify the ICC and what factors influence state behavior. It also puts those results in context by statistically examining state commitment to 13 other international human rights treaties, articles, and protocols, which are categorized according to five different levels of enforcement mechanism from the weakest (self-reporting) to the strongest (an independent ICC and prosecutor). The chapter concludes with a discussion of some implications of the findings.

The book then turns to the case studies. Chapters 3, 4, and 5 explore the commitment decisions of powerful states with good human rights practices and how the ICC's enforcement mechanism influenced those decisions. Chapter 3 examines the United States' decision to refuse to join the court. The evidence shows that while the United States was behind the idea of an international criminal court, it wanted a court that was essentially under the control of the UN Security Council. When the remaining states instead decided to create a strong and independent court, the United States refused to vote to adopt the ICC treaty. The evidence suggests that cost of compliance concerns and the credible threat of the ICC's relatively strong enforcement mechanism influenced the United States to err on the side of guarding its sovereignty. Even though it generally has good human rights practices, it expressed concerns that the ICC may try to prosecute its citizens, particularly since it has a large military presence abroad and the court has jurisdiction over war crimes.

Chapters 4 and 5 provide a contrast to the case study of the United States and examine the decisions to join the court by four powerful states with good human rights practices. Chapter 4 looks at Germany's decision to ratify the ICC treaty and its leadership role in pushing for the ICC's strong enforcement mechanism. The evidence suggests that Germany was motivated to adopt this leadership role because of some strong individuals who took the opportunity to distance the country from its genocidal past. However, the evidence also shows that Germany was aware of the strength of the ICC's enforcement mechanism and only joined the court after determining that Germany could comply with treaty terms and not risk having its citizens prosecuted by the ICC. Chapter 5 puts the ratification behavior of the other two powerful states in context by examining the commitment decisions of Canada, France, and the United Kingdom and their reactions to the ICC's enforcement mechanism. Unlike the United States, all three of these states joined. Canada was more like Germany in that it was an early supporter of a strong and independent court and prosecutor. France and the United Kingdom were eventually persuaded to support a strong court, but both initially took positions similar to that of the United States in favoring a much weaker court and prosecutor.

To explore the ratification behavior of weaker states and those with weak domestic law-enforcement institutions that may be incapable of prosecuting potential mass atrocities in the future, Chapter 6 examines Trinidad and Tobago's decision to ratify the ICC treaty promptly. Trinidad and Tobago is credited with reinvigorating the idea of an international criminal court. Many of the country's statements suggest it committed because it felt pride in being part of the court's creation and because it believed in the norms advanced by the ICC treaty. However, the record also shows that Trinidad and Tobago did not commit for normative reasons only and without concern for compliance costs: the country carefully guards its sovereignty and does not commit to treaties that run counter to its domestic interests or with which it has no intention of complying. It understood the ICC treaty's enforcement mechanism and ratified the treaty only after concluding it could comply so that the country would not have to surrender its citizens to the ICC for prosecution.

Chapters 7 and 8 study the ICC commitment decisions of two states with poor human rights practices and weak domestic legal institutions, with a particular focus on whether and how these types of states view and respond to the ICC's enforcement mechanism. Chapter 7 examines Rwanda's decision to refuse to commit to the court and concludes that the credible threat theory—not credible commitment—best explains Rwanda's behavior. The evidence shows that Rwanda's leader President Kagame has not wanted to commit to the ICC's strong enforcement mechanism and risk punishment so as to tie his hands to comply with the provisions of an international treaty. He appears instead to want no constraints on his power to rule, even if that means using violence and allowing perpetrators of certain acts of violence to escape justice.

Chapter 8 examines Kenya's decision to ratify the ICC treaty in 2005 despite its poor human rights practices. Kenya's behavior is seemingly inconsistent with the credible threat theory because Kenya's poor practices should have indicated that it might run afoul of treaty terms and risk punishment for bad and noncompliant behavior. Why did Kenya join at that time? Kenya joined the court only three years after it elected President Kibaki. Kibaki ran on a platform promising democratic and judicial reforms, and he joined the court when he was under a lot of pressure from both the international community and Kenya's own civil society to demonstrate more fully his commitment to those promised reforms. In short, the evidence suggests that Kenya ratified the ICC treaty in spite of its poor prospects for compliance because other factors appeared to outweigh the threat to its sovereignty at that moment. However, the evidence also suggests that Kenya did not join the court to tie its hands and credibly commit to better human rights practices or a better record of holding abusers accountable. Kenya continued its poor human rights practices, and after it failed to prosecute the perpetrators, the ICC decided to open an investigation against several of its leaders for committing mass atrocities.[8] Moreover, Kenya has not embraced the ICC treaty's hand-tying effects and instead has tried to release itself from its commitment: for example, its parliament voted to withdraw from the ICC;[9] and it has lobbied the Security Council, among others, to keep the case against its citizens from going forward.[10]

The final chapter of the book pulls together the evidence from the quantitative analyses and case studies and addresses the implications of the findings as they relate to the likely success of the ICC in realizing its goals. The evidence does indicate that the court's strong enforcement mechanism may be discouraging "bad" states from regularly and readily committing to the ICC. However, as the Kenya case demonstrates, there is hope that the ICC can realize its goals because when "bad" states join, the court can hold them accountable.

Notes

1 Portions of the Introduction, Chapters 1 and 2 and the Conclusion draw on work that appeared in Yvonne M. Dutton, "Commitment to International Human Rights Treaties: The Role of Enforcement Mechanisms," *University of Pennsylvania Journal of International Law* 34 (2012); and Yvonne M. Dutton, "Explaining State Commitment to the International Criminal Court: Strong Enforcement Mechanisms as a Credible Threat," *Washington University Global Studies Law Review* 10 (2011).

2 In fact, all but one of the 193 states that ratified the Convention on the Rights of the Child did so within 10 years of the treaty being available for signature. See the United Nations Treaty Collection, treaties.un.org.

3 Belgian authorities arrested the former vice-president of the Democratic Republic of the Congo—who was the subject of a sealed arrest warrant—during his visit to the country. "Congo Ex-Official is Held in Belgium on War Crimes Charges," *Agence France-Presse*, 25 May 2008. In November 2011, Côte d'Ivoire authorities surrendered Laurent Gbagbo pursuant to an ICC arrest warrant. "New Suspect in the ICC's Custody: Laurent Gbagbo Arrived at the Detention Centre," ICC Press Release, 30 November 2011.

4 Two alleged Darfur rebel commanders surrendered themselves to the court to face charges. "New Suspects in the Situation in Darfur, Sudan Arrive Voluntarily at the ICC: First Appearance Scheduled for Tomorrow," ICC Press Release, 16 June 2010. Six Kenyans charged with committing mass atrocities in the aftermath of the country's 2007 elections voluntarily appeared before the court. Human Rights Watch, "Kenya: Q&A on Pre-Trial Hearing in First ICC Case," www.hrw.org/news/2011/08/30/kenya-qa-pre-trial-hearin g-first-icc-case.

5 Beth A. Simmons and Allison Danner, "Credible Commitments and the International Criminal Court," *International Organization* 64, no. 2 (2010): 233–36.

6 Michael Struett, *The Politics of Constructing the International Criminal Court: NGOs, Discourse, and Agency* (New York: Palgrave MacMillan, 2008), 6–7.

7 Christine M. Wotipka and Kiyoteru Tsutsui, "Global Human Rights and States Sovereignty: State Ratification of International Human Rights Treaties, 1965–2001," *Sociological Forum* 23, no. 4 (2008): 734–35; Emilie Hafner-Burton, "Trading Human Rights: How Preferential Trade Agreements Influence Government Repression," *International Organization* 50, no. 3 (2005): 593–94.

8 Steve Inskeep, "ICC Case Accuses 6 Prominent Kenyans of Violence," *NPR*, 16 December 2010, www.npr.org/news/World/132101160.
9 Sarah Wambui, "Anger Over MPs Vote Against ICC," *Capital News*, 25 December 2010.
10 Benjamin Muindi, "Minister Says Kenya a 'Laughing Stock' over ICC Deferral," *All Africa & Daily Nation*, 25 March 2011, allafrica.com/stories/201103110913.html.

1 The ICC

A new kind of institution in the international human rights regime

- **The creation of the ICC in the context of the international human rights regime**
- **The evolution of the ICC's institutional design: a weak court becomes strong**
- **The ICC's enforcement mechanism in context**
- **Conclusion**

This chapter sets the stage for the following chapters by providing background information on the International Criminal Court (ICC) and its institutional design as relates to holding states to their commitment to protect against and punish genocide, crimes against humanity, and war crimes. It first briefly describes the court's creation in the context of the international human rights regime. It then traces the evolution of the ICC's institutional design from its original conception as a weak institution that would allow states to guard their sovereignty since states and the United Nations (UN) Security Council would retain significant control over the ability of the prosecutor and court to act. Finally, the chapter provides additional context for understanding the ICC's enforcement mechanism by comparing the court's powers to those typically granted to the committees overseeing compliance with international human rights treaties and to those associated with the ad hoc international criminal tribunals.

The creation of the ICC in the context of the international human rights regime

The existence of the ICC is the result of a journey that commenced with the Nuremberg trials after World War II. Motivated by the destruction caused by the war, the international community began the process of creating a regime to protect the basic human rights of all individuals.[1] In 1948, the UN General Assembly adopted the Universal Declaration of Human Rights (UDHR), a document that expressed the somewhat revolutionary idea that human rights were universal and the international community had an obligation to ensure those rights were protected without regard to state boundaries or states' sovereign rights.[2] Although the UDHR was only declaratory, it paved the way for a host of binding international human rights treaties to which states were encouraged to commit.[3]

The two main treaties at the foundation of the international human rights regime are the International Covenant on Civil and Political Rights (ICCPR) and the International Covenant on Economic, Social and Cultural Rights (ICESCR). Additional international human rights treaties followed, and the regime now boasts six main treaties, to which the great majority of states have committed.[4] For example, the International Convention on the Elimination of All Forms of Racial Discrimination (CERD) entered into force in 1969. The Convention Against Torture and Other Cruel, Inhuman or Degrading Treatment or Punishment (CAT) was adopted in December 1984 and entered into force in 1987. The Convention on the Elimination of All Forms of Discrimination Against Women (CEDAW) opened for signature in 1980 and entered into force in 1981. Finally, the Convention on the Rights of the Child (CRC) entered into force in 1990. By their terms and provisions, all six primary treaties have in common the goal and focus of encouraging governments to improve their domestic legal practices as they relate to protecting against and punishing human rights abuses—for all citizens and particular groups that historically have received less protection.

The idea of a permanent international criminal court was also first raised decades ago. The experience of the war made only too clear that some governments may not abide by international human rights norms. In those cases where governments or leaders continued to abuse their citizens, the trials at Nuremberg provided a model for holding individuals criminally liable for abuses they committed on their own citizens as well as others.[5] Thus, beginning in 1951, the International Law Commission (ILC) was tasked with preparing draft statutes for the creation of a permanent international criminal court.[6] However, the process of creating the court stalled thereafter with the commencement of the Cold War and was not again revisited until four decades later.

A 1990 request submitted by Trinidad and Tobago[7] for an international criminal court to help it prosecute narcotics traffickers caused the world community once again to turn its attention to the possibility of a permanent court that could hold individuals criminally accountable for human rights abuses.[8] By July 1994, the ILC produced a draft statute that was adopted and recommended to the General Assembly.[9] Thereafter, the General Assembly adopted a resolution to establish an Ad Hoc Committee to review the 1994 ILC Draft, and they invited states to submit comments to the draft and participate in Committee debates.[10] A Preparatory Committee took over between 1996 and 1998 with the object of negotiating the precise statutory language that would govern the court and its functions.[11] By April 1998, based on input from various state representatives, the Preparatory Committee had produced a draft statute with 116 articles and many bracketed optional provisions that the international community decided to use as the basis for negotiations during a diplomatic conference of plenipotentiaries in the summer of 1998 in Rome—the Rome Conference.[12]

After five weeks of negotiations, at the conclusion of the conference in July 1998, states voted to adopt the Rome Statute—the treaty creating the world's first permanent treaty-based international criminal court. Attending the conference were 160 states, 33 international governmental coalitions, and a coalition of over 200 nongovernmental organizations (NGOs).[13] Of the states in attendance, 120 voted in favor of adoption of the statute, seven voted against, and 21 abstained.[14] On 1 July 2002, after the required 60 states had ratified the statute, the ICC came into existence and began operating in The Hague, The Netherlands.

The Rome Statute's preamble states that the ICC was created in order to end impunity for perpetrators of the most serious crimes of genocide, crimes against humanity, war crimes, and aggression (which will come under the court's jurisdiction after January 2017).[15] By ratifying the treaty, states agree to grant the court automatic jurisdiction over their citizens who commit one of the core crimes with no further consent from the state party, as long as the crimes were committed after ratification.[16] In fact, the ICC may exercise jurisdiction over nationals of states that are not parties to the treaty without their consent where the nationals of those states commit covered crimes within the territory of states parties.[17] In addition, according to the terms of the treaty, an independent ICC prosecutor elected by a majority of signatory nations has *proprio motu* powers to commence investigations on his own or based on referrals from a state party.[18] The Security Council can also refer investigations, but it has no direct oversight powers and no veto power over what situations are investigated or prosecuted.[19] Moreover, the ICC's powers to investigate and prosecute extend to all individuals since the treaty does not recognize any immunity that states may otherwise grant to heads of state who engage in criminal activity.[20]

Although the ICC has a broad jurisdictional mandate, it operates based on a system of "complementarity," meaning that it functions as a court of last resort. By the provisions of the Rome Statute, the ICC will obtain jurisdiction over the nationals of states parties where the state is "unwilling or unable genuinely" to proceed with a case.[21] "Unwillingness" includes instances where national proceedings are a sham or are inconsistent with an intention to bring the person to justice.[22] The "unwillingness" provision is designed to preclude the possibility of prosecutions aimed at shielding perpetrators due to, for example, government participation in, or complicity with, the offense.[23] A nation's "inability" to prosecute includes instances where, because of the collapse or unavailability of its national judicial system, the nation cannot obtain the accused or the necessary evidence, or is otherwise incapable of carrying out the proceedings.[24] The ICC, as opposed to the states that are parties to the treaty creating the court, is charged with determining whether the "unwilling or unable" bases for proceeding before the court have been met.

The evolution of the ICC's institutional design: a weak court becomes strong

That the ICC was created and that it has the powers it has is nothing short of remarkable. The original conception for the court reflected state sovereignty concerns and envisaged a weak institution with circumscribed jurisdiction and which vested much control over the decision to commence prosecutions in the states themselves or the UN Security Council.

For example, early ILC drafts allowed states to limit or extend their acceptance of the ICC's jurisdiction over particular crimes and/or for particular time periods—an "opt-in" regime.[25] The 1994 ILC Draft provided that for crimes other than genocide, the international criminal court could not exercise jurisdiction unless *all* states that could otherwise assert jurisdiction (such as the state where the acts were committed or the state with custody over the accused) specifically consented.[26] By contrast, under the Rome Statute, the prosecutor and court have automatic jurisdiction over any of the covered crimes committed by the citizens of a state party unless the pertinent state itself is prosecuting the offenses.

Not only did the 1994 ILC Draft significantly limit the scope of the court's jurisdiction, but it also limited the role of the court and prosecutor in triggering investigations. That draft only permitted states or the Security Council to commence proceedings.[27] The Security Council's power did not end with its ability to suggest cases, however. According to the 1994 ILC Draft, any permanent member of the Security Council would be able to use its veto power to prevent the ICC from exercising jurisdiction over a matter since no prosecution could be commenced without Security Council approval.[28]

In fact, during the 1998 Rome Conference, this same core set of issues about the ICC's jurisdiction over crimes, the mechanism for triggering prosecutions, and the role of the Security Council was the subject of intense debate. NGOs and about 60 states known as the like-minded group were aligned from the start of the conference in pushing for a stronger and more independent prosecutor and court with broad powers to exercise jurisdiction over mass atrocities. Some other states initially pressed for a court with more limited powers, but were persuaded during the conference to vote for a stronger court. For example, France eventually voted for the adoption of the Rome Statute, but it had previously called for a jurisdictional regime whereby all states affected by a case would have to give their consent in order for the ICC to proceed.[29] On the other hand, some permanent members of the Security Council (the P-5), namely the United States, China, and Russia, never wavered from arguing for a court with more limited powers.[30]

Nevertheless, at the conclusion of the Rome Conference on 17 July 1998 a majority of states rejected the idea of a weak institution based on state consent and Security Council control. They voted to design an international criminal court with strong powers to enforce compliance with treaty terms and punish noncompliant behavior. Upon ratification, states agreed that the ICC prosecutor and court may investigate, arrest, prosecute, and punish state nationals who commit mass atrocities if the state fails to prosecute those atrocities domestically—without any separate, additional state consent.

That the 1998 ICC negotiations produced a stronger institution than was originally anticipated is interesting, but this book's primary focus is not to question why the international community decided at that time to create such a powerful institution. Rather, this book's focus is on the very existence of the ICC's ultimate enforcement mechanism, how that enforcement mechanism affects state membership in the institution, and the likelihood that the treaty will realize its goal of ending impunity for mass atrocities. Tracing the evolution of the court's institutional design shows the relative strength of the ICC's enforcement mechanism by situating it within the context of the earlier-conceived court, which essentially would have had no independent power.

The ICC's enforcement mechanism in context

The strength of the ICC's ultimate enforcement mechanism is also evident when one considers the court and its powers in the context of the international human rights regime as a whole. The discussion that follows describes the typically weak powers states have granted to the committees that oversee compliance with international human rights treaties and compares those to the powers states granted to the ICC pursuant to the Rome Statute. It also compares the ICC's powers and functions to those of the ad hoc international criminal courts created by the Security Council since the early 1990s.

International human rights treaties: under the control of committees without the authority to sanction bad and noncompliant behavior

The treaties that form the foundation of the international human rights regime typically delegate the power and duty to monitor compliance with treaty terms to some committee of experts. Table 1.1 lists the six main treaties and the rights they generally protect.

The six main international human rights treaties are characterized by the weakest enforcement mechanisms because they rely on a system

Table 1.1 Six main international human rights treaties

Treaty	*Rights protected*
International Covenant on Civil and Political Rights (ICCPR)	Life, liberty, freedom from torture and slavery
International Covenant on Economic, Social and Cultural Rights (ICESCR)	Economic, social, and cultural rights
International Convention on the Elimination of All Forms of Racial Discrimination (CERD)	Fundamental and human rights for persons of all races
Convention on the Elimination of All Forms of Discrimination Against Women (CEDAW)	Fundamental and human rights for women
Convention Against Torture and Other Cruel, Inhuman or Degrading Treatment or Punishment (CAT)	Freedom from torture and other forms of punishment
Convention on the Rights of the Child (CRC)	Fundamental and human rights for children

of self-reporting: states must file reports with the committee describing their efforts to comply with the treaty's provisions. States can bind themselves to additional committee oversight of their practices—and hence purportedly greater enforcement mechanisms—by ratifying some of the optional articles and protocols connected to the six main treaties. First, states can agree on the committee's competence to hear complaints by other states claiming that they are not living up to their treaty obligations.[31] Some optional articles and protocols permit states to agree on the committee's competence to hear complaints by individuals alleging that the state has violated rights protected by the treaty—if the individuals have, among other things, exhausted available domestic remedies.[32] Finally, by joining the Optional Protocol to the Convention against Torture, states can authorize a committee to visit their territory and also grant it access to relevant information about potential violations of the rights protected by the treaty.[33] Yet, even these enforcement mechanisms by which states can agree to greater oversight of their domestic human rights practices are relatively weak when compared to the ICC treaty's enforcement mechanism: in no case have states granted the committees overseeing compliance any powers to issue legally binding decisions or provided them with resources to punish bad and noncompliant behavior.

Rather, the committees' oversight and enforcement powers are limited to questioning states about the matters in their reports and commenting on the states' level of treaty compliance. Thus, states can fail to file reports, file their reports late, file perfunctory reports, or even fail to ensure that their domestic practices are consistent with treaty terms without risking any real sanctions. Indeed, a review of committee records shows that many states do not file the required reports or file them late[34]—an indication that treaty enforcement mechanisms are too weak to hold states to their treaty commitments. Thus, as Jack Donnelly notes, the committees overseeing the process are not empowered with any mechanism to force recalcitrant states into actually improving their behavior.[35]

The powers granted to the committees overseeing the complaint procedures are also limited as regards holding states accountable to improving their domestic practices. States do agree to subject themselves to more oversight than they do by the self-reporting procedure since treaty terms require them to submit to a grievance procedure before an independent committee. But if the matter cannot be resolved via negotiation, the committee is generally limited to summarizing its activities in a report.[36] Moreover, according to the website for the Office of the UN High Commissioner for Human Rights, as of August

2010, the procedures for interstate complaints had never been used[37]—likely because states do not want to risk the diplomatic and political fallout should they reach out to get involved in other states' affairs.

The individual complaint procedure may appear more costly to state sovereignty than the interstate complaint procedure. States may expect they would receive more complaints from individuals than from other states because there are more individuals in a state than there are other states. Individuals are also more likely than other states to actually know of, and be willing to challenge, the state's human rights practices. Yet, this enforcement mechanism is also lacking because the committees considering the complaints have no "authority to act punitively against the offending state, or impose any sanctions."[38] The committees' powers are essentially limited to attempting to persuade the state to follow their recommendations.[39]

Finally, the CAT Optional Protocol appears to bind states to a stronger enforcement mechanism than those previously described: states agree that a committee of experts may enter their sovereign territory and privately interview persons the state is holding in detention.[40] However, here too the committee has no power to punish bad and noncompliant behavior—or even to sanction a state that refuses to cooperate with the committee. Pursuant to Article 16 of the CAT Optional Protocol, the committee is authorized to publish reports of its investigations, together with any comments the state party may wish to include. If the state party does not cooperate, the committee is limited to making a public statement or publishing a report commenting on the state's behavior.[41]

The enforcement mechanisms typically associated with international human rights treaties certainly can play a helpful and meaningful role in inducing state compliance with international human rights norms. The reports, decisions, and comments by the committees on state noncompliance can be used by NGOs or individuals in an effort to shame the state into compliance. Other states may also use the evidence contained in those reports as ammunition to force a state to improve its human rights record if it wants to continue to receive aid or trade. However, regarding the level of the enforcement mechanisms to which states bind themselves pursuant to the treaty's terms, the committees do not have legally binding adjudicatory power coupled with resources to compel compliance with their comments, views, and recommendations.[42] Moreover, even had the state not joined the particular treaty, NGOs, states, or civil society could still likely find evidence about the state's poor human rights practices to use against it in an effort to shame it into improving.

In contrast to the committees overseeing compliance with the international human rights treaties, the ICC has a relatively strong enforcement mechanism: states have granted the prosecutor and court the power to issue legally binding orders and provided resources to punish noncompliant behavior. As mentioned in the Introduction, the ICC may issue arrest warrants in order to bring individuals or groups to stand trial for their crimes before judges at the ICC in The Hague. The ICC may also prosecute and punish the suspects that are brought before the court. In March 2012, in fact, the ICC rendered its first verdict.[43] Although the ICC may not have the same ability to follow through on its enforcement powers as domestic institutions overseeing compliance with domestic criminal law, in the context of the international human rights regime, its powers are significant.

In fact, the significance of its powers is shown by the fact that states and individuals have complied with ICC orders—even though the court has no police force to carry out its orders. In Brussels, Belgian authorities arrested Jean-Pierre Bemba, who had been charged by the ICC with committing war crimes in the Central African Republic.[44] In Paris, French authorities arrested Callixte Mbarushimana, who was charged by the ICC with committing crimes in the Democratic Republic of the Congo.[45] Côte d'Ivoire surrendered former President Laurent Gbagbo to the ICC based on a sealed arrest warrant.[46] Other suspects, including some charged in cases concerning violence in Darfur and Kenya, have appeared in response to the ICC's orders without a need to be arrested.[47] Although this may not sound like a significant number of arrests, it bears noting that the ICC is still a very young institution. The fact that even some states and individuals have complied with this young institution's orders suggests that its powers are viewed as legitimate and significant.

Of course, even though the ICC has these powers to effectuate arrests and prosecute those who commit mass atrocities, the evidence also shows that not all states have complied with the court's orders. As a result, some suspects, like President Omar Bashir of Sudan, have thus far escaped justice. Indeed, the ICC has informed the UN Security Council of the failure of ICC states parties Djibouti, Chad, Kenya, and Malawi to execute on the ICC's warrant for the arrest of President Bashir during his visits to their countries.[48] Nevertheless, the power delegated to the ICC is still legally binding. Suspects may be able to escape arrest by staying in their own state, hiding, or visiting only friendly states, but those who are subject to an arrest warrant are not completely free to do as they please, as President Bashir no doubt knows. Bashir is not travelling to Western Europe where he likely fears he would be arrested and sent to The Hague to be tried. Bashir may not even be able to travel to other formerly "friendly" countries. In fact, Malawi's new President Joyce Banda publicly announced in June 2012 that her country will not host an African Union summit if Bashir must be invited, noting how strained ties with key donors in the international community became after her predecessor allowed Bashir to visit.[49] The fact of Malawi's change in position towards hosting Bashir provides some evidence that many in the international community believe the ICC's orders have the power of law and that states and individuals should comply with them or at least not flout them.

The ad hoc international criminal tribunals: limited, after-the-fact enforcement

Even when compared to the ad hoc international criminal tribunals that have been established since the early 1990s, the ICC stands out as having especially strong powers. It is true that the ad hoc tribunals also have powers to investigate, arrest, prosecute, and punish individuals who commit mass atrocities. However, the ICC has all of those powers, and it is also a permanent institution that can investigate and punish offenses as they occur. Indeed, the very fact of the ICC's permanence provides it with the kind of threat that should be able to deter acts before they occur. It stands ready to prosecute those who commit mass atrocities if the state is unable or unwilling to prosecute them domestically. It can prosecute atrocities committed by the nationals of any state party or by others should they occur on the territory of a state party. All states that join the ICC—even if they are strong and powerful—agree that their citizens can be the subject of an ICC prosecution. Moreover, the ICC can commence investigations and prosecutions without Security Council approval.

This is not the case with the ad hoc tribunals, which are only created in certain circumstances, after the fact, and to deal with atrocities in particular states. Their powers are limited to influencing behavior only after a mass atrocity has occurred. Furthermore, the ad hoc tribunals must be authorized by the Security Council and, thus far, only a few have been created and they have been imposed only on weaker states.

In short, the ICC has the powers of the ad hoc tribunals, but its permanence and its structure make it even more powerful. The ICC has powers to influence state behavior and hold states accountable from the moment the state commits to the treaty. By committing to the ICC, states agree in advance to surrender their sovereign rights to an international institution to manage their domestic affairs as it relates to identifying and punishing mass atrocities. In the case of ad hoc tribunals, states need not make such an advance commitment, and the international community would not have any basis to hold them to one.

Conclusion

In conclusion, in the context of the international human rights regime, the ICC has a strong enforcement mechanism designed to enforce compliance and to punish bad and noncompliant behavior. The treaty states enacted to create the ICC envisions a powerful and independent prosecutor and court that can significantly affect state sovereignty: states committing to the ICC accept the risk that their nationals will be prosecuted by the ICC if they commit mass atrocities.

How will the ICC's strong enforcement mechanism influence treaty membership? Will the states that most need to improve their domestic human rights practices view the ICC's enforcement mechanism as a credible threat and refuse to join? If those states that most need to improve their practices do not join the court, is there any hope that the threat of punishment by the ICC can play a role in bettering states' human rights practices and ending impunity for mass atrocities? Chapter 2 explores these questions by quantitatively examining the reasons why states commit or refuse to commit to the treaty creating the ICC.

Notes

1 Thomas Buergenthal, "The Normative and Institutional Evolution of International Human Rights," *Human Rights Quarterly* 19, no. 4 (1997): 705.
2 Jack Donnelly, "International Human Rights: A Regime Analysis," *International Organization* 40, no. 3 (1986): 606; James Raymond Vreeland, "Political Institutions and Human Rights: Why Dictatorships Enter into the United Nations Convention Against Torture," *International Organization* 62, no. 1 (2008): 71.
3 Treaties are adopted and opened for signature by the UN General Assembly and require some number of countries to sign and ratify them before they enter into force. States are only bound to a treaty's terms if they ratify or accede to the treaty. States each have their own domestic rules regarding ratification and some permit the executive to make ratification decisions, while others require the approval of a legislative body or bodies. Finally, until they enter into force, treaties have no binding effect.
4 Treaty texts and information about their membership are on file with the Secretary-General of the UN at the UN Treaty Collection, treaties.un.org.
5 See Lawyers Committee for Human Rights, *Establishing an International Criminal Court: Major Unresolved Issues in the Draft Statute*, coalitionfortheicc.org/documents/LCHRUnresolvedIssues.pdf.

6 Antonio Cassese, *International Criminal Law* (Oxford: Oxford University Press, 2nd edn, 2008), 323.
7 *Letter dated August 21, 1989 from the Permanent Representative of Trinidad and Tobago to the Secretary-General* (UN Doc. A/44/195), 21 August 1989.
8 Cassese, *International Criminal Law*, 323–28.
9 The ILC's 1994 Draft is available at Report of the International Law Commission on the Work of its 49th Session, UN GAOR, Supp. 10, at 44, UN Doc. A/49/10 (1994) (hereafter 1994 ILC Draft).
10 Lawyers Committee for Human Rights, *Establishing an International Criminal Court: Major Unresolved Issues in the Draft Statute*, 7.
11 Adriaan Bos, "From the International Law Commission to the Rome Conference (1994–98)," in *The Rome Statute of the International Criminal Court: A Commentary, Volume 1*, ed. Antonio Cassese, Paola Gaeta, John R.W.D. Jones (Oxford: Oxford University Press, 2002), 37.
12 *Preparatory Committee Draft Statute* (A/CONF.183/2/Add.2), 14 April 1998.
13 Caroline Fehl, "Explaining the International Criminal Court: A 'Practice Test' for Rationalist and Constructivist Approaches," *European Journal of International Relations* 10, no. 3 (2004): 362.
14 Mahnoush H. Arsanjani, "The Rome Statute of the International Criminal Court," *American Journal of International Law* 93, no. 1 (1999): 23.
15 *Rome Statute of the International Criminal Court* (UN Doc. A/CONF 183/9), 17 July 1993, Preamble, paras. 4 and 5 (hereinafter, *Rome Statute*). The ICC will have jurisdiction over aggression after 1 January 2017, and after the parties vote to amend the Rome Statute to include the agreed-upon definition of the crime. See Resolution RC/Res. 6 at Annex 1, paras. 2 and 3(3), www.icc-cpi.int/iccdocs/asp_docs/Resolutions/RC-Res.6-ENG.pdf.
16 *Rome Statute*, art. 11.
17 Ibid., art. 12.
18 Ibid., arts. 13–15.
19 Christopher Rudolph, "Constructing an Atrocities Regime: The Politics of War Crimes Tribunals," *International Organization* 55, no. 3 (2001): 679–80; Lionel Yee, "The International Criminal Court and The Security Council: Articles 13(b) and 16," in *The International Criminal Court: The Making of the Rome Statute: Issues, Negotiations, Results*, ed. Roy S. Lee (The Hague, The Netherlands: Kluwer Law International, 1999), 143–52.
20 *Rome Statute*, art. 27.
21 Ibid., Preamble, para. 10 and art. 17(1)(a).
22 Ibid., art. 17(2).
23 John T. Holmes, "The Principle of Complementarity," in *The Making of the Rome Statute*, 50.
24 *Rome Statute*, art. 17(3).
25 Hans-Peter Kaul, "Preconditions to the Exercise of Jurisdiction," in *The Rome Statute of the International Criminal Court: A Commentary*, 593.
26 1994 ILC Draft, art. 21.
27 Ibid., arts. 23 and 25.
28 Adriaan Bos, "From the International Law Commission to the Rome Conference (1994–98)," in *The Rome Statute of the International Criminal Court: A Commentary*, 49–50.

29 Draft Statute of the International Criminal Court, Working Paper Submitted by France (UN Doc. A/AC 249/L.3, art. 34), 6 August 1996.
30 For a detailed discussion of the debate concerning the court's jurisdiction, see Hans P. Kaul and Class Kress, "Jurisdiction and Cooperation in the Statutes of the International Criminal Court," *Yearbook of International Humanitarian Law* 2 (1999): 143–75.
31 For example, under Article 41 of the ICCPR states may authorize the Human Rights Committee to hear interstate complaints if both state parties have formally acknowledged the committee's competence to receive and consider inter-state communications. The provisions of Article 21 of the CAT are similar.
32 By committing to the First Optional Protocol to the ICCPR, states agree that individuals can bring complaints against them alleging violations of the ICCPR. Similar provisions are contained in Article 14 of the CERD, Article 22 of the CAT, and in the Optional Protocol to the CEDAW.
33 By the CAT Optional Protocol, states agree to recognize the competence of a Subcommittee on Prevention regularly to visit any place under its jurisdiction and control where persons are held in detention by the government or with its acquiescence. CAT Optional Protocol, arts. 4, 11.
34 State reporting data for all six main treaties can be obtained from the website maintained by the Office of the UN High Commissioner for Human Rights.
35 Jack Donnelly, *International Human Rights* (Boulder, CO: Westview Press, 2007), 87.
36 See ICCPR, art. 41(h) and CAT, art. 21(h).
37 See www.2.ohchr.org/english/bodies/petitions/index.htm.
38 Henry J. Steiner, "Individual Claims in a World of Massive Violations: What Role for the Human Rights Committee," in *The Future of UN Human Rights Monitoring*, ed. Philip Alston and James Crawford (Cambridge: Cambridge University Press, 2000), 37 (discussing the ICCPR Human Rights Committee).
39 For example, see the ICCPR Optional Protocol, arts. 5 and 6 and the CEDAW Optional Protocol, arts. 7 and 12.
40 CAT Optional Protocol, arts. 4, 11, 12, and 14.
41 Ibid., art. 16.
42 Achene Boulesbaa, *The U.N. Convention on Torture and the Prospects for Enforcement* (Leiden, The Netherlands: Martinus Nijhoff Publishers,1999), 63 (discussing the Committee Against Torture); Steiner, "Individual Claims in a World of Massive Violations: What Role for the Human Rights Committee," 37 (noting that the Human Rights Committee has no authority to act punitively against any state offending against the ICCPR or to impose sanctions against it).
43 "ICC First Verdict: Thomas Lubanga Guilty of Conscripting and Enlisting Children Under the Age of 15 and Using Them to Participate in Hostilities," ICC Press Release, 14 March 2012.
44 "Congo Ex-Official is Held in Belgium on War Crimes Charges," *Agence France-Presse*, 25 May 2008.
45 "New ICC Arrest: Leader of Movement Involved in Massive Rapes in the DRC is Apprehended in Paris," ICC Press Release, 11 October 2010.

46 "New Suspect in the ICC's Custody: Laurent Gbagbo Arrived at the Detention Centre," ICC Press Release, 30 November 2011.
47 "As Darfur Rebel Commanders Surrender to the Court, ICC Prosecutor 'Welcomes Compliance with the Court's Decisions and with Resolution 1593 (2005) of the Security Council,'" ICC Press Release, 16 June 2010; "Kenya: Q&A on Pre-Trial Hearing in First ICC Case," *Human Rights Watch* (discussing the voluntary appearance of six Kenyans charged by the ICC with committing mass atrocities in the aftermath of the country's 2007 elections).
48 "Pre-Trial Chamber I Informs the United Nations Security Council and the Assembly of States Parties About Chad's Non-cooperation in the Arrest and Surrender of Omar Al Bashir," ICC Press Release, 13 December 2011.
49 "Malawi Cancels AU Summit Hosting Over Bashir Invite," *Radio Netherlands Worldwide*, 8 June 2012.

2 Testing state commitment to the ICC

- **Treaty design and commitment to international human rights treaties**
- **The credible threat argument and its implications**
- **Empirical analyses of state commitment to the ICC in the context of other international human rights treaties**
- **Conclusion**

This chapter begins by situating the book's credible threat argument in the context of several prominent theories seeking to explain why states join international human rights treaties. It then tests the explanatory power of those theories by quantitatively examining state decisions to commit to the International Criminal Court (ICC). The quantitative tests also examine state commitment in the context of the 13 other international human rights treaties discussed in Chapter 1 in an effort to analyze further the role differing levels of enforcement mechanisms play in influencing ratification behavior. To conclude, the chapter addresses some implications of the findings regarding the ICC's likelihood of realizing its goal of ending impunity for mass atrocities.

Treaty design and commitment to international human rights treaties

What causes states to join an international human rights treaty? Some scholars suggest that states will act in their rational self-interest and ratify treaties where the benefits of commitment appear to outweigh the costs of complying with treaty terms.[1] This initially raises the question of what benefits states might obtain from commitment. Unlike other treaties, like those governing arms and trade, human rights treaties do not require their members to provide each other with reciprocal benefits.[2] They purport only to place constraints on the state's ability to manage its domestic political affairs. Yet, a rational state could still view commitment as providing benefits to it—even if such benefits may be difficult to quantify or measure. States may join because they believe in the norm of protecting against human rights abuses and may obtain a moral benefit from supporting an institution that exists to spread that norm. More tangibly, if that norm is spread, the world may become a more peaceful place with fewer disruptions to commerce and less need for costly interventions to stop mass atrocities or manage the damage they produce. In addition, by committing to the ICC, states can hope to entice others to join and thereby hold those *other* states accountable to protecting against human rights abuses. Finally, some states can likely obtain benefits in the form of foreign aid or trade contracts if they appear to be embracing international human rights norms. There is a rich history of more powerful states providing such benefits to states in exchange for their commitment to human rights treaties. As Emilie M. Hafner-Burton notes, many states are required to commit to improving certain domestic human rights practices to be eligible for certain preferential trade agreements.[3] In short, states may join human rights treaties because they believe in the principles of the institution, because they want to constrain others, or because they are pressured to do so.

States proceeding from a rationalist perspective, however, will still have to assess whether those benefits outweigh the costs of commitment. Downs, Rocke, and Barsoom argue that commitment costs will be lowest for states that can already easily comply with treaty terms. They suggest the primary reason we may see widespread compliance with many treaties is because states have a tendency to join only those treaties that do not require them to depart from what they would have otherwise done.[4] Jana von Stein makes a similar point about treaty selection effects, noting that "institutional design is at least in part endogenous" because states may not want to invest their time and resources in creating agreements with which they do not intend to comply.[5] As von Stein argues, we may find that treaties will actually screen out potentially bad and noncompliant members, rather than inducing them to join and thereafter alter their behavior to conform to treaty terms.[6]

Under this rationalist perspective states with policies and practices that are already consistent with treaty terms will be the most likely to conclude that commitment is not overly costly since there is little risk that the state will be punished for failing to comply.[7] In the case of international human rights treaties, state determinations about policy and practice similarity should center on the state's domestic political configuration and its past and present human rights practices. For example, much literature suggests that democracies are more likely than autocracies to commit to treaties requiring them to protect against human rights abuses. For democratic states, commitment should not change the *status quo ante* since these states generally protect basic human rights, apply the rule of law fairly, and limit state power.[8] By contrast, autocratic regimes may find ratification quite costly because they tend not to place legal restraints on the leader's power. To avoid running afoul of treaty terms, autocratic states may have to implement significant policy change.[9] Aside from the state's general political configuration, its specific human rights policies and practices should also enter into rational compliance cost calculations. States with a recent history of better human rights practices should find commitment less costly than states with a history of worse practices.[10]

However, commitment can also be less costly where treaty mechanisms to enforce compliance are weak or nonexistent.[11] Even for rights-abusing states, the benefits of commitment—perhaps the benefits associated with sending an insincere signal that the state embraces international norms—can outweigh what is essentially costless commitment since the state cannot be punished even if it fails to change its policies and practices. Some empirical evidence supports the notion that state commitment decisions are influenced at least in part by states' perceptions about the strength of the treaty's enforcement mechanisms. In her study examining state commitment to four different human rights treaties requiring only that states report their level of compliance, Oona Hathaway found that non-democracies with poor human rights ratings were just as likely, and sometimes even more likely, than non-democracies with better human rights ratings to ratify. Hathaway attributed this finding to the treaties' weak enforcement mechanisms and also the absence of domestic mechanisms, such as a vocal civil society, that push for better practices in democracies.[12]

Other scholars, however, proceed from a different premise and emphasize the benefits of strong enforcement mechanisms and costly commitment. Under this thinking, states without compliant practices and policies may embrace costly commitments so they can send a credible signal to act differently—and in accordance with treaty terms—in the future.[13] For example, Beth Simmons argues that a primary reason states bind themselves to Article VIII of the International Monetary Fund Treaty is to tie their hands and commit to a future policy course.[14] Indeed, Beth Simmons and Allison Danner advance their credible commitment theory to explain ICC ratification behavior, arguing that autocracies with poor prospects for compliance will join the court to send a costly signal and credibly commit to their domestic audiences to protect better against human rights abuses in the future.[15] Accordingly, some states may wish to ratify international treaties because the potential for incurring costs can actually prove beneficial.[16]

Finally, other theories about commitment to international human rights treaties are less focused on rational cost/benefit analyses, emphasizing instead how states may be enticed into ratifying international human rights treaties because of external pressures from others, such as powerful states, nongovernmental organizations (NGOs), and civil society.[17] Even if these states would prefer to guard their sovereignty and avoid domestic constraints, they may be persuaded that joining a human rights treaty will make them appear more legitimate and more worthy of extra-treaty benefits, like investment, aid, and trade.[18] States may also be pressured directly or indirectly to commit to the treaties their neighbors ratify in order to signal that they are legitimate members of the region. In short, states may conclude that despite the inability to comply with treaty terms, treaty ratification is necessary if the state is to fit in with its neighbors and also obtain the benefits of being a good neighbor—such as being able to participate in regional trade arrangements.[19]

The credible threat argument and its implications

This book approaches state commitment to international human rights treaties from a rationalist perspective. It suggests that although all states may have many reasons to want to join the ICC treaty, states should be wary of committing to the ICC and its stronger enforcement mechanism. Therefore, unlike the credible commitment theory and the external pressures theories which focus on the reasons why some states—even those with bad practices—might be encouraged to join international human rights treaties, the credible threat theory focuses on the role that enforcement mechanisms might play in discouraging ratification. Indeed, slightly more than 100 states had ratified the ICC by the end of 2008 (the data cut-off date for this project). By contrast, more than 190 states had ratified the Convention on the Rights of the Child (CRC) within the first 10 years that treaty was available for signature.

The credible threat argument has two main components: 1 the strength of the anticipated enforcement mechanism; and 2 the state's ability to comply with the terms of the treaty. The first component focuses on enforcement mechanisms because they ostensibly exist so as to hold states to their commitment to abide by treaty terms. This book defines an enforcement mechanism[20] as the formal grant of power from states to an institution with authority to oversee state compliance. The weakest enforcement mechanisms lack clear obligations, precision, and/or a precise delegation of authority or responsibility—"soft law" according to the language of Kenneth Abbott and Duncan Snidal.[21] Stronger, "hard law" enforcement mechanisms are precise and binding and, for example, will contain a formal grant of power to a committee or court to engage in authoritative, institutionalized, and legally binding decision making.[22] As Darren Hawkins argues, strong enforcement mechanisms provide for authorized decision makers who are "officially empowered by states to interpret and apply the rule of law, and control resources that can be used to prevent abuses or to punish offenders."[23] States should view strong enforcement mechanisms as a credible threat because failure to comply with treaty terms can result in punishment to them or their citizens—namely, a costly loss of sovereignty.

The credible threat argument's second component about compliance focuses primarily on a state's record of human rights practices. States rationally calculating their ability to comply with treaty terms should consider their past and present human rights practices because that record can provide information about how the state, its leaders, and its citizens will likely behave in the future. According to the credible threat theory, states with better human rights practices should be most likely to conclude that ratifying international human rights treaties with stronger enforcement mechanisms is in their rational self-interest. Those states with good current and past practices should be confident that they can comply with treaty terms, whereas states with bad practices should not have that same level of confidence. Where enforcement mechanisms are weak, however, the credible threat theory predicts that even states with bad practices can rationally conclude that the benefits of ratification outweigh the risks because punishment for noncompliance is not an option.

Although the credible threat theory may seem intuitive, the predictions generated by the theory about state ratification behavior are quite different from those that follow from the credible commitment and external pressures theories. According to the credible commitment theory advanced by Simmons and Danner, autocracies with bad human rights practices will not run from the ICC's stronger enforcement mechanisms. These states will instead embrace the opportunity to use an international enforcement mechanism to tie leaders' hands and force them to be better in the future. The external pressures theories also predict that "bad" states will ratify—not because they want to be "good," but rather because they are pressured to ratify by more powerful states upon which they depend for extra-treaty benefits. By contrast, the credible threat theory expects that the ICC's relatively strong enforcement mechanism will not generally discourage states with good practices from joining the court, but that it will discourage these "bad" states from joining because they will fear the possibility of an ICC prosecution.

Of course, no one theory likely explains the ratification behavior of all states, and this book also considers whether other theories and factors influence ICC ratification behavior. Nevertheless, it bears noting at this juncture why the other two prevailing theories are problematic. First, as to the credible commitment theory, although some autocratic states with bad practices have joined the ICC, it seems unlikely most would want to join an institution that can prosecute the state's leaders or citizens if policy change does not come promptly. Indeed, autocratic regimes typically have refused to implement domestic restraints on their power—for example, by appointing an independent judiciary. One can question why they would want to bind themselves to international restraints when they have not imposed domestic restraints. Finally, even if states with bad practices sincerely want to be "better" in the future, they likely know that change takes time and also that efforts to change an entrenched set of policies can even result in a backlash. Theories predicting states will ratify treaties with strong enforcement mechanisms because of external pressures are problematic for the same reasons. Even if "bad" states can obtain some extra-treaty benefits from ratifying, those benefits are likely outweighed by the risk of prosecution.

In sum, the credible threat theory predicts that "bad" states will generally refuse to join the court because they are not ready or able to comply with treaty terms and do not want to risk sovereignty losses by having their leaders or citizens prosecuted by the ICC. This means that the ICC treaty's institutional design may have the negative effect of discouraging ratification by the very states that most need to be held accountable to improving their domestic practices and institutions so that mass atrocities do not occur and do not go unpunished. Nevertheless, even though fewer "bad" states may join the ICC, the institution can still realize its goals. States with bad practices are not constrained to be bad forever. They may experience certain "windows of opportunity"—such as a change in leadership or a point where external or internal calls for commitment can no longer be ignored—where the benefits of joining may seem to outweigh costs. This does not mean that these "bad" states join because they are necessarily also committed to changing their policies for the better—at that moment at least. However, the good news is that when "bad" states join the ICC, they may actually be *required* to change unless they want to see their citizens tried in The Hague.

Empirical analyses of state commitment to the ICC in the context of other international human rights treaties

This section now turns to the empirical tests of the explanatory power of the credible threat theory and the hypotheses advanced to explain state commitment to international human rights treaties. The tests consider ICC commitment individually and also in the context of state commitment to 13 other human rights treaties with weaker but varying levels of enforcement mechanisms, all of which were described in Chapter 1. Table 2.1 lists those treaties, together with the date they were available for signature, according to their enforcement mechanisms from weakest to strongest.

Examining state ratification patterns

Examining ratification patterns provides preliminary support for the credible threat theory and the idea that states will avoid joining treaties with stronger enforcement mechanisms unless they can comply with treaty terms. Table 2.2[24] shows that states with worse human rights practices constitute only about 30 percent of the ICC membership. On the other

Table 2.1 14 human rights treaties and levels of enforcement mechanisms

Level of enforcement	*Description of mechanism*	*Human rights treaty*
1 – weakest	State must file reports	ICCPR (1966); ICESCR (1966); CERD (1966); CEDAW (1980); CAT (1984); CRC (1989)
2 – weak	States make complaints to committee	Article 41 ICCPR (1966); Article 21 CAT (1984)
3 – moderate	Individuals file complaints with committee	Optional Protocol ICCPR (1966); Article 14 CERD (1966); Article 22 CAT (1984); Optional Protocol CEDAW (1999)
4 – stronger	Committee may visit state	Optional Protocol CAT (2003)
5 – strongest	Independent prosecutor investigations and prosecutions	ICC (1998)

Table 2.2 Ratification of the 14 different treaties based on human rights ratings

Treaty	*Total number ratified*	*Number ratified with better human rights*	*Number ratified with worse human rights*
ICCPR	157	83	74
ICESCR	154	80	74
CERD	162	86	76
CEDAW	171	95	76
CAT	139	73	66
CRC	174	95	79
ICCPR Art. 41	47	31	16
CAT Art. 21	56	39	17
ICCPR Optional	96	60	36
CERD Art. 14	47	31	16
CAT Art. 22	60	37	23
CEDAW Optional	89	57	32
CAT Optional	41	29	12
ICC	98	66	32

hand, states with worse human rights practices comprise about half of the membership in the six treaties that only require self-reporting.

Figure 2.1 illustrates these ratification patterns.

In fact, as Table 2.3 shows, states with the worst human rights practices[25] readily and regularly commit to international human rights treaties with the weakest enforcement mechanisms, but they tend to

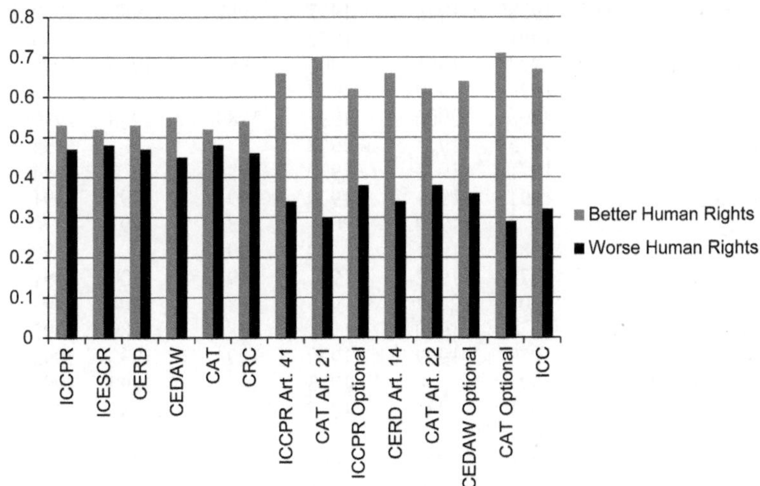

Figure 2.1 Ratification of the 14 different treaties based on average human rights ratings

Table 2.3 Worst human rights countries and ratifications

Country	*ICC*	*ICCPR*	*ICESCR*	*CERD*	*CEDAW*	*CAT*	*CRC*
Afghanistan	2003	1983	1983	1983	2003	1987	1994
Albania	2003	1991	1991	1994	1994	1994	1992
Algeria	–	1989	1989	1972	1996	1989	1993
Andorra	2001	2006	–	2006	1997	2006	1996
Bangladesh	2010	2000	1998	1979	1984	1998	1990
Brazil	2002	1992	1992	1968	1984	1989	1990
Burundi	2004	1990	1990	1977	1992	1993	1990
Cambodia	2002	1992	1992	1983	1992	1992	1992
Cameroon	–	1984	1984	1970	1994	1986	1993
Central African Rep.	2001	1981	1981	1971	1991	–	1992
Chad	2006	1995	1995	1977	1995	1995	1990
China	–	–	2001	1981	1980	1988	1992
Colombia	2002	1969	1969	1981	1982	1987	1991
Congo (Brazzaville)	2004	1983	1983	1988	1982	2003	1993
DRC (Kinshasa)	2002	1976	1976	1976	1986	1996	1990
Cuba	–	–	–	1972	1980	1995	1991
Egypt	–	1982	1982	1967	1981	1986	1990
Equatorial Guinea	–	1987	1987	2002	1984	2002	1992
Eritrea	–	2002	2001	2001	1995	–	1994
Ethiopia	–	1993	1993	1976	1981	1994	1991
Georgia	2003	1994	1994	1999	1994	1994	1994
Guatemala	–	1992	1988	1983	1982	1990	1990
Guinea	2003	1978	1978	1977	1982	1989	1990
Haiti	–	1991	–	1972	1981	–	1995
Honduras	2002	1997	1981	2002	1983	1996	1990
India	–	1979	1979	1968	1993	–	1992
Indonesia	–	2006	2006	1999	1984	1998	1990
Iran	–	1975	1975	1968	–	–	1994
Iraq	–	1971	1971	1970	1986	–	1994
Israel	–	1991	1991	1979	1991	1991	1991
Kenya	2005	1972	1972	2001	1984	1997	1990
North Korea	–	1981	1981	–	2001	–	1990
Lebanon	–	1972	1972	1971	1997	2000	1991
Liberia	2004	2004	2004	1976	1984	2004	1993
Libya	–	1970	1970	1968	1989	1989	1993
Morocco	–	1979	1979	1970	1993	1993	1993
Mozambique	–	1993	–	1983	1997	1999	1994
Mexico	2005	1981	1981	1975	1981	1986	1990
Myanmar	–	–	–	–	1997	–	1991
Nigeria	2001	1993	1993	1967	1985	2001	1991
Pakistan	–	–	2009	1966	1996	–	1990

Table 2.3 (continued)

Country	*ICC*	*ICCPR*	*ICESCR*	*CERD*	*CEDAW*	*CAT*	*CRC*
Papua New Guinea	–	2008	2008	1982	1995	–	1993
Paraguay	2001	1992	1992	2003	1987	1990	1990
Peru	2001	1978	1978	1971	1982	1988	1990
Philippines	–	1986	1974	1967	1981	1986	1990
Russia	–	1973	1973	1969	1981	1987	1990
Rwanda	–	1975	1975	1975	1981	2008	1991
Saudi Arabia	–	–	–	1997	2000	1997	1996
Sierra Leone	2000	1996	1996	1967	1988	2001	1990
Somalia	–	1990	1990	1975	–	1990	–
South Africa	2000	1998	–	1998	1995	1998	1995
Sri Lanka	–	1980	1980	1982	1981	1994	1991
Sudan	–	1986	1986	1977	–	–	1990
Syria	–	1969	1969	1969	2003	2004	1993
Tajikistan	2000	1999	1991	1995	1993	1995	1993
Thailand	–	1996	1999	2003	1985	2007	1992
Togo	–	1984	1984	1972	1983	1987	1990
Tunisia	–	1969	1969	1967	1985	1988	1992
Turkey	–	2003	2003	2002	1985	1988	1995
Uganda	2002	1995	1987	1980	1985	1986	1990
Ukraine	–	1973	1973	1969	1981	1987	1991
Uzbekistan	–	1995	1995	1995	1995	1995	1994
Venezuela	2000	1978	1978	1967	1983	1991	1990
Yemen	–	1987	1987	1972	1984	1991	1991
Zambia	2002	1984	1984	1972	1985	1998	1991
Zimbabwe	–	1991	1991	1991	1991	–	1990

avoid committing to the ICC with its stronger enforcement mechanism. Of the 66 countries with the worst human rights ratings, 65 (all except Myanmar) ratified at least four of the six main international human rights treaties. All but 18 ratified all six treaties. By contrast, 39 of the 66 countries with the worst ratings did not ratify the ICC treaty. Amongst the 39 countries that did not ratify the ICC treaty, 23 nevertheless ratified all six main international human rights treaties.

In sum, the evidence from examining ratification patterns is consistent with the predictions of the credible threat theory because it shows that states with worse human rights practices are regularly joining treaties with the weakest enforcement mechanisms, but are more often avoiding the ICC and its stronger enforcement mechanism. In addition, although no theory can explain the behavior of all states, this evidence also tends to discredit the explanatory power of the credible commitment theory and the external pressures theories: states with worse practices do not seem to be embracing strong enforcement mechanisms in order to tie their leaders' hands to act differently in the future. Nor are they regularly succumbing to external pressures and ignoring the threat of the ICC's stronger enforcement mechanism.

Event history analyses

Research design and data

The book now turns to event history analysis (also called "survival" analysis),[26] to test more fully the explanatory power of the credible threat theory and to test it against the credible commitment and the external pressures theories. Event history analysis tests each state's "time until" the *event* of treaty ratification and the factors that influence state decision making—including the role of stronger or weaker enforcement mechanisms. I use the Cox proportional hazards model because it can accommodate necessary time-varying covariates, such as a state's yearly human rights or democracy ratings.[27]

The primary focus is on state decisions to join or refuse to join the ICC. To provide context for understanding ICC commitment, additional tests examine state commitment to the 13 other international human rights treaties which are arranged according to their different enforcement levels, as set out in Table 2.1. Ratification data for all treaties were coded from the United Nations. The data are assembled at yearly intervals for more than 190 countries between 1966 and 2008. Appendix A lists the 14 different treaties and shows the states that are parties to each.

The main explanatory variable in the models measures each state's level of human rights protection. While each treaty does have its own terms and particular rights that it is designed to protect, all have in common the goal of encouraging states and their leaders to protect against and punish any human rights abuses. Thus, to test consistently commitment across the various treaties, I measure the human rights protection concept using the Political Terror Scale (described in note 24), which captures a country's tendency to protect against human rights abuses using a scale that ranges from 1 to 5—with 1 representing the best practices.[28] The Political Terror data are available beginning in 1976 and are reported from each year thereafter until 2008.[29]

If the credible threat theory is correct, the statistical evidence should show that states with poor human rights practices will be just as likely as states with good human rights practices readily to ratify international human rights treaties containing the weakest enforcement mechanisms. States with poorer records, however, should be much less likely to ratify the ICC treaty because it has a strong enforcement mechanism that can be used to punish bad and noncompliant behavior. The predictions of the credible commitment theory and the external pressures theories are quite different. The credible commitment theory proceeds from the premise that states with poor human rights records that are also non-democracies will join the court in order to signal to their domestic audiences their intention to be better in the future. The external pressures theories predict that even states with poor past and present human rights practices will commit to treaties with stronger enforcement mechanisms because they are enticed into believing that commitment may bring extra-treaty benefits.

The models also include some control variables. One measures a state's level of democracy using the Polity IV dataset.[30] Protection of human rights is consistent with democratic values, and democracies are better at protecting them than autocracies. If the credible threat theory is correct, states that are more democratic should be more likely to commit to international human rights treaties since compliance should be relatively costless. The credible commitment theory also predicts that democracies will ratify human rights treaties since democracies do not need an external enforcement mechanism to tie their hands in order to act better in the future. Along those same lines, a measure of each state's gross domestic product (GDP) per capita captures the idea that states that are economically more developed are likely also better to protect human rights at home. Compliance with human rights treaties should be easier for more developed states and increase those states' likelihood of commitment.

The models also include variables to control for how a state's domestic practices or processes impact the difficulty it faces in ratifying international human rights treaties. For example, Beth Simmons argues that states with more onerous treaty ratification processes may be less likely to ratify treaties quickly and readily. I measure this concept using Simmons's data which code ratification processes using a four-category scale of difficulty.[31] Simmons also suggests that states following a common law tradition may find treaty commitment more costly because common law courts may have more flexibility than civil law courts to apply treaty law in a way that creates new government obligations to the state's citizens and others.[32] Thus, the model contains a control variable to measure whether a state follows the common law tradition or not.

To account for Andrew Moravcsik's "lock-in" theory which predicts that states transitioning to democracy will embrace strong external commitment mechanisms, the model includes a dummy variable derived from the Polity IV democracy measure. According to Moravcsik, states in transition to democracy are likely to commit to treaties with strong enforcement mechanisms to lock-in democratic principles and thereby constrain the activities of future governments that may seek to subvert democracy.[33]

Finally, the models also include two variables to measure the influence of external pressures on state ratification behavior. First, to capture the idea that less developed states may ratify treaties so as to receive extra-treaty benefits from more powerful and wealthier nations, the model includes a measure for net official development assistance and official aid (ODA).[34] ODA consists of loans and grants made to developing countries. The model also includes a measure for the proportion of states in a state's region that have ratified each of the treaties. This measure captures the competition or diffusion effect from neighboring states, which can lead states to ratify a treaty that many of their neighbors have ratified. Appendix B describes the nature and source of the control variables in more detail.

Discussion of results

The event history analysis of ICC commitment reported in Table 2.4 provides additional support for the idea that states view the treaty's enforcement mechanism as a credible threat and will be more likely to commit when their policies and practices are already such that they can likely avoid being punished for bad and noncompliant behavior. The results are reported as hazard ratios, which indicate the particular factor's proportionate influence on the decision to ratify. Numbers greater than one indicate an increase in the hazard rate of ratification, while numbers less than one indicate a decrease.

That a state's level of human rights practices is a highly significant predictor of whether the state will join the ICC supports the credible threat theory.[35] The hazard ratio of 0.523 means that states are about 50 percent less likely to ratify the ICC treaty with each unit decrease in their human rights practices.[36] The democracy indicator is also significant for ICC treaty ratification, a fact that is consistent with the credible threat theory since democracies also tend to follow the rule of law, limit government power, and have the types of policies and practices enabling them to comply with international human rights treaties. With each unit improvement in its democracy rating, a state is about 20 percent more likely to ratify the ICC.

These findings regarding ICC commitment also tend to discredit the explanatory power of the credible commitment theory and the external

Table 2.4 Level 5 enforcement mechanism: independent prosecutor and court

Explanatory variables	*Hazard ratios* *International Criminal Court*
Level of human rights	0.523**
Level of democracy	1.230**
Level of economic development	0.743*
Difficulty of ratification process	1.127
Common law or not	0.939
Transitioning democracy or not	0.673
Level of aid	0.134
Regional ratifications	7.389*
Number of countries	135
Number of ratifications	74
Number of observations	848

Note: *significant at 0.05; **significant at 0.01.

pressures theories. The evidence does not show that states with poor human rights practices or non-democratic states are overwhelmingly binding themselves to a treaty with which they cannot comply because they either want to tie their hands to act better in the future or because they have been lured by the promise of extra-treaty benefits. As to the credible commitment theory in particular, again, one might question why an autocratic state which has declined to subject itself to domestic accountability mechanisms would willingly subject itself instead to an international accountability mechanism that could result in government leaders being tried in The Hague. On the contrary, the evidence suggests that, consistent with the credible threat theory, states with poor human rights practices and non-democracies—the very states that are likely to conclude that compliance with the ICC may be difficult and, hence, costly to their sovereignty—are wary of joining the court and will avoid its strong enforcement mechanisms.

Regarding the other theories for which control variables were added, the results provide some limited support for the idea that states are influenced by their neighbors' behavior. The regional ratification variable is a positive and significant predictor of ICC ratification. The only other variable that significantly predicts ICC ratification is the economic development variable. The hazard rate there indicates as states become more developed, they are less likely to commit to the court. One interpretation of these results is that some less-developed states are avoiding the ICC's strong enforcement mechanism. It bears noting, however, that the United States and China are two very wealthy states that have not committed to the court. Importantly, however, the addition of all of these control variables to account for other theories did not alter the significance of the human rights variable, thus lending additional support for the explanatory power of the credible threat theory.

Comparing state decisions to commit to the ICC treaty with state decisions to commit to other international human rights treaties with differing levels of enforcement mechanisms provides an important test of the implications of the credible threat theory. If the credible threat theory is correct, we should see that states behave very differently where enforcement mechanisms are weak. Even states with poor domestic human rights practices should readily commit to treaties with weak enforcement mechanisms because those states will have no reason to fear punishment.

The results of these additional tests of state ratification behavior do, indeed, provide support for the explanatory power of the credible threat theory. Table 2.5 shows that where enforcement mechanisms are

Table 2.5 Level 1 enforcement mechanisms: state reporting

Explanatory variables	*Hazard ratios*					
	ICCPR	*ICESCR*	*CERD*	*CEDAW*	*CAT*	*CRC*
Level of human rights	1.024	0.903	0.827	1.066	0.917	0.961
Level of democracy	1.20**	1.20**	1.030	1.107*	1.043	1.109*
Level of economic development	0.737*	0.680**	0.938	0.773	1.119	0.620**
Difficulty of ratification process	0.792	0.489**	0.547*	0.837	0.849	0.702
Common law or not	0.603	0.287**	0.576	.412**	0.340**	0.438**
Transitioning democracy or not	0.389	0.296*	1.079	0.892	0.986	0.917
Level of aid	0.132	0.042	0.178	0.023*	0.096	0.405
Regional ratifications	13.0**	7.93**	5.682*	1.28	6.35**	0.647
Number of countries	74	73	57	69	107	82
Number of ratifications	57	55	51	65	80	81
Number of observations	1,051	1,056	610	491	1,003	213

Note: *significant at 0.05; **significant at 0.01.

weakest and require only self-reporting, a state's level of human rights practices is not a significant predictor of ratification: states with worse practices are no less likely on the whole than states with better practices to commit to any of the six main international human rights treaties. This finding is consistent with Cole's regarding state commitment to the International Covenant on Civil and Political Rights (ICCPR) and International Covenant on Economic, Social and Cultural Rights (ICESCR)—the two main international human rights treaties he examined in his study testing state ratification behavior.[37]

In fact, state ratification of these six main international human rights treaties appears indiscriminate. Various factors did influence commitment in some cases, but their influence was not in any way uniform across these treaties with the same enforcement mechanism. The results show that democracies are more likely than autocracies quickly to ratify each of the ICCPR, ICESR, the Convention on the Elimination of All Forms of Discrimination Against Women (CEDAW), and CRC. States with more difficult ratification procedures are less likely to ratify the ICESCR and the International Convention on the Elimination of All Forms of Racial Discrimination (CERD). Common law states are less likely to commit to the ICESCR, CEDAW, Convention Against Torture and Other Cruel, Inhuman or Degrading Treatment or Punishment (CAT), and CRC. Regional ratification patterns positively influence ratification of the ICCPR, ICESCR, CERD, and CAT. Only ratification of the ICESCR is significantly influenced by all four of these factors, however.

Table 2.6 Level 2 enforcement mechanism: interstate complaints

Explanatory variables	*Hazard ratios*	
	Art. 41 ICCPR	*Art. 21 CAT*
Level of human rights	1.042	1.008
Level of democracy	1.155	1.170*
Level of economic development	1.245	1.585
Difficulty of ratification process	0.653	0.734
Common law or not	1.632	0.473
Transitioning democracy or not	0.707	1.220
Level of aid	0.789	0.120
Regional ratifications	14.775	8.368*
Number of countries	121	129
Number of ratifications	18	34
Number of observations	2,594	1,910

Note: *significant at 0.05; **significant at 0.01.

The results of the tests of the treaties grouped in enforcement level 2 (interstate complaints) similarly lend support to the credible threat theory. Table 2.6 shows that a state's level of human rights practices did not significantly predict the state's decision to ratify either Article 41 of the ICCPR or Article 21 of the CAT. In those models, only the democracy and regional ratifications variables are significant and then only with respect to ratification of CAT Article 21. Indeed, the treaty terms associated with the treaties grouped in enforcement level 2 make clear that committee power will be limited to trying to negotiate a resolution to any interstate complaints. Moreover, it seems the interstate complaint practice is not really used in any event—a fact that states ratifying the treaty likely knew when they decided to bind themselves to this mechanism. For example, 26 of the 48 states that have ratified Article 41 of the ICCPR did not do so until 1990 or after (even though many could have ratified beginning in 1966), by which time states likely realized the provision for interstate complaints was not being invoked.[38]

Results are mixed where enforcement mechanisms are in the middle range (enforcement levels 3 and 4), however. Supportive of the credible threat theory are the findings regarding commitment to the ICCPR Optional Protocol. As shown in Table 2.7, and consistent with Cole's

Table 2.7 Level 3 enforcement mechanism: individual complaints

Explanatory variables	*Hazard ratios*			
	ICCPR Opt. Protocol	*Art. 14 CERD*	*Art. 22 CAT*	*CEDAW Opt. Protocol*
Level of human rights	0.630*	0.813	1.129	0.832
Level of democracy	1.212**	1.156	1.137	1.198**
Level of economic development	0.622**	0.826	1.335	0.815
Difficulty of ratification process	0.943	1.191	0.683	1.064
Common law or not	0.325**	0.236*	0.217**	0.554
Transitioning democracy or not	1.113	0.885	1.225	0.890
Level of aid	0.056	1.62	0.001	0.007*
Regional ratifications	1.010	17.867*	9.400*	2.828
Number of countries	102	131	129	138
Number of ratifications	50	27	35	72
Number of observations	1,862	2,766	1,922	846

Note: *significant at 0.05; **significant at 0.01.

findings,[39] states with better human rights practices and democracies do seem more likely than states with bad practices and autocracies to ratify the ICCPR Optional Protocol. On the other hand, a state's human rights ratings did not predict ratification of the other three treaties allowing individual complaints. Instead, the only compliance cost measure that significantly predicted ratification of these three treaties was the democracy measure. However, that measure only predicted ratification of the CEDAW Optional Protocol.

In addition, as to this individual complaint enforcement mechanism there is some limited support for the explanatory power of the external pressures theories. Regional ratification rates positively and significantly influenced ratification of CERD Article 14 and CAT Article 22. However, the findings on the effect of regional ratifications are not consistent across all of the four treaties in this category. Furthermore, the other relevant external pressures variable—level of aid—is not a significant predictor of ratification of any of these treaties. Thus, on the whole, the empirical evidence as to this level of enforcement mechanisms is rather inconclusive.

Another interpretation of these null results as to enforcement level 3, though, is that states do not view the individual complaint procedure as a very strong enforcement mechanism. If the individual complaint mechanism poses no credible threat, then states can commit without having to concern themselves with their ability to comply—meaning that the state's level of human rights ratings need not be figured into the ratification calculation. After all, the committees to which these individual complaints are referred are only empowered to attempt to persuade states to adopt their views and recommended remedies. Furthermore, there is evidence that, at least with regard to the CERD and the CEDAW, the individual complaint procedure mechanism is of little significance in practice. Jack Donnelly characterizes the procedure for considering individual complaints under the CERD as "largely moribund." He notes that the CEDAW committee has only issued several decisions under the individual complaint procedure since it was empowered to consider such complaints in 2000.[40]

The null findings regarding the CAT Optional Protocol (enforcement level 4), which are reported in Table 2.8, may be explained similarly. States may simply not view the treaty's enforcement mechanism as a credible threat since the committee overseeing that treaty is not empowered to act punitively or impose any sanctions for noncompliance.[41] Furthermore, as Henry Steiner notes regarding the Human Rights Committee, it is unlikely to pose a great threat to states as it thus far is able to consider only a small number of communications, most of its decisions receive little publicity or attention, and the suggested remedies—compensation,

Table 2.8 Level 4 enforcement mechanism: committee visits

Explanatory variables	*Hazard ratios*
	CAT Optional Protocol
Level of human rights	0.732
Level of democracy	1.215
Level of economic development	0.691
Difficulty of ratification process	0.832
Common law or not	1.71
Transitioning democracy or not	1.443
Level of aid	0.008
Regional ratifications	7.349
Number of countries	135
Number of ratifications	30
Number of observations	600

Note: *significant at 0.05; **significant at 0.01.

release of a prisoner, or changes to legislation—do not likely threaten state interests sufficiently.[42] Those same issues presumably prevail in connection with committees for each of the main international human rights treaties and affect how states view the enforcement mechanisms associated with treaty ratification.

Conclusion

Both the positive and null results from the quantitative analyses provide support for the explanatory power of the credible threat theory. The evidence shows that on the whole states with worse human rights practices act rationally and tend to avoid committing to the ICC and its stronger enforcement mechanism. However, those states quite readily embrace costless commitment and are just as likely as states with better human rights practices to join treaties that have weak enforcement mechanisms which cannot be used to punish the state for bad and noncompliant behavior.

The remaining chapters of the book use in-depth case studies to explore further the power of the credible threat theory and competing theories to explain state commitment to the ICC treaty and how enforcement mechanisms influence state ratification behavior.

Notes

1 George W. Downs, David M. Rocke, and Peter M. Barsoom, "Is the Good News about Compliance Good News about Cooperation?" *International*

Organization 50, no. 3 (1996): 383; Oona A. Hathaway, "The Cost of Commitment," *Stanford Law Review* 55, no. 5 (2003): 1856–57.

2 Hathaway, "The Cost of Commitment," 1823.

3 Emilie M. Hafner-Burton, "Trading Human Rights: How Preferential Trade Agreements Influence Government Repression," *International Organization* 59, no. 3 (2005): 593–94.

4 Downs, Rocke and Barsoom, "Is the Good News about Compliance Good News about Cooperation?" 383.

5 Jana von Stein, "Do Treaties Constrain or Screen? Selection Bias and Treaty Compliance," *American Political Science Review* 99, no. 4 (2005): 611.

6 Ibid.

7 Downs, Rocke and Barsoom, "Is the Good News about Compliance Good News about Cooperation?" 383.

8 Wade M. Cole, "Sovereignty Relinquished? Explaining Commitment to the International Human Rights Covenants, 1966–99," *American Sociological Review* 70, no. 3 (2005): 475–76.

9 Ibid.

10 Ibid.; Christine M. Wotipka and Kiyoteru Tsutsui, "Global Human Rights and State Sovereignty: State Ratification of International Human Rights Treaties, 1965–2001," *Sociological Forum* 23, no. 4 (2008): 737.

11 Downs, Rocke, and Barsoom, "Is the Good News about Compliance Good News about Cooperation?" 373, 388–92; Hathaway, "The Cost of Commitment," 1832, 1834–36.

12 Hathaway, "The Cost of Commitment," 1856–57.

13 Beth A. Simmons, "International Law and State Behavior: Commitment and Compliance in International Monetary Affairs," *American Political Science Review* 94, no. 4 (2000): 819–20.

14 Ibid.

15 Beth A. Simmons and Allison Danner, "Credible Commitments and the International Criminal Court," *International Organization* 64, no. 2 (2010): 233–36.

16 Andrew Moravcsik also posits a hand-tying theory to explain commitment to international human rights treaties, suggesting that new, transitioning democracies can outweigh the sovereignty costs associated with joining by locking in the treaty's democratic principles and thereby constraining the activities of future governments that may seek to subvert democracy. Andrew Moravcsik, "The Origins of Human Rights Regimes: Democratic Delegation in Postwar Europe," *International Organization* 54, no. 2 (2000): 225–30.

17 Wotipka and Tsutsui, "Global Human Rights and State Sovereignty," 736. For a specific argument about the influence of NGOs, see Michael J. Struett, *The Politics of Constructing the International Criminal Court: NGOs, Discourse, and Agency* (New York: Palgrave Macmillan, 2008), 6–7.

18 Hafner-Burton, "Trading Human Rights," 593–94; Wotipka and Tsutsui, "Global Human Rights and State Sovereignty," 734–35.

19 Wotipka and Tsutsui, "Global Human Rights and State Sovereignty," 735 (discussing states' tendencies to be concerned about appearing like their neighbors).

20 For this discussion about enforcement and legalization, I draw on the work of several scholars, including Darren Hawkins, "Explaining Costly

Institutions: Persuasion and Enforceable Human Rights Norms," *International Studies Quarterly* 48, no. 4 (2004): 781; Kenneth W. Abbott, Robert O. Keohane, Andrew Moravcsik, Anne-Marie Slaughter and Duncan Snidal, "Legalization and World Politics: An Introduction," *International Organization* 54, no. 3 (2000): 385; Jack Donnelly, "International Human Rights: A Regime Analysis," *International Organization* 40, no. 3 (1986): 606.

21 Kenneth W. Abbot and Duncan Snidal, "Hard and Soft Law in International Governance," *International Organization* 54, no. 3 (2000): 422–24.

22 Ibid.

23 Hawkins, "Explaining Costly Institutions," 781.

24 Human rights practices are measured using the Political Terror Scale, which is a generally recognized human rights measure obtained from reports issued by Amnesty International and the US Department of State. The reports assign country scores from 1 to 5 (with 1 being the best practices) by considering the presence of government practices that include murder, torture, forced disappearances, and political imprisonment. For this study, states with "better" human rights include those states with average human rights ratings of 2.5 and below, during the relevant time periods in which the various treaties could be ratified. States with "worse" human rights include those with average human rights ratings above 2.5 during the relevant time periods. The relevant time periods for ratification are 1965–2008 (ICCPR, ICESCR, and CERD); 1979–2008 (CEDAW); 1983–2008 (CAT); 1988–2008 (CRC); and 1997–2008 (ICC).

25 States with the worst ratings are those that consistently averaged above 2.5 on the Political Terror Scale (see note 24) during each of the five time periods relevant to the seven treaties.

26 For a comprehensive description of event history analysis, see Paul D. Allison, *Event History Analysis: Regression for Longitudinal Event Data* (Thousand Oaks, CA: Sage Publications, 1984).

27 Ibid.

28 This Political Terror Scale measure of a state's tendency to commit human rights violations better targets the concept than the measure Simmons and Danner used in their study of ICC commitment: namely, whether the state had experienced a civil war within the several-year period before the ICC treaty was available for ratification. "Credible Commitments and the International Criminal Court," 233–34, 237. First, Simmons and Danner counted civil wars as those with 25 battle deaths per year, notwithstanding that the widely used Correlates of War dataset classifies civil wars as those having over 1,000 yearly war-related casualties. In addition, the civil war data do not account for whether those deaths were the result of "criminal" action or other poor human rights practices by the government. Furthermore, in this instance I concluded it was more beneficial to use the Political Terror Scale measure, rather than the similar Cingranelli-Richards Physical Integrity Rights measure. First, Cingranelli-Richards do not report data until 1981—some five years after the Political Terror dataset begins reporting. Using the Political Terror Scale facilitates a comparison to the two other studies testing state commitment also to international human rights treaties which used that measure. See Wotipka and Tsutsui, "Global Human Rights and State Sovereignty," 743; Cole, "Sovereignty Relinquished?" 480.

29 Mark Gibney, L. Cornett, and R. Wood, "Political Terror Scale 1976–2008," politicalterrorscale.org. When possible, I averaged the two scores reported in an effort to mitigate any possible bias from using only one of the two. In addition, as did Cole in his study of state commitment to some human rights treaties, for the period between 1966 and 1976 (a time period relevant to the examination of several of the treaties), I extrapolate missing data points using a state's median score over the period 1976–84 if data are available. Cole, "Sovereignty Relinquished?" 475–76.

30 Monty G. Marshall, Ted Robert Gurr, and Keith Jaggers, *Dataset Users' Manual, Polity IV Project: Political Regime Characteristics and Transitions, 1800–2009*, 30 April 2010, www.systemicpeace.org/inscr/p4manualv2009.pdf.

31 Beth A. Simmons, *Mobilizing for Human Rights* (Cambridge: Cambridge University Press, 2009), 68.

32 Ibid., 71.

33 Moravcsik, "The Origins of Human Rights Regimes," 225–30.

34 See Simmons, *Mobilizing for Human Rights*, 385 (using ODA to capture the idea that states might be influenced to ratify human rights treaties because of the hope that by doing so they may obtain more access to aid).

35 Judith Kelley similarly found that a state's human rights ratings were a positive and significant predictor of ICC ratification in her examination of state decisions to sign bilateral immunity agreements with the United States exempting military personnel from surrender to the ICC. Judith Kelley, "Who Keeps International Commitments and Why? The International Criminal Court and Bilateral Nonsurrender Agreements," *American Political Science Review* 101, no. 3 (2007): 578–80. On the other hand, Goodliffe and Hawkins found little evidence that a state's human rights practices predicted whether the state supported a strong and independent ICC based on statements made during Rome Statute negotiations. That study, however, did not look at state ratification decisions, but instead quantified state positions regarding the court and commitment to it by coding statements state representatives had made during various negotiations of the Rome Statute. Jay Goodliffe and Darren Hawkins, "A Funny Thing Happened on the Way to Rome: Explaining International Criminal Court Negotiations," *Journal of Politics* 71, no. 3 (2009).

36 Substituting the Cingranelli-Richards human rights measure for the Political Terror measure produced similar results. States with better human rights practices were still significantly more likely than states with poor practices to commit to the ICC, but human rights practices did not predict state commitment to the treaties with the Level 1 enforcement mechanism.

37 See Cole, "Sovereignty Relinquished?" 483. On the other hand, Wotipka and Tsutsui found that state's human rights practices were significantly and negatively related to their tendency to ratify the six main human rights treaties. "Global Human Rights and State Sovereignty," 744–47. However, those scholars did not separately test commitment to each of the human rights treaties as this study does—and as Cole did for the two main treaties in his study. Rather, in Wotipka and Tsutsui's study the event examined was whether a state ratified any one of seven human rights treaties in a given year between 1965 and 2001. Ibid., 739.

38 Some 34 of the 60 states that have ratified Article 21 of the CAT similarly did not do so until 1990 or after.

39 Cole, "Sovereignty Relinquished?" tested the influence of enforcement mechanisms on ratification decisions, but only as to the ICCPR, the ICESCR, and the ICCPR Optional Protocol. He found that a state's level of human rights ratings did not predict ratification of the ICCPR (even as to Article 41 which allows state complaints) or the ICESCR. However, states with better human rights ratings were more likely to join the optional protocol—a fact that he attributed to the differing enforcement mechanisms between the main treaties and the optional protocol. Ibid., 485.

40 Donnelly, *International Human Rights* (Boulder, CO: Westview Press, 3rd edn, 2007), 87.

41 Henry J. Steiner, "Individual Claims in a World of Massive Violations: What Role for the Human Rights Committee?" in *The Future of UN Human Rights Treaty Monitoring*, ed. P. Alston and J. Crawford (Cambridge: Cambridge University Press, 2000), 37.

42 Ibid., 36–37.

3 The United States

For justice, but against relinquishing sovereignty

- **The United States and the international human rights regime**
- **Supporting the creation of an international criminal court, but one with limited powers**
- **Refusal to join the ICC**
- **Recent evidence of cooperation, but no treaty ratification**
- **The United States and the ICC: assessing the explanatory power of the credible threat theory**
- **Conclusion**

There are limits to what one can learn from large statistical analyses about why states commit to the International Criminal Court (ICC). Those analyses provide information about trends, but they cannot fully explain why any state or type of state joins the court or precisely how the ICC's stronger enforcement mechanism influences commitment decisions. This chapter, exploring in detail the United States' refusal to ratify the Rome Statute, is the first of several case study chapters tracing the ICC ratification behavior of particular states.

Studying the United States' ICC ratification behavior is critical to exploring the explanatory power of the credible threat theory. It shows how stronger enforcement mechanisms can discourage even a powerful state with relatively good human rights practices and good domestic law enforcement institutions from committing to an international human rights institution with powers to punish bad and non-compliant behavior.[1] The evidence shows that the United States backed the idea of an international criminal court, but it wanted a court that was more under the control of the United Nations (UN) Security Council. When the majority of states instead decided to support creating an ICC with broader powers, the United States refused to vote for the adoption of the Rome Statute. Given the United States' military presence abroad and significant role in worldwide peacekeeping efforts, it especially expressed concerns that the ICC might try to prosecute its military personnel for war crimes. The United States thereafter went on a campaign discouraging states from ratifying the ICC treaty and encouraging them to sign bilateral immunity agreements stating that they would refuse to surrender American military personnel to the ICC. Although the United States is a leader in promoting better human rights practices and accountability mechanisms, the evidence suggests that it viewed, and continues to view, the ICC's strong enforcement mechanism as a credible threat to state sovereignty.

The chapter begins with a brief discussion of the United States' involvement with the international human rights regime. It then explores the United States' role in the creation of the ICC and the positions it took on several core issues relating to the court's powers. The chapter follows by examining the country's refusal to ratify the ICC treaty and its relationship with the court since states adopted the Rome Statute. To conclude, the chapter assesses the explanatory power of the credible threat theory and the other theories discussed in Chapter 2 as they relate to the United States' ICC ratification behavior.

The United States and the international human rights regime

The United States' relationship to the international human rights regime is somewhat complicated. The country has relatively good domestic human rights practices and is a leader in promoting the spread of good human rights practices internationally. It uses its power and economic strength to encourage other states to improve their human rights practices and provides peacekeepers and conducts military interventions to aid in situations where human rights are being abused. Also, it took the lead in the Nuremburg prosecutions after World War II. Later in the 1990s, as the dominant power on the Security Council, the United States provided the key political support necessary to create the first ad hoc criminal tribunals. The United States advocated creating these institutions, prodded other states to cooperate with them, donated significant funds to operate them, and provided significant staff to the institutions.[2]

Yet, as Table 3.1 shows, the United States is also reluctant to commit itself to international human rights institutions. Unlike even states with bad practices, it has not ratified all of the main treaties with the weakest enforcement mechanisms. Of those six, the United States has ratified the International Covenant on Civil and Political Rights (ICCPR), the

Table 3.1 US commitment to the six primary international human rights treaties

Treaty	*Enforcement mechanism*	*Date open*	*Ratification date*
ICCPR	Reports	1966	1992
ICESCR	Reports	1966	–
CERD	Reports	1966	1994
CEDAW	Reports	1980	–
CAT	Reports	1984	1994
CRC	Reports	1989	–
ICCPR Art. 41	State complaints	1966	1992
CAT Art. 21	State complaints	1984	1994
ICCPR Opt.	Individual complaints	1966	–
CERD 14	Individual complaints	1966	–
CAT Art. 22	Individual complaints	1984	–
CEDAW Opt.	Individual complaints	1999	–
CAT Opt.	Committee visits	2003	–

International Convention on the Elimination of All Forms of Racial Discrimination (CERD), and the Convention Against Torture and Other Cruel, Inhuman or Degrading Treatment or Punishment (CAT). Even then, however, it ratified those treaties many years after they were available for signature. Regarding the treaties with stronger enforcement mechanisms, the United States has ratified none allowing for individual complaints. While the United States did ratify two treaties allowing for state complaints, it also likely knew that states were not using the mechanism. It may also have suspected that other states would be reluctant to risk retaliation by bringing a formal complaint against the world's superpower. Thus, the United States may ultimately have concluded that committing to these two treaties allowing for state complaints posed little threat to its sovereign rights to manage its domestic affairs.[3]

The reluctance of the United States to commit itself to these institutions is somewhat surprising given its apparent commitment to the cause of improving human rights practices. It also has relatively good human rights practices and should not generally expect to run afoul of treaty terms. Its behavior, though, shows that it carefully guards its sovereignty even in cases where it likely can comply with treaty terms and even where enforcement mechanisms are too weak effectively to punish bad and noncompliant behavior. As a world leader the United States may want to join international human rights treaties in order to set an example to other states, but as a superpower it may not feel the need to succumb to any external pressures to join an institution that may pose even a minimal threat to its sovereignty.

Supporting the creation of an international criminal court, but one with limited powers

In the early days of drafting the ICC treaty, the United States supported the idea of creating a permanent international criminal court. Indeed, commentators have noted that the court would not likely have become a reality had the United States been unwilling to engage in negotiations for its creation.[4] However, the United States backed the idea of a much weaker court and one over which it would be able to exercise some control. The discussion below describes the positions the United States took on the core issues of the court's exercise of jurisdiction, the role of the Security Council, and the powers granted to the prosecutor.

The issue of the court's jurisdiction

As mentioned in Chapter 1, early International Law Commission (ILC) drafts reflected state sovereignty concerns and allowed states to limit or extend their acceptance of the ICC's jurisdiction over particular crimes and/or for particular time periods. The 1994 ILC Draft only provided for "inherent" jurisdiction over the crime of genocide. For other crimes, states that could otherwise assert jurisdiction would have to consent specifically to the ICC's exercise of jurisdiction even if those states were parties to the court.[5]

By the Rome Conference, it became clear that states had differing views on when the court should be able to exercise jurisdiction over the several core crimes. Some states still favored a type of "opt-in" regime even for states parties. On the other hand, nongovernmental organizations (NGOs) and the like-minded group of states supported allowing the court to exercise automatic jurisdiction over all of the core crimes as to nationals of states parties. The United States was in the camp that favored less power for the court. It would allow the court to exercise automatic jurisdiction over genocide for states parties, but for other crimes it supported an opt-in regime.[6] When it became clear that many states were moving away from an opt-in regime, in the final week of the Rome Conference, the United States proposed a compromise position which was supported by the other permanent members of the Security Council. By that proposal, states parties would be permitted for a 10-year transitional period to opt out of the ICC's automatic jurisdiction over war crimes and crimes against humanity. The proposal, however, was not successful in garnering significant support from other states.[7] States instead agreed on Article 12 which grants the court "automatic" jurisdiction over genocide, crimes against humanity, and war crimes as regards states parties.

States also had differing views about whether the court should be able to exercise jurisdiction over the nationals of states that were not parties to the Rome Statute. One proposal submitted by the Republic of Korea (South Korea) obtained substantial support as time wore on.[8] The Korean proposal allowed the ICC to exercise jurisdiction over the nationals of states not party to the court as long as one of the following states with a connection to the crime had ratified the treaty: 1 the territorial state; 2 the custodial state; 3 the state of the accused's nationality; or 4 the state of the victim's nationality.[9]

However, the United States was not among the states favoring the approach proposed by South Korea. Instead, it argued that permitting the ICC to have jurisdiction over nationals of non-states parties would violate the Vienna Convention on the Law of Treaties, which provides that treaties cannot be binding on those not party to them.[10] It thus proposed limiting the court's exercise of jurisdiction over acts committed in the territory of non-states parties or by officials or agents of non-states parties to cases where the state or states in question consented to ICC jurisdiction.[11] Although others tried to convince the United States that the ICC treaty's complementarity provision would sufficiently protect it and other non-states parties from potentially politically motivated prosecutions, the United States was not persuaded. It explained that complementarity would not aid it in situations where other states accused the United States of wrongdoing in connection with humanitarian intervention or peacekeeping operations it had already authorized: the United States would likely conclude such actions did not merit prosecution, yet the ICC could decide thereafter to launch its own investigation.[12] At the conclusion of the Rome Conference, the majority of states rejected the United States' arguments and voted to allow ICC jurisdiction over nationals of non-states parties as long as either the territorial state or the state of the nationality of the accused had joined the court.[13]

The role of the Security Council

The 1994 ILC Draft also gave significant control over the ICC's docket to the Security Council. It contemplated that the Security Council could refer matters to the ICC acting under Chapter VII of the UN Charter without any requirement for state consent. It also provided that the ICC could not commence a prosecution without the approval of the Security Council if the matter arose out of a situation being dealt with by the Council under Chapter VII.[14]

As it turned out, permitting the Security Council to have a role in referring matters was a relatively uncontroversial concept. Early in the Rome Conference, the majority of states made clear they supported permitting the Council to refer cases to the ICC pursuant to its Chapter VII powers.[15] The final version of the Rome Statute codifies in Article 13(b) the Security Council's power to refer situations to the ICC.

The issue of whether and how the Security Council could defer matters that the ICC might otherwise pursue, though, proved to be quite controversial. The United States favored the 1994 ILC Draft position which read: "No prosecution may be commenced under this Statute arising from a situation which is being dealt with by the Security Council as a threat to or breach of the peace or an act of aggression under Chapter VII of the Charter, unless the Security Council otherwise decides."[16] The United States argued that the 1994 ILC Draft properly recognized the Security Council's primary responsibility for maintaining international peace and security which meant granting the Council the power to approve prosecutions.[17]

On the other hand, the like-minded group of states was concerned about granting too much power to the Security Council. They worried about curtailing the judicial independence of the ICC and also that the Council might seek to prevent referrals that were not in the interest of the Council's permanent members.[18] Indeed, William Schabas has argued that because matters threatening the peace would likely also constitute the kinds of atrocities that would interest the ICC prosecutor, this provision would effectively have given the Security Council a veto on potential prosecutions.[19] Ultimately, the majority of states ended up voting for a provision that was based on a proposal by Singapore—the Singapore Compromise—which allowed the Security Council to defer cases, but not to act as a gatekeeper for the ICC's docket.[20] With some revisions, the Singapore Compromise formed the basis for Article 16 of the Rome Statute which empowers the Security Council to defer an ICC prosecution for a renewable 12-month period by way of a resolution under Chapter VII.

The powers granted to the prosecutor

Finally, the 1994 ILC Draft did not grant the prosecutor power to initiate investigations on his own motion (*proprio motu*).[21] Instead, cases could only be commenced based on referrals from a state party or the Security Council. The pros and cons of allowing the prosecutor *proprio motu* powers were debated during the Ad Hoc Committee meetings in 1995 and during the 1996 Preparatory Committee, and eventually states clearly divided into two camps. By 1997, NGOs and the like-minded group of states were strongly behind the idea of *proprio motu* powers. They argued that these powers were essential to a strong and independent court which otherwise could face a situation where significant and important matters were not referred for political or diplomatic reasons.[22] Opponents, on the other hand, argued that an independent prosecutor might be tempted to initiate cases frivolously or for political reasons.[23] The United States was decidedly in the opponents' camp. It argued that the prosecutor should not be able to commence investigations or prosecutions unless the overall situation had been referred by either an ICC state party or the Security Council.[24]

Refusal to join the ICC

The vote against adopting the Rome Statute

When states decided to create an ICC that was not subject to significant Security Council control and that also had the potential to bring cases against the nationals of non-states parties, the United States joined only six other states in voting against the treaty's adoption.[25] It later explained that it would not support a treaty that would allow its soldiers to be potentially subjected to politically motivated prosecutions because of accidents that happen while those soldiers are abroad engaging in humanitarian or peacekeeping efforts.[26] The possibility that nationals of non-states parties could be subjected to ICC jurisdiction remained a primary concern that the United States continued to seek to address after the treaty was adopted. For example, on 7 December 2000, it presented a proposal to the Preparatory Commission that referenced the need to encourage states to contribute to world peacekeeping efforts. In the absence of a Security Council referral, that proposal would have allowed the ICC to determine the admissibility of any cases involving the surrender of a suspect charged with a crime that occurred outside the suspect's state of nationality.[27]

The United States signs the treaty while referencing its "significant flaws"

While that 7 December proposal was under review, and on the last day the Rome Statute was open for signature, on 31 December 2000 the United States nevertheless signed the treaty. President Bill Clinton explained that by signing, the United States was reaffirming its "strong support for international accountability and for bringing to justice perpetrators of genocide, war crimes, and crimes against humanity." On the other hand, the president also stated that the United States remained convinced the Rome Statute had "significant flaws." He emphasized "that when the Court comes into existence, it will not only exercise authority over personnel of states that have ratified the Treaty, but also claim jurisdiction over personnel of states that have not." Although President Clinton said signing the treaty was the appropriate action at that point, he also said that he could not recommend his successor (President George W. Bush was soon to take office) submit the treaty to the Senate for advice and consent until the United States' concerns about the treaty's significant flaws were satisfied.[28]

The United States "unsigns" the treaty and wages a campaign to exempt service personnel from ICC jurisdiction

When President Bush took office, he began addressing the "significant flaws" that President Clinton had referenced. However, instead of addressing the flaws by engaging with the court, the Bush Administration addressed them in a more actively hostile manner. First, it took the unusual step of "unsigning" the treaty in 2002. By a letter dated 6 May 2002, Under Secretary of State for Arms Control and International Security John Bolton informed UN Secretary-General Kofi Annan that the United States would not ratify the Rome Statute and that it accordingly "has no legal obligations arising from its signature on 31 December 2000."[29] Defense Secretary Donald Rumsfeld released a statement that same day stating that "[t]he United States will regard as illegitimate any attempt by the court or state parties to the treaty to assert the ICC's jurisdiction over American citizens."[30]

The United States followed the "unsigning" by stepping up its efforts to ensure that US service personnel could not be subjected to an ICC prosecution because of any acts committed by its troops abroad. In June 2002, just one month before the ICC came into being, the United States began lobbying the Security Council to adopt a resolution that would exempt from the ICC's jurisdiction any nationals of non-states parties taking part in missions established or authorized by the UN. When other Security Council members voiced their initial opposition to the idea, the United States responded by vetoing the renewal of the UN Peacekeeping Mission in Bosnia-Herzegovina and threatened to veto the renewal of all peacekeeping missions. On 12 July 2002, the Security Council ceded to the United States' wishes and adopted Resolution 1422, which grants ICC immunity to UN peacekeepers of states that had not ratified the Rome Statute for a 12-month renewable period.[31] In a press release, the UN Permanent Representative for the United States expressed pleasure over the adoption of Resolution 1422, stating that it was only a first step in protecting the country's citizens from the ICC. He noted that the country is "especially concerned that Americans sent overseas as soldiers, risking their lives to keep the peace or to protect us all from terrorism and other threats, be themselves protected from unjust or politically motivated charges."[32]

The United States followed the resolution with domestic legislative action and also a campaign to obtain agreements from states exempting US officials and military personnel from the court's jurisdiction. In July 2002, the United States enacted the American Service-Members' Protection Act of 2002 (ASPA).[33] While it is subject to certain exceptions, ASPA prohibits cooperation with the ICC; authorizes military action to secure the release of any American service members taken into ICC custody; and prohibits military assistance to states parties to the ICC that refuse to sign bilateral immunity agreements precluding the state from surrendering American officials or military personnel to the court.[34] Simultaneous with the passage of ASPA, the United States began encouraging states to sign bilateral immunity agreements. Though some states resisted the pressure to sign, the United States succeeded in negotiating agreements with more than 100 countries.[35]

Recent evidence of cooperation, but no treaty ratification

In recent years, the relationship between the United States and the ICC has become less overtly hostile and more cooperative. On the other hand, even with increased cooperation, the evidence shows that the United States remains wary of the court's powers. It has not revoked its decision to "unsign" the Rome Statute, nor has it joined the court. Its statements and actions also show that any increase in cooperation with the court must not infringe on state sovereignty or risk subjecting its military personnel to ICC prosecutions. The section below describes the turn away from hostility and the new era of cooperation in greater detail.

The second Bush Administration: an end to overt hostility

The United States' decision in 2005 to refrain from vetoing the Security Council's referral of the Darfur situation to the ICC provides some concrete evidence that the Bush Administration was backing away from any position of overt hostility.[36] The resolution supporting the referral was backed by 11 states, with the United States, China,

Algeria, and Brazil abstaining from the vote.[37] In a statement accompanying the passage of the resolution, the United States praised the international community for establishing "an accountability mechanism for the perpetrators of crimes and atrocities in Darfur" by adopting the resolution.[38] At the same time, though, it reiterated its fundamental objection "to the view that the Court should be able to exercise jurisdiction over the nationals, including government officials, of States not party to the Rome Statute." In fact, at the United States' request, the resolution included "a provision that exempted persons of non-Party States in the Sudan from the ICC prosecution."[39]

The Bush Administration's position on providing military aid to countries that had not signed bilateral immunity agreements with the United States also began to soften by the mid-2000s. Officials within the administration had criticized the policy stance, suggesting that it was actually negatively affecting the country's national security. Secretary of State Condoleezza Rice, in fact, commented in early 2006 on the risks to the United States of blocking military aid to nations seeking to combat terrorism.[40] In response to the criticism, by October 2006, the United States had amended ASPA to remove restrictions on providing military training to all nations.[41] By January 2008, the prohibitions on any kind of military assistance to countries that had not signed bilateral immunity agreements were repealed.[42]

The Obama Administration: increased cooperation, but continued sovereignty concerns

Since President Barack Obama assumed office in 2009, the United States has become more cooperative and engaged with the court. Yet, the evidence still shows a country that closely guards its sovereignty and is wary of the ICC's powers to punish bad and noncompliant behavior. President Obama's comment during his presidential campaign is illustrative of this position. He said that "the US should cooperate with ICC investigations in a way that reflects American sovereignty and promotes our national security interests."[43]

First, early in the Obama Administration, the United States began engaging with the ICC's Assembly of States Parties. The evidence shows that the United States saw a role for the court in holding individuals accountable for committing mass atrocities. However, the United States also knew that the states parties were moving towards a Review Conference wherein they would decide on the definition of aggression and related issues of how investigations of that crime would be triggered.[44] Thus, the United States had a selfish reason for participating in meetings of the ICC parties: it had not abandoned its concerns about the court's broad jurisdictional reach and it wanted to ensure that aggression was defined and triggered in a way that would least impinge on state sovereignty.

In fact, the United States sent one of the largest country delegations to the Kampala Review Conference in May 2010, despite the fact that it had still not ratified the Rome Statute. It built good will among the states parties to the court by formally pledging to: 1 continue to help build the legal capacity of some countries to prosecute mass atrocities; and 2 renew President Obama's commitment to support the ICC's efforts in its case involving Uganda to bring members of the Lord's Resistance Army to justice.[45] However, in addition, the United States actively sought to convince states that the Security Council should continue to play the primary role in making determinations of aggression and that non-states parties should not be subjected to ICC aggression investigations or prosecutions.[46] Statements made after the conclusion of the Kampala Review Conference suggest the United States believed it had been successful in convincing other states of the merits of its arguments. State Department Legal Advisor Harold Koh reported that "[t]he outcome on aggression … served [the United States'] core interests." He explained that US armed forces and other nationals could not be subjected to an aggression prosecution since the prosecutor cannot charge nationals of non-states parties with that crime. As to the triggering mechanism, the ICC would not be able to pursue an aggression case unless: 1 the Security Council determines aggression has occurred; or 2 the prosecutor otherwise offers a reasonable basis for the proceeding that is confirmed by the majority vote of six ICC judges. While Mr Koh indicated that the final resolution on aggression did not take sufficient "account of the Security Council's assigned role on aggression," he suggested the United States could continue to work on that issue going forward.[47]

That the United States was beginning to accept the court's existence and its usefulness—at least in regards to holding others accountable—is also evidenced by its vote to refer the Libya situation to the ICC for investigation.[48] In fact, the United States proposed adopting the resolution referring the matter to the court, along with France, Germany, and the United Kingdom.[49] However, the United States' support came with a requirement similar to that it had insisted upon in order to abstain from the vote on the Darfur referral: a special provision carving out from the ICC's jurisdiction any alleged crimes committed by non-parties to the ICC stemming from operations in Libya authorized by the Security Council.[50]

Finally, although it is still taking no steps to subject itself to the court's jurisdiction, the United States has recently made other small and large gestures to support the court. It issued a statement disapproving of Kenya's decision to invite President Omar Bashir of the Sudan (under an ICC arrest warrant) to attend Kenya's celebration of its new constitution in 2010.[51] President Obama also indicated the country's support for the prosecutor's decision to open an investigation against persons who had instigated Kenya's 2007 post-election violence, urging Kenya's leaders to cooperate fully with the ICC investigation.[52] The United States thereafter refused to back Kenya's bid to the Security Council to intervene to halt the ICC processes.[53] It has also offered to help protect witnesses who testify against Kenyan officials at the court.[54] In addition, the United States is supporting the collection of evidence for possible ICC prosecutions in connection with the conflict which began in 2011 in Syria. Furthermore, President Obama has dispatched 100 military advisors to help in the hunt for Lord's Resistance Army leader Joseph Kony, who has been the subject of an ICC arrest warrant since 2005.[55]

The United States and the ICC: assessing the explanatory power of the credible threat theory

That the United States has not committed to the ICC is, on its face, inconsistent with the credible threat theory. Nevertheless, the evidence indicates that cost of compliance concerns and the threat of the ICC's strong enforcement mechanism influenced the United States' decision to refuse to ratify the ICC treaty. The United States generally has good human rights practices, but since 2004 and its commitment to the "war on terror," the country's human rights ratings have been only average or below. Indeed, many have criticized the United States for some of the tactics it has allegedly used against suspects detained in connection with the war on terrorism.[56] The United States is also a country with a large military presence abroad—a fact that means it could be subjected to more potential war crimes claims than countries without such an international military presence. Thus, despite its generally good human rights practices, the United States' behavior is in many ways consistent with the credible threat theory since it could reasonably fear that its nationals could commit acts contrary to treaty terms or at least be accused of having done so.

Of course, the United States does have very good independent and capable domestic law enforcement institutions it could use to punish offenders. This fact should lessen any of its concerns about compliance costs and risks to its sovereignty should it join the court. However, as it has noted, under the ICC's system of complementarity, the ICC prosecutor and court make the final determination about whether a state's domestic processes are sufficient to avoid ICC jurisdiction. Therefore, even if the United States concludes that particular conduct does not warrant prosecution, the ICC could still conclude that its citizens should be prosecuted in The Hague. Also, the United States is not just any state. As Ruth Wedgewood explains, "[t]he worry of the United States is that in an unpopular conflict, there is a real chance that an adversary or critic will choose to misuse the ICC to make its point." She further notes, "The role of the United States in balance of power structures in Asia and Europe, and in support of transcontinental peacekeeping and peace enforcement operations, together with the deployment of 200,000 American troops abroad, may leave the United States in a unique position in regard to the Court."[57]

Indeed, the record is replete with evidence that the United States views the ICC's enforcement mechanism as a credible threat. During negotiations, it favored positions that would limit the independence of the court and the prosecutor and instead place them under the control of the Security Council where it is a permanent member. When it did not succeed in convincing other states to back a weaker court, it refused to vote for the adoption of the Rome Statute and thereafter "unsigned" the treaty. Its actions since the court has come into existence continue to demonstrate its concern that the court might seek to assert jurisdiction over its citizens. It lobbied the Security Council for Resolution 1422 exempting personnel of non-states parties who participate in authorized interventions and peacekeeping missions from ICC jurisdiction. It enacted ASPA and waged a campaign to encourage states to sign bilateral immunity agreements granting its military personnel immunity from ICC prosecutions. Even more recently, the United States remains careful to cooperate in a way that does not risk exposing its citizens to the court. For example, in connection with both the Darfur and Libya referrals, it negotiated an escape clause for non-states party personnel. Its stance during the negotiations over the definition and triggering mechanism for aggression further shows that the United States remains uncomfortable with an independent court and prosecutor with a broad jurisdictional reach.

It is true that the United States is in many ways unique. It is a world superpower, which adds to its concerns about being subjected to political prosecutions. It sends substantial troops abroad, increasing the risk that its citizens will be accused of committing war crimes even though the United States has generally good human rights practices.

Its status as a superpower also means that it may be better able than other states to disregard criticisms regarding its failure to bind itself and its people more fully to the international human rights regime. Nevertheless, this case study illustrates how even some powerful states with relatively good human rights practices may view the ICC's strong enforcement mechanism as a credible threat. Indeed, as the case studies in Chapter 5 show, the United Kingdom and France also expressed concerns about a strong and independent court and prosecutor outside of Security Council control. While these states did join the court, the case studies show that they did not do so without considering the ICC treaty's enforcement mechanism or the costs of complying with treaty terms.

Conclusion

This case study shows that the United States guards its sovereignty very closely and also prefers to have some control over the international institutions in which it participates. It has not broadly committed to international human rights treaties, even those with the weakest enforcement mechanisms. It has backed the international criminal ad hoc tribunals, but they pose no threat to state sovereignty. While the United States was behind the idea of an international criminal court, it wanted a much weaker court; since states instead decided to create a strong and independent court, the United States has refused to join.

What are the implications of the United States' refusal to join the ICC in terms of the court's legitimacy and ability to carry out its orders and aid in ending impunity for mass atrocities? Since the court depends on its members to enforce its orders, having the United States as a member would certainly be helpful. However, the evidence also shows that the United States is no longer actively opposing the court and in fact is lending its diplomatic, military, and other resources to help the court enforce its orders. The fact of the United States' changed position towards the court should not be lightly disregarded: it tends to show that the court is establishing itself as a legitimate institution in the fight against human rights abuses even without the United States' membership—so much so that the United States has been persuaded to assist in its functioning.

Notes

1 The United States scored a 1 on the Political Terror Scale between 1996 and 2001; a 2 between 2001 and 2003; and a 3 between 2004 and 2008. See Chapter 2, note 24 for an explanation of the scale. Between 1996 and 2008,

it scored an average of about 1.5 on the World Bank's Rule of Law Scale, which ranges between about -2.5 and 2.

2 Vijay Padmanabhan, "From Rome to Kampala: The U.S. Approach to the 2010 International Criminal Court Review Conference," *Council on Foreign Relations Special Report* (April 2010), 4, secure.www.cfr.org/publication/21934/from_rome_to_kampala.html.

3 The United States did not even ratify the Genocide Convention until 1986, and its reservations seek to eliminate the possibility that US citizens would be tried before an international court. Michael J. Struett, *The Politics of Constructing the International Criminal Court: NGOs, Discourse, and Agency* (New York: Palgrave Macmillan, 2008), 69.

4 Lee Feinstein and Tod Lindberg, *Means to an End: U.S. Interest in the International Criminal Court* (Washington, DC: Brookings Institution Press, 2009), 37 (noting that signals of American willingness to support the creation of a court helped reinvigorate negotiations).

5 See Elizabeth Wilmshurst, "Jurisdiction of the Court," in *The International Criminal Court: The Making of the Rome Statute: Issue, Negotiations, Results*, ed. Roy S. Lee (The Hague, The Netherlands: Kluwer Law International, 1999), 128.

6 Ibid., 135–36.

7 See David J. Scheffer, "Staying the Course with the International Criminal Court," *Cornell International Law Journal* 35, no. 1 (2001): 71.

8 Wilmhurst, "Jurisdiction of the Court," 136.

9 *Proposal of the Republic of Korea*, art. 8 (A/CONF.183/C.1/L.6), 1998.

10 Sharon A. Williams and William A. Schabas, "Article 12: Preconditions to the Exercise of Jurisdiction," in *Commentary on the Rome Statute of the International Criminal Court: Observers' Notes, Article by Article*, ed. Otto Triffterer (Baden-Baden, Germany: Nomos Verlagsgesellschaft, 2008), 553.

11 *Proposal Submitted by the United States of America* (Article 7 ter, UN Doc. A/CONF.183/C.1/L.90), 1998.

12 General Assembly, Summary record of the 9th meeting, para. 55 (A/C.6/53/SR.9), 21 October 1998.

13 Wilmhurst, "Jurisdiction of the Court," 138 (describing Article 12).

14 Lionel Yee, "The International Criminal Court and The Security Council: Articles 13(b) and 16," in *The International Criminal Court: The Making of the Rome Statute: Issue, Negotiations, Results*, 144.

15 Yee, "The International Criminal Court and The Security Council," 146–47.

16 1994 ILC Draft, art. 23(3).

17 Morten Bergsmo and Jelena Pejic, "Article 16: Deferral of Investigation or Prosecution," in *Commentary on the Rome Statute of the International Criminal Court* (Munich, Germany: Nomos Verlagsgesellschaft, 1999), 596.

18 Yee, "The International Court and The Security Council," 146–47; William A. Schabas, "United States Hostility to the International Criminal Court: It's All About the Security Council," *European Journal of International Law* 15, no. 4 (2004): 715.

19 Schabas, "United States Hostility to the International Criminal Court," 715.

20 Bergsmo and Pejic, "Article 16: Deferral of Investigation or Prosecution," 597.

21 Sharon A. Williams and William A. Schabas, "Article 13: Exercise of Jurisdiction," in *Commentary on the Rome Statute of the International Criminal Court*, 564.

22 Williams and Schabas, "Article 13: Exercise of Jurisdiction," 567.
23 Morten Bergsmo and Jelena Pejic, "Article 15: Prosecutor," in *Commentary on the Rome Statute of the International Criminal Court*, 583.
24 "The Concerns of the United States Regarding the Proposal for a *Proprio Motu* Prosecutor (June 22, 1998)," reprinted in "Is a U.N. International Criminal Court in the U.S. National Interest? Hearing Before the Subcomm. on International Operations of the Senate Comm. on Foreign Relations," 105th Cong. 129 (1998) [Senate Hearing], 147.
25 The other states voting against the treaty's adoption were China, Libya, Iraq, Israel, Qatar, and Yemen.
26 (A/C.6/53/SR.9), 21 October 1998.
27 *US Proposal* PCNICC/2000/WGICC-UN/DP.17. See Scheffer, "Staying the Course with the International Criminal Court," 60–63 (describing, as former head of the US delegation to the UN talks on the ICC, the reasons for the proposal and how the George W. Bush Administration failed to pursue it).
28 Statement by President Clinton: Signature of the International Criminal Court Treaty (31 December 2000), clinton4.nara.gov/textonly/library/hot_releases/December_31_2000.html.
29 State Department Press Release: "International Criminal Court: Letter to UN Secretary General Kofi Annan," 6 May 2002.
30 DoD News Release "Secretary Rumsfeld Statement on the ICC Treaty," www.defenselink.mil/releases/release/aspx?releaseid=3337.
31 S/RES/1422 (2002), 12 July 2002.
32 UN Press Release, "Vote About the International Criminal Court," 12 July 2002, 2001-9.state.gov/p/io/rls/rm/2002/11846.htm.
33 22 U.S.C., section. 7421 et seq. (2002).
34 For example, ASPA gives the president authority to waive the withdrawal of military aid if deemed necessary for the national interest. See H.R. 4475, Public Law 107–206, art. 2007. In addition, by the Dodd Amendment, the United States may still render "assistance to international efforts to bring to justice ... foreign nationals accused of genocide, war crimes or crimes against humanity." H.R. 4475, Public Law 107–206, art. 2015.
35 The website for the Coalition for the International Criminal Court lists the states that had signed bilateral immunity agreements with the United States as of 2006. See *Status of Bilateral Immunity Agreements*, www.iccnow.org/documents/CICCCFS_BIAstatus_current.pdf.
36 S.C. Res. 1593 (UN Doc. S/RES/1593), 31 March 2005.
37 Press Release, "Security Council Refers Situation in Darfur, Sudan to Prosecutor of the International Criminal Court," (SC/8351), 31 March 2005.
38 Ibid.
39 Ibid. See also S.C. Res. 1593, at para. 6.
40 Department of State, "Trip Briefing: Secretary Condoleezza Rice en Route to San Juan, Puerto Rico," 10 March 2006, www.state.gove/secretary/rm/2006/63001.htm.
41 John Warner National Defense Authorization Act for Fiscal Year 2008, H. R. 4986, art. 1212.
42 See H.R. 4775, Public Law 107–206 (as amended by the John Warner National Defense Authorization Act for Fiscal Year 2007, H.R. 5122, S.2766, signed into law 17 October 2006); and H.R. 4986, the National

Defense Authorization Act for Fiscal Year 2008, signed into law 28 January 2008, www.amicc.org/docs/ASPA_2008.pdf.

43 Statements of US Presidential Candidates on the International Criminal Court, AMICC (August 2008), www.amicc.org/docs/2008%20Candidates%20on%20ICC.pdf?tr=y&auid=3003692.

44 Although the UN Charter grants the Security Council the power to determine whether an act of aggression has occurred, the Charter does not define the crime of aggression. UN Charter, art. 39. Thus, at the Rome Conference, states had differing views on how the crime should be defined. At the conclusion of the conference when states failed to agree on a consensus definition for aggression, states adopted Resolution F, which among other things, provides that states would reconvene at a later date to renew those discussions. UN Doc. A/CONF.183/10 (1998).

45 US Pledges at the Review Conference, amicc.org/docs/Review_Conference_Pledges_by_the_US.pdf.

46 Harold Koh and Stephen Rapp, Briefing on the International Criminal Court Conference in Kampala, Uganda (June 2010), m.state.gov/md142585.htm.

47 Harold Koh and Stephen Rapp, "The U.S. and the International Criminal Court: Report From the Kampala Review Conference," ASIL/CFR Seminar (June 2010), 5, www.asil.org/files/Transcript_ICC_Koh_Rapp_Bellinger.pdf.

48 S.C. Res. 1970 (UN Doc. S/RES/1970), 26 February 2011.

49 Helene Cooper and Mark Landler, "Following U.S. Sanctions, U.N. Security Council to Meet on Libya," *The New York Times*, 27 February 2011.

50 See S.C. Res. 1970, para. 6 (exempting from the ICC's jurisdiction for the purposes of the referral "nationals, current or former officials or personnel from a State outside the Libyan Arab Jamahiriya which is not a party to the Rome Statute"). See also Marion Wong, "U.S. Support for the War Crimes Investigation of Libya Hinged on Exemption for Americans," *The Washington Current*, 2 March 2011 (reporting that the provision exempting nationals of non-ICC parties from prosecution was a "deal breaker" for the United States to support the Libya referral).

51 "Obama 'Disappointed' Kenya Hosted Sudan's Bashir," *Agence France-Presse*, 27 August 2010.

52 White House, "Statement by President Obama on the International Criminal Court Announcement," 15 December 2010.

53 Tom Odula, "US Opposes Kenya's Bid to Defer Int'l Trials of 6 Accused of Vote Violence that Killed 1,000," *AP*, 10 March 2011.

54 Alan Boswell, "U.S. to Help Protect Kenyan Violence Witnesses," *VOA News*, 11 February 2010.

55 "International Criminal Court Prosecutor: Kony will be Arrested in 2012," NDTV.com, 7 April 2012.

56 See Paul Reynolds, "Water-boarding as Torture—or Not," *BBC News*, 11 December 2007, news.bbc.co.uk/2/hi/americas/7138144.stm; "Rendition: Tales of Torture," *BBC News*, 7 December 2005, news.bbc.co.uk/2/hi/americas/4502986.stm.

57 Ruth Wedgewood, "The International Criminal Court: An American View," *European Journal of International Law* 10, no. 1 (1999): 102–4.

4 Germany

A strong country leads the way to a strong court

- **International human rights norms and accountability: the German evolution in attitude and behavior**
- **Strong leadership role in negotiations and support for a strong court**
- **Germany's record on ICC commitment and compliance**
- **Germany and the ICC: assessing the explanatory power of the credible threat theory**
- **Conclusion**

This chapter traces Germany's decision to commit to the International Criminal Court (ICC) and the role the court's strong enforcement mechanism played in influencing Germany's ratification behavior. Germany is like the United States in that it is a powerful, wealthy democracy with generally good human rights practices and domestic institutions that follow the rule of law.[1] However, unlike the United States, Germany took a leadership role by pushing for a strong and independent ICC. It also promptly signed and ratified the ICC treaty, and it has been a leader in encouraging other states to ratify and to comply with treaty terms. Germany also went on record opposing the United States' decision to seek bilateral immunity agreements.

Because Germany enjoys high human rights ratings and has good domestic law enforcement institutions, its decision readily to ratify the Rome Statute may not seem surprising. Germany should not expect to suffer a significant sovereignty loss by joining the court since its practices and policies are already consistent with treaty terms. Yet, that Germany would be a leader in pushing for a strong and independent ICC was not a foregone conclusion. Germany was responsible for a horrendous genocide in connection with World War II, and for decades after Germany rejected the idea of international accountability for acts committed by its leaders and soldiers. During those same decades Germany also avoided joining international human rights treaties with stronger enforcement mechanisms. Only in the late 1990s with generational change and after it had improved its own domestic human rights practices did Germany's attitude towards international mechanisms of accountability change. The evidence shows that Germany's decision to take a leadership position in backing a strong and independent ICC was colored by its desire to distance itself from its shameful past. However, it also shows that Germany understood the strength of the ICC's enforcement mechanism and committed only after ensuring that its own citizens would not be subjected to international criminal prosecution.

This chapter begins with background on Germany's past human rights abuses and the evolution of its attitudes and behavior as relates to international human rights norms and accountability for human rights abuses. The chapter then traces Germany's role in the creation of the ICC and its leadership position in arguing for a strong and independent court and prosecutor. It follows by looking at Germany's decision to ratify the Rome Statute in December 2000 and the actions it has taken to comply with the treaty. The chapter concludes by assessing the power of the credible threat theory and other competing theories to explain Germany's ratification decision.

International human rights norms and accountability: the German evolution in attitude and behavior

World War II crimes and Nuremberg: sovereign rights, not international accountability

It took several decades for Germany to evolve from the country it was during World War II to the rights-respecting nation it is today. During World War II, German soldiers waged war on civil populations, destroyed much of Europe, and massacred prisoners of war. The war also served as a cover for the Nazi plan to exterminate Europe's Jewish population (as well as its Gypsy and gay population)—committing what British Prime Minister Winston Churchill later called "probably the greatest and most horrible single crime ever committed in the whole history of the world."[2] Indeed, the Allied powers that won the war—the United States, Great Britain, France, and Russia—concluded that the conduct of Germany's leaders and soldiers was so heinous that it required international punishment. The Allies established the Nuremberg Tribunal and charged Germans with having committed crimes against peace, war crimes, and crimes against humanity.[3] The Nuremberg trials against 22 indicted defendants commenced on 20 November 1945.[4] Judgment was rendered on 1 October 1946. Twelve defendants received the death sentence, three were acquitted, and the remaining defendants were sentenced to varying terms of imprisonment.[5]

The evidence, however, suggests that Germany and many of its people were resentful of the Nuremberg trials and unconvinced that the atrocities committed by Germans were deserving of international punishment. First, many argued that the Nuremberg Tribunal was without jurisdiction because the crimes Germans were charged with committing were not in fact crimes under international or domestic law at the time they were committed.[6] In addition, many believed that the justice dispensed at Nuremberg and thereafter was "victor's justice"—and thus a form of injustice—in that it focused only on German wrongdoing while ignoring crimes committed by the Allies.[7] The fact that the Allies prosecuted Germans for some acts that occurred solely within Germany was a particularly sore point: at least some Germans viewed charging the defendants with criminal acts on this basis as a unique invasion of their sovereign rights to conduct their domestic affairs as they saw fit. Hitler's deputy Goering, in fact, declared at the Nuremberg trials: "But that was our right! We were a sovereign State and that was strictly our business."[8]

Although these arguments about the unjustness of the Nuremberg trials do not excuse German atrocities or make them any less deserving of international approbation, it bears noting that some scholars have also criticized the Nuremberg trials for similar reasons. There is significant debate about whether by charging and convicting Germans of crimes against humanity, the Tribunal applied law retroactively since that crime had not been clearly defined by international law when the acts were committed.[9] Even the crime of genocide was not clearly defined as an international crime until 1948 with the adoption of the Genocide Convention.[10] On the other hand, others defend the Allied decision to prosecute the German genocidal acts against Jews as crimes against humanity, noting that in the absence of the Nuremberg trials, the acts would have likely gone unpunished.[11] Moreover, although some of the acts with which the defendants were charged may not have been specifically criminalized, the Nuremberg trials proceeded on the theory that the acts were so heinous that the defendants could not claim they did not know they were committing crimes in the opinion of the world community.

For the purposes of this study, however, the point is not whether the Nuremberg trials properly applied international law, but rather how Germany perceived the conduct of its people and how it responded to the idea of international accountability. Here, the evidence suggests that Germans on the whole did not acknowledge their own culpability. The US State Department came to a similar conclusion in 1953:

> The German position on the trials of war criminals is a problem which has continued to trouble us ever since the trials were held. The Germans have failed to accept the principles on which the trials were based and do not believe that those convicted were guilty. Their attitude is very much sentimental and cannot be influenced by arguments or an objective statement of the facts. They adhere to the view that the majority of the war criminals were soldiers who were punished for doing what all soldiers do in war, or indeed were ordered to do.[12]

In fact, the German government later negotiated its non-recognition of the judgments in the various Nuremberg follow-up trials in the Convention on the Settlement of Matters Arising out of the War and the Occupation, further evidencing Germany's refusal to view its soldiers' actions as illegal under international law.[13] Later, Germany went even further when it sought to pardon persons who had been convicted in the follow-up trials conducted by the occupying powers. Many of those prisoners were released—apparently in exchange for Germany's promise to agree to take the side against the rising threat of communism.[14]

A shift in attitude: embracing international human rights norms

Although Germany resisted the efforts of the international community to hold its citizens accountable for acts committed during World War II, the evidence shows that after the war, Germany began a decades-long process of reforming its domestic policies and practices to conform to international human rights norms. In 1958, the government established the Central Investigative Agency for Nazi Crimes, which was tasked with carrying out investigations of crimes against humanity Germans allegedly committed outside Germany during the war.[15] A new generation of younger prosecutors, determined to ensure crimes did not go unpunished, brought charges against some 6,000 Nazi defendants over two decades. In doing so, they waged battle against an older, largely former Nazi judiciary willing to turn a blind eye to Nazi injustice. The battle was hard fought and some defendants were found not guilty or convicted of lesser crimes (murder instead of crimes against humanity).[16] Yet, with these prosecutions over two decades, attitudes about what behavior was criminal and the need for accountability began to change.

A real change in attitude and behavior commenced in the 1990s with German reunification and in response to the abuses that East Germans had suffered while under Russian rule. Following the fall of the Berlin

Wall, West German courts were called upon to judge the criminality of various acts that had occurred in East Germany—such as fatal shootings at the Berlin Wall or alleged miscarriages of justice that occurred during political trials under communism. During the trials, West German judges were presented with many of the same defenses the defendants had raised at the Nuremberg trials—most particularly, the defense of superior orders and the principle of non-retroactivity of the criminal law. In the 1990s, however, West German judges rejected such defenses, concluding that inhumane laws permitting state-sponsored crime would have to yield to justice and a respect for human rights.[17]

Also in the 1990s, the government finally and more fully made attempts to remedy the injustices that had been done within Germany and against Germans using state laws under Nazism. True, the government did act to repeal the most heinous of the Nazi laws immediately after World War II. Thus, the laws allowing for persecution on racial and religious grounds, allowing for arbitrary death sentences and the like, were promptly taken off the books. However, immediately after the war, Germany was under the influence of the Allied powers which were working to dismantle the Nazi regime, including the discriminatory laws against the Jewish people. Only many years later, however, did Germany finally void the judgments that were entered during the period of Nazi rule by which persons were convicted for their race or status or because they acted against the regime. For example, not until 1998 did the state dismiss the criminal judgments carried out during the Nazi period by the Nazi SS (*SchutzStaffel*, or special police force) courts.[18]

None of the above evidence demonstrates that there was an exact point at which German attitudes towards human rights and their Nazi past changed or that the change was an unequivocal one or without inconsistencies. The evidence does suggest, though, that with a generational shift, and also because of learning based on experiences in East Germany under Russian rule, German behavior and attitudes towards protecting individuals against human rights abuses changed for the better. Younger Germans who had not participated in World War II and who had not been indoctrinated into Nazi ideology seemed most eager to confront Germany's past atrocities and ensure that at least some of its Nazi criminals were brought to justice.

Germany and the international human rights regime: commitment follows domestic reforms

Table 4.1 shows how Germany's commitment to the international human rights regime mirrored its domestic shift in behavior and

Table 4.1 Germany's commitment to the six primary international human rights treaties

Treaty	*Enforcement mechanism*	*Date open*	*Ratification date*
ICCPR	Reports	1966	1973
ICESCR	Reports	1966	1973
CERD	Reports	1966	1969
CEDAW	Reports	1980	1985
CAT	Reports	1984	1990
CRC	Reports	1989	1992
ICCPR Art. 41	State complaints	1966	2001
CAT Art. 21	State complaints	1984	2001
ICCPR Opt.	Individual complaints	1966	1993
CERD 14	Individual complaints	1966	2001
CAT Art. 22	Individual complaints	1984	2001
CEDAW Opt.	Individual complaints	1999	2002
CAT Opt.	Committee visits	2003	2008

attitudes toward human rights abuses and accountability. It also suggests that Germany's ratification behavior is influenced by compliance cost concerns. In the early decades after World War II and when Germany was still transitioning to a country that respected international human rights norms, Germany joined only several international human rights treaties with the weakest enforcement mechanisms. Because the treaties only required states to file reports about their behavior to a committee with non-binding powers, Germany could ratify them without worrying that a failure to comply with treaty terms would result in punishment.

However, Germany did not ratify most of the treaties containing procedures for state complaints, individual complaints, or committee visits until the 2000s—until after reunification and after it had put in place domestic policies and practices to punish human rights abuses. By the 2000s, in fact, Germany's human rights practices were among the very best.[19] Thus, it could rationally conclude that committing to treaties with stronger enforcement mechanisms would not be costly since it could expect to be able to comply with treaty terms.

Strong leadership role in negotiations and support for a strong court

At the same time it was increasingly binding itself to international human rights treaties with stronger enforcement mechanisms, Germany also began playing a leadership role in the creation of the ICC. Germany was an early member and a leader of the like-minded group of states that supported a strong and independent ICC.[20] Indeed, it submitted and supported proposals to create an even stronger international criminal court than the one that was created. The discussion below describes the positions Germany took on several core issues that were the subject of ICC negotiations, including: 1 the court's exercise of jurisdiction; 2 the powers of the prosecutor to commence cases; and 3 the issue of surrendering state nationals to the ICC.

The issue of the court's jurisdiction

First, and in great contrast to the position taken by the United States on the court's jurisdictional scope, Germany argued for a court that could exercise universal jurisdiction over genocide, crimes against humanity, and war crimes. By its February 1996 proposal and its March 1998 discussion paper, Germany argued that the ICC should be able to exercise universal jurisdiction over all of the core crimes with no further state consent necessary.[21] It based its position on customary international law, which it noted permitted all states to exercise universal jurisdiction over those crimes. It explained that since ratifying states officially and formally would be accepting the ICC's jurisdiction over the core crimes, the ICC should also "be competent to prosecute persons which have committed one of these core crimes, regardless of whether the territorial State, the custodial State or any other State has accepted jurisdiction of the Court."[22] Germany remained committed to the idea of universal jurisdiction through the Rome Conference.[23]

Although the German universal jurisdiction proposal was supported by nongovernmental organizations (NGOs) and many of the like-minded group, it was eliminated from consideration as an option by 6 July 1998 after it had become clear that many powerful states—the United States being one—would not vote for it.[24] Thus, Germany accepted a compromise position on jurisdiction and agreed to the jurisdictional framework outlined in Article 12 of the Rome Statute. Although Germany's representatives later expressed disappointment that states did not agree to an ICC with universal jurisdiction, they also suggest that Germany helped broaden the ICC's jurisdictional scope from what was originally contemplated by the 1994 International Law Commission (ILC) Draft.[25]

The role of the prosecutor

Regarding the mechanism for triggering ICC prosecutions, Germany's position again differed significantly from that of the United States.

Germany was consistently in the camp of the like-minded group of states and favored an independent prosecutor with *proprio motu* powers to commence prosecutions without any input from states or the United Nations (UN) Security Council. As discussed in Chapter 3, opponents, including the United States, argued that an independent prosecutor might be tempted to initiate cases frivolously or for political reasons.[26] Like the issue of jurisdiction, the issue of the prosecutor's powers became so contentious that it became clear a compromise was necessary. Germany and Argentina proposed the compromise solution which eventually became Article 15 of the Rome Statute.[27] To assuage their opponents, they suggested some limited controls on the prosecutor's powers to mount investigations: the prosecutor would initially be able to conduct a preliminary investigation, but could proceed further only with the court's approval. Eventually, states agreed to this proposal because it reduced the power held in the hands of one individual, while at the same time ensuring another triggering mechanism in addition to a state or Security Council referral.[28]

The issue of surrendering state nationals

Another great debate concerned the surrender of state nationals to the court. Here, again, Germany's position was counter to that of the United States. At the time of the Rome Conference, Germany's constitution prohibited the extradition of nationals. Nevertheless, Germany favored the conclusion of the like-minded group—namely, that the prohibition would be inapplicable in the context of handing persons over to the ICC.[29] Germany also took a leading role in persuading other states to adopt this same view.[30] Its representatives, Hans-Peter Kaul and Claus Kress, argued that an ordinary "horizontal" approach to cooperation, whereby states guarded their sovereignty in response to extradition requests from other states, was inappropriate "in the context of an international judicial body responsible for judging international core crimes."[31] They stressed the importance of prosecuting international crimes and the need to support that goal by supporting the court's complementarity regime, which Kaul and Kress suggested states should view as an extension of their own national jurisdictions.[32] Eventually, states were persuaded of the correctness of Germany's position, and the Rome Statute requires states to surrender their own nationals to the court should they be unwilling or unable to prosecute them domestically.[33]

Germany's record on ICC commitment and compliance

Germany not only argued for a strong and powerful ICC, but also promptly ratified the ICC treaty and has been vocal in encouraging other states to ratify and also comply with their treaty obligations. Furthermore, by its actions, Germany has shown that its commitment is sincere and that it understands the strength of the ICC's enforcement mechanism. It committed to the court knowing that it had the kinds of policies and practices that should not cause it to run afoul of treaty terms. It also passed domestic implementing legislation—meaning that it can now domestically prosecute any mass atrocities should they occur. Finally, it resisted the United States' request to sign a bilateral immunity agreement and sought to discourage other states from signing such agreements.

The section that follows elaborates on each of these points.

Signing and ratification

Germany promptly committed to the ICC. It signed the treaty on 10 December 1998. Thereafter, it began the process of passing a bill allowing it to ratify the Rome Statute. On 27 October 2000, at the third reading of the ratification bill, Germany's legislature unanimously approved ratifying the Rome Statute. At the invitation of Hans-Peter Kaul, Whitney R. Harris, a member of the US prosecuting team at Nuremberg, attended that reading. He has confirmed that after extensive discussion, the bill was approved without a single dissenting vote, a fact he suggests shows Germany's "approval of the principles of the Nuremberg Trial."[34] Thereafter, on 11 December 2000, Germany became the 25th state to join the court.

National implementing legislation

Germany did not cease its commitment to the court upon ratification. It also amended its national laws to allow it to: 1 prosecute the ICC crimes domestically; and 2 cooperate with the court in various ways, including by surrendering its own nationals.

First, in June 2002, the German legislature implemented the substantive provisions of the Rome Statute by passing the Code of Crimes Against International Law (CCAIL).[35] By the CCAIL, and for the first time in its history, Germany criminalized "war crimes" and "crimes against humanity." Further, although Germany had criminalized genocide under its domestic laws after it ratified the Genocide Convention, by the CCAIL, Germany updated terminology regarding that crime to make it consistent with the Rome Statute.[36] Thus, the CCAIL allows Germany to prosecute any of the ICC's core crimes domestically should they occur.

It is worth noting that compliance with the Rome Statute does not by its terms specifically require states to incorporate prohibitions against the covered crimes into domestic law. But by choosing to implement such legislation, Germany has made itself better able to comply with treaty terms and avoid sovereignty losses since it can prosecute any treaty violations domestically, rather than having its citizens tried in The Hague. As Hans-Peter Kaul explained, without amending its domestic laws, Germany would not have been able to punish war crimes or crimes against humanity per se.[37] Its charging choices would have been restricted to crimes such as murder or inflicting grave bodily harm. In addition, the state wanted to clarify that universal jurisdiction covered these mass atrocities by including that provision in a new draft code for international crimes since Germany's judiciary had previously interpreted restrictively universal jurisdiction in its criminal code for genocide. Furthermore, Kaul explained that Germany had to reformulate these crimes in order to satisfy the constitutional requirement that a crime must have been determined clearly and specifically prohibited at the time the act was committed.[38]

Germany also amended its constitution and laws in order to allow it to cooperate with the ICC. On 4 December 2000, Germany amended its constitution (Basic Law 16) to permit German nationals to be surrendered to the ICC.[39] Contemporaneously with the passage of the CCAIL, Germany also passed the Law on Cooperation with the International Criminal Court (ICC Cooperation Act).[40] That Act governs, among other things, Germany's obligations to cooperate with the ICC in surrendering suspects.[41] It addresses other aspects of cooperation as well, such as enforcing any orders of forfeiture issued by the ICC.[42]

Germany's global leadership role in advancing commitment and compliance

Germany's commitment to the court also extends to using its leadership role to call on other states to commit and comply. In a ratification press release, Hans-Peter Kaul "reiterated his country's firm hope that States that had not done so would sign and ratify the Rome Statute as early as possible." Post-ratification, Kaul has also encouraged states to promote the universal character of the ICC and to persuade other states to join.[43] He has particularly beseeched the United States promptly to join the court.[44] Kaul continues to appeal to the United States, arguing that the court needs American support politically, morally, and materially.[45]

In addition, Germany has demonstrated its commitment to the ICC and treaty goals by voicing opposition to the bilateral immunity agreements the United States was asking states to sign.[46] Recall that those agreements require states to refuse to surrender American government or military personnel to the jurisdiction of the ICC—even if those states are already members of the ICC. Although numerous states ultimately signed such agreements, Germany went on record opposing them on the grounds that they appeared to undermine the court and state obligations to the court.

All of the above actions demonstrate Germany's commitment to the ICC and its intention to comply with treaty terms. They also evidence a country that is determined to ensure that its commitment will not result in a costly sovereignty loss by having its citizens prosecuted in The Hague.

Germany and the ICC: assessing the explanatory power of the credible threat theory

Based on the evidence outlined above, Germany's behavior in ratifying the Rome Statute is consistent with the credible threat theory and the argument that states that are more able to comply with treaty terms are also more likely to commit to treaties with strong enforcement mechanisms. Germany's human rights and rule of law ratings suggest that its costs of complying with the treaty will be minimal, and it will face little risk that its citizens will be subjected to an ICC prosecution for having committed mass atrocities. Moreover, Germany has gone further to minimize that risk by passing the CCAIL. The very fact that it passed that law is also evidence that Germany views the ICC's enforcement mechanism as a credible threat since Germany has responded to the ICC treaty by ensuring that it can domestically prosecute any mass atrocities in the event they occur.

This is not to say that Germany does not expect some benefits as a result of joining the ICC. By being a leader in pushing for the court, Germany has helped to distance itself from its shameful past. Germany also benefits if by self-binding it also manages to encourage other weaker states to join the court. Like other wealthy and powerful states, Germany has the potential of saving money and other resources in the long run if there is an organization in place that is set up to prosecute *the citizens of other states* for mass atrocities—particularly one that might be able to deter those atrocities before they even occur. Yet, the evidence still shows that Germany did not commit to the ICC without ensuring that its leaders and citizens would not be the subject of an ICC investigation and prosecution.

Germany's role in creating the ICC and also committing to the court is striking given its history of human rights abuses and its earlier refusal to accept that the international community should be able to hold perpetrators of human rights abuses accountable for their actions. However, those times have passed. This case study has shown that beginning in the 1960s and continuing through the 1990s, a new generation of younger Germans began playing a greater role in shaping state policy. As a result, Germany revised its domestic policies and practices so that they were more in line with international human rights norms. That the human rights ratings assigned to Germany by outside entities were also very high during the 1990s provides additional evidence that Germany had evolved into a state that respected and protected human rights. Accordingly, an exogenous change in Germany's own practices and policies caused it to be the kind of state that would support a strong and independent ICC to which it promptly committed. Because Germany had good human rights practices and good domestic law enforcement institutions by the time it participated in ICC negotiations and thereafter, Germany acted consistently with the credible threat theory and ratified the ICC treaty.

Although compliance costs related to ICC treaty terms and the credible threat theory may not completely explain all aspects of Germany's ratification behavior, it better explains Germany's swift commitment to the ICC than do the other relevant theories. First, this is not a case where the credible commitment theory is even relevant, since at the time of ratification, Germany possessed, and continues to possess, good human rights ratings.

Second, the evidence shows that Germany did not ratify because of external pressures. Even amongst the like-minded group, Germany was a leader in pushing for a strong and independent court. It proposed the court have universal jurisdiction over the ICC crimes, taking a position contrary to the United States. While NGOs tended to favor the same positions as those advocated by Germany and the like-minded group, the evidence does not suggest that Germany blindly followed the suggestions of NGOs or committed to the court because of NGO pressures. Further, this is not a situation where Germany took positions or ratified the ICC treaty in order to please other nations that might be able to provide it with benefits. In fact, it repeatedly stood up to the United States, a powerful country which it counts amongst its greatest allies and supporters.

In addition, by committing to the court so promptly, Germany acted contrary to the predictions of some of the other rationalist view theories. Unlike other powerful nations with large military presences like the United States and China, Germany ratified the ICC treaty. By its negotiating presence and the fact that it passed domestic legislation codifying into its national laws the crimes covered by the ICC treaty, Germany obviously knew that the treaty covers war crimes. However, because its domestic human rights practices are good and because it has the domestic institutions and laws to enable it to prosecute any war crimes domestically, Germany could still act rationally in concluding the costs of ICC commitment would be minimal from a sovereignty standpoint.

Furthermore, Germany promptly ratified the ICC treaty despite its difficult domestic ratification processes—and by unanimous vote. Recall that theory predicts that states with more difficult ratification processes will be less likely or slower to ratify international treaties. Even though Hans-Peter Kaul and Claus Kress, among others, played great leadership roles during ICC negotiations, and even though they may have acted to persuade others within Germany to accept the idea of the ICC, the record shows that Germany's entire government was behind ICC ratification. Accordingly, this is not a case where rational concerns fell by the wayside because of the interests of a few individuals. Instead, the evidence suggests that Germany's ratification decision was based on rational cost-of-compliance concerns. It committed knowing that it had good human rights practices and good domestic law enforcement institutions, and it passed domestic implementing legislation to ensure further compliance. Not only does this show that Germany's support for the court expands well beyond the individuals who were engaged in ICC negotiations, but it also shows that the German government as a whole was well aware of the commitment it was making by joining the court.

Finally, theories about locking in state behavior for newly democratizing countries or hand-tying for states that have recently experienced civil wars cannot explain Germany's decision to ratify the ICC treaty. Germany was not a new democracy when it joined the ICC. Nor had it very recently experienced civil wars or a situation where its government was inclined to respond violently in response to challenges to its power. Moreover, the evidence does not suggest Germany would have joined the court if its practices were not already consistent with treaty terms. After all, Germany acted swiftly to pass domestic legislation criminalizing the exact conduct covered by the ICC treaty. It did so absent a requirement for implementing legislation and even though some states have concluded such legislation is not necessary.

Nevertheless, while Germany's behavior in ratifying the ICC treaty is consistent with the credible threat theory, this case study reveals that individuals—in particular Hans-Peter Kaul—may have played a role in causing Germany to become a leader in pushing for a strong and independent ICC. Kaul was a leader in Germany's delegation in ICC negotiations from the very beginning, and he is a person who shares his views about the importance of the ICC with the world community through his speaking engagements and written works. In fact, Claus Kress has credited Kaul as being instrumental in shaping Germany's new approach towards international criminal law.[47] Because of Kaul and Kress, Germany may have taken on an even greater leadership role in pushing for a strong and independent ICC than one might ordinarily expect from a country with good human rights practices—even from a country like Germany that has reasons to distance itself from its past. The evidence, however, still shows that Germany committed to the ICC rationally and with knowledge that for it, ratification would pose few risks that its citizens would face an ICC prosecution.

Conclusion

From the beginning of ICC negotiations, Germany pushed for a strong and independent court with significant powers to ensure that states ratifying the ICC treaty are also held accountable for respecting and furthering treaty goals and terms. It has also used its influence to encourage states to commit to the court and comply with its terms. The evidence shows that Germany's behavior has been influenced by some strong individuals who took the opportunity to distance the country from its genocidal past and demonstrate that it could take a leadership role in protecting against human rights abuses. However, the evidence also shows that Germany committed to the ICC only after concluding that it could comply with treaty terms and not risk having its citizens prosecuted in The Hague.

To put Germany's commitment decision in greater context, the next chapter examines the ratification behavior of three other wealthy and powerful states: Canada, France, and the United Kingdom. All three states have joined the court, but as the case studies show, not all three demonstrated Germany's leadership and constant support for creating an international human rights institution with a strong enforcement mechanism to punish bad and noncompliant behavior.

Notes

1 Germany scored between 1 and 2 on the Political Terror Scale between 1998 and 2008 (see Chapter 2, note 24 for an explanation of the scale). During those same years, it typically scored about 1.7 on the World Bank's Rule of Law Scale (see Chapter 3, note 1 for an explanation of this).
2 Gary Jonathan Bass, *Stay the Hand of Vengeance: The Politics of War Crimes Tribunals* (Princeton, NJ: Princeton University Press, 2000), 193.
3 Herman von Hebel, "An International Criminal Court—A Historical Perspective," in *Reflections on the International Criminal Court: Essays in Honour of Adriaan Bos*, ed. H.A.M. von Hebel, J.G. Lammers and J. Schukking (The Hague, The Netherlands: T.M.C. Asser Press, 1999), 19–20; Antonio Cassese, "From Nuremberg to Rome: International Military Tribunals to the International Criminal Court," in *The Rome Statute of the International Criminal Court: A Commentary*, ed. Antonio Cassese, Paola Gaeta, and John R.W.D. Jones (Oxford: Oxford University Press, 2002), 7.
4 Von Hebel, "An International Criminal Court—A Historical Perspective," 19; Whitney R. Harris, "A World of Peace and Justice Under the Rule of Law," in *The Nuremberg Trials: International Criminal Law Since 1945*, ed. H.R. Reginbogin and C.J.M. Safferling (Munich, Germany: K.G. Saur Verlag GmbH, 2006), 690.
5 Harris, "A World of Peace and Justice Under the Rule of Law," 695.
6 Harry M. Rhea, "Setting the Record Straight: Criminal Justice at Nuremberg," *Journal of the Institute of Justice and International Studies*, no. 7 (2007): 255–56.
7 Claus Kress, "Germany and International Criminal Law: Continuity or Change?" in *The Nuremberg Trials: International Criminal Law Since 1945*, 235–36.
8 Herbert R. Reginbogin, "Confronting 'Crimes Against Humanity' from Leipzig to the Nuremberg Trials," in *The Nuremberg Trials: International Criminal Law Since 1945*, 118.
9 Von Hebel, "An International Criminal Court—A Historical Perspective," 20–21; Rhea, "Setting the Record Straight: Criminal Justice at Nuremberg," 255–56.
10 Reginbogin, "Confronting 'Crimes Against Humanity' from Leipzig to the Nuremberg Trials," 118.
11 Bass, *Stay the Hand of Vengeance*, 179–80.
12 Kress, "Germany and International Criminal Law," 235.
13 Ibid.
14 "Justice on Trial, The Legacy of Nuremberg," *American Radio Works*, July 2002, americanradioworks.publicradio.org/features/justiceontrial/index.html.
15 Kress, "Versailles-Nuremberg-The Hague: Germany and International Criminal Law," *International Lawyer* 40, no. 1 (2006): 23–24.
16 Rebecca Wittman, The Normalization of Nazi Crime in Postwar West German Trials," in *The Nuremberg Trials: International Criminal Law Since 1945*, 209.
17 Christoph Burchard, "The Nuremberg Trial and its Impact on Germany," *Journal of International Criminal Justice* 4, no. 4 (2006): 821–22.
18 Wittmann, "The Normalization of Nazi Crime in Postwar West German Trials," 214.

19 From 1990 forward, Germany scored between 1 and 2 on the Political Terror Scale.
20 *Comments of Governments on the Report of the Working Group on a Draft Statute for an International Criminal Court* (A/CN.4/458, Addendum 3, 7–10), 7 April 1994.
21 Hans-Peter Kaul, "Preconditions to Exercise of Jurisdiction," in *The Rome Statute of the International Criminal Court: A Commentary*, 595; *Report of the Preparatory Committee on the Establishment of an International Court, Vol. II (Compilation of Proposals)*, 73, Proposal 1, (UN Doc. A51/22, Supp. No. 22 A); (UN Doc. A/AC/249/1998/DP.2), 23 March 1998.
22 UN Doc. A/AC/249/1998/DP.2, 23 March 1998.
23 "Role of United Nations Security Council in International Criminal Court Among Issues Discussed this Afternoon at UN Conference" (Press Release L/2877), Statement of Edzard Schmidt-Jortzig, Minister of Justice of Germany, 16 June 1998.
24 Kaul, "Preconditions to Exercise of Jurisdiction," 598–99.
25 Hans-Peter Kaul and Claus Kress, "Jurisdiction and Cooperation in the Statute of the International Criminal Court: Principles and Compromises," in *Yearbook of International Humanitarian Law* (1999): 171–72. Hans-Peter Kaul was the Head of Germany's Delegation to the Preparatory Committee and Deputy Head of Germany's Delegation to the Rome Conference and Claus Kress was a member of Germany's Delegation to the Preparatory Committee and the Rome Conference.
26 Morten Bergsmo and Jelena Pejic, "Article 15: Prosecutor," in *Commentary on the Rome Statute of the International Criminal Court: Observers' Notes, Article by Article*, ed. Otto Triffterer (Baden-Baden, Germany: Nomos Verlagsgesellschaft, 1999), 359–62.
27 *Proposal by Argentina and Germany*, reflected in A/AC.249/1998/WG.4/DP.35, 25 March 1998.
28 Phillipe Kirsch and Darryl Robinson, "Initiation of Proceedings by the Prosecutor," in *The Rome Statute of the International Criminal Court*, 660.
29 Phakiso Mochochoko, "International Cooperation and Judicial Assistance," in *The International Criminal Court: The Making of the Rome Statute: Issues, Negotiations, Results*, ed. Roy S. Lee (The Hague, The Netherlands: Kluwer Law International, 1999), 310–11. Mochochoko (Lesotho) was the Chairman of the working group on cooperation at the Rome Conference.
30 Ibid.
31 Kaul and Kress, "Jurisdiction and Cooperation in the Statute of the International Criminal Court," 158.
32 Ibid., 158–60.
33 *Rome Statute*, art. 89.
34 Whitney R. Harris, "Tyranny on Trial—Trial of Major German War Criminals at Nuremberg, Germany, 1945–46," in *The Nuremberg Trials: International Criminal Law Since 1945*, ed. H.R. Reginbogin and C.J.M. Safferling (Munich: K.G. Saur Verlag GmbH, 2006), 110.
35 The full text of the law is available in English at www.iuscomp.org/gla/statutes/VoeStGB.pdf.
36 Michael P. Hatchell, "Note and Comment: Closing the Gaps in United States Law and Implementing the Rome Statute: A Comparative

Approach," *ILSA Journal of International & Comparative Law* 12, no. 1 (2005): 202.

37 Hans-Peter Kaul, "International Criminal Law in Germany: The Drafts of the International Crimes Code and the Rome Statute Implementation Act," German Delegation to the PrepCom, presented at the Ninth Session of the Preparatory Commission for the International Criminal Court at the UN on 18 April 2002.

38 Ibid., 2–4.

39 Ibid.

40 An English version of the text of the ICC Cooperation Act is available at www.legislation.gov.uk/ukpga/1990/5/contents.

41 ICC Cooperation Act, arts. 2–33.

42 ICC Cooperation Act, art. 44.

43 Hans-Peter Kaul, "Construction Site for More Justice: The International Criminal Court After Two Years," *American Journal of International Law* 99, no. 2 (2005): 379–80.

44 Press Release, "South Africa, Germany Announce Ratification of Statute to Establish International Criminal Court" (L/2966), 27 November 2000.

45 Hans-Peter Kaul, "The International Criminal Court: Current Challenges and Perspectives," *Washington University Global Studies Law Review* 6, no. 3 (2007): 582.

46 Paul Meller, "EU [European Union] Exempts U.S. from War Crimes Trials," *Chicago Tribune*, 1 October 2002; Mark S. Ellis and Richard J. Goldstone, *The International Criminal Court: Challenges to Achieving Justice and Accountability in the 21st Century* (New York: The International Debate Education Association, 2008), 137.

47 Kress, "Germany and International Criminal Law," 239.

5 Canada, France, and the United Kingdom

A study in contrasts

- **Relationship with the international human rights regime generally**
- **Role in the creation of the ICC**
- **Commitment and compliance**
- **ICC commitment: assessing the explanatory power of the credible threat theory**
- **Conclusion**

This chapter expands on the prior case study chapters by exploring the International Criminal Court (ICC) ratification behavior of Canada, France, and the United Kingdom. Unlike the United States, but like Germany, all three states promptly committed to the ICC. Their decisions to join the court are consistent with the expectations of the credible threat theory because they all have domestic policies and practices that should enable them to comply with treaty terms. Indeed, they are all powerful democratic states with good human rights practices and strong domestic law enforcement institutions that follow the rule of law.[1]

On the other hand, even though all three states joined the court, the evidence shows differences in their ratification behavior. Like Germany, Canada was an early member and leader of the like-minded group of states favoring a court with a broad jurisdictional reach, independent of United Nations (UN) Security Council control, and with *proprio motu* powers for the prosecutor.[2] France and the United Kingdom, by contrast, often sided with the United States and other permanent Security Council members to support proposals limiting the court's jurisdictional scope and powers. The United Kingdom eventually became a member of the like-minded group of states, but it initially favored granting the Security Council more control over the court's docket and proposed that the court only be able to exercise jurisdiction over non-states parties based on the consent of both the territorial and custodial state.[3] France was even more forceful in pushing for a court with a smaller jurisdictional reach based on a system of state consent. Its 1996 proposal to the Preparatory Committee called for a jurisdictional regime whereby all states affected by a case would have to give their consent in order for the ICC to proceed (for example, the state of the territory where the crime was committed, the state of the nationality of the victim, and the state of the nationality of the offender).[4] France was finally persuaded to join the European Union (EU) states and support an automatic jurisdiction regime for states parties. However, it first insisted on Article 124, which allows states to opt out of the court's jurisdiction over war crimes for a period of seven years.[5] France invoked Article 124 when it ratified the Rome Statute.

The chapter begins with a discussion of each country's relationship with the international human rights regime in general. It follows with a description of the positions each took during Rome Statute negotiations on the core issues of the court's jurisdiction, the role of the Security Council, and the powers granted to the prosecutor. The chapter then examines each country's decision to ratify the ICC treaty and some evidence relating to its compliance with treaty terms. The conclusion assesses the power of the credible threat theory and other competing theories to explain the ICC ratification behavior of Canada, France, and the United Kingdom.

Relationship with the international human rights regime generally

Canada, France, and the United Kingdom have broadly committed to the international human rights regime as one might expect of countries with good human rights practices and good domestic law enforcement institutions that enforce the rule of law. Their broad commitment is also consistent with each country's tendency over the past decades to support mechanisms to hold individuals accountable for human rights abuses. Though Canada's strong commitment to that norm is more recent, France and the United Kingdom have actively participated in the spread of international human rights norms from the time they actively backed the Nuremberg prosecutions. Canada's soldiers fought in World War II, but the country was not active in pushing for the Nuremberg trials, and for several decades thereafter it had a reputation as a safe haven for European war criminals since it was not particularly proactive in prosecuting them. In the 1980s, however, Canada's tendency towards inaction and indifference changed, and since that time the country has adopted legislation permitting the prosecution of international war criminals.[6] As discussed below, Canada's role in the creation of the ICC is more evidence that it is now a leader in promoting the spread of international human rights norms.

Yet, even though these countries share similarities with the United States and Germany because of their good practices and tendency to support international justice, Tables 5.1, 5.2 and 5.3 show that they differ somewhat in whether and when they commit to international human rights treaties. Each of Canada, France, and the United Kingdom has more broadly committed to the regime than has the United States (which did not even commit to all the main treaties). As to these three states, only the United Kingdom stands out as less likely to commit to treaties with stronger enforcement mechanisms: it only joined one allowing for individual complaints against it. Yet, it did join the Convention Against Torture and Other Cruel, Inhuman or Degrading Treatment or Punishment (CAT) Optional Protocol allowing for committee visits on its territory.

Further, while none of these states has committed as broadly as Germany, the timing of their commitment is different. Germany only ratified the treaties with stronger enforcement mechanisms in the last decade or so after it had completed the process of transforming itself into a country that protected against human rights abuses. These countries, by contrast, ratified quite rapidly and usually only within a few years of the treaties' availability for signature. Even their ratification of the International Covenant on Civil and Political Rights (ICCPR) and International Covenant on Economic, Social and

Table 5.1 Canada's commitment to the six primary international human rights treaties

Treaty	*Enforcement mechanism*	*Date open*	*Ratification date*
ICCPR	Reports	1966	1976
ICESCR	Reports	1966	1976
CERD	Reports	1966	1970
CEDAW	Reports	1980	1981
CAT	Reports	1984	1987
CRC	Reports	1989	1991
ICCPR Art. 41	State complaints	1966	1979
CAT Art. 21	State complaints	1984	1987
ICCPR Opt.	Individual complaints	1966	1976
CERD 14	Individual complaints	1966	–
CAT Art. 22	Individual complaints	1984	1987
CEDAW Opt.	Individual complaints	1999	2002
CAT Opt.	Committee visits	2003	–

Table 5.2 France's commitment to the six primary international human rights treaties

Treaty	*Enforcement mechanism*	*Date open*	*Ratification date*
ICCPR	Reports	1966	1980
ICESCR	Reports	1966	1980
CERD	Reports	1966	1971
CEDAW	Reports	1980	1983
CAT	Reports	1984	1986
CRC	Reports	1989	1990
ICCPR Art. 41	State complaints	1966	–
CAT Art. 21	State complaints	1984	1988
ICCPR Opt.	Individual complaints	1966	1984
CERD 14	Individual complaints	1966	1982
CAT Art. 22	Individual complaints	1984	1988
CEDAW Opt.	Individual complaints	1999	2000
CAT Opt.	Committee visits	2003	2008

Table 5.3 The UK's commitment to the six primary international human rights treaties

Treaty	*Enforcement mechanism*	*Date open*	*Ratification date*
ICCPR	Reports	1966	1976
ICESCR	Reports	1966	1976
CERD	Reports	1966	1969
CEDAW	Reports	1980	1986
CAT	Reports	1984	1988
CRC	Reports	1989	1991
ICCPR Art. 41	State complaints	1966	1976
CAT Art. 21	State complaints	1984	1988
ICCPR Opt.	Individual complaints	1966	–
CERD 14	Individual complaints	1966	–
CAT Art. 22	Individual complaints	1984	–
CEDAW Opt.	Individual complaints	1999	2004
CAT Opt.	Committee visits	2003	2003

Cultural Rights (ICESCR) was relatively prompt since those treaties were the first created and did not come into existence until 1976. For the most part, these three countries even committed promptly to the treaties with stronger enforcement mechanisms. Of course, Canada, France, and the United Kingdom did not have Germany's more recent history as a rights-abusing state. Thus, it makes sense that these countries might commit more promptly than Germany to treaties permitting state or individual complaints.

Role in the creation of the ICC

Despite their similarities, Canada, France, and the United Kingdom did not initially all agree on how the ICC should be structured. Early on, Canada demonstrated a commitment to a strong and independent court and prosecutor. It was part of the like-minded group, and senior Canadian diplomat Philippe Kirsch served as Chair of the Committee of the Whole and played a pivotal role in drafting the final proposal for the ICC treaty.[7] While both France and the United Kingdom ultimately voted for the adoption of the Rome Statute, both at times showed a tendency to be more protective of state sovereignty and favored proposals to limit the court's power. Both states backed some of the proposals advanced by the permanent members of the Security Council—the P-5—which tended to favor granting the Security Council some control over the ICC's docket and a more circumscribed jurisdictional realm for the court.[8] In fact, the United Kingdom was sometimes criticized for being a stalking horse for the United States.[9] As to France, it only agreed to vote for the adoption of the Rome Statute after states agreed to an opt-out provision for war crimes.

The section below details the positions of these three countries on the core issues of the court's jurisdiction, the role of the Security Council, and the powers of the prosecutor.

The issue of the court's jurisdiction

At first, Canada, France, and the United Kingdom did not all agree on whether and how the court should be able to exercise jurisdiction over the core crimes as to states parties or non-states parties. Canada and the United Kingdom both favored permitting the court to exercise automatic jurisdiction over the covered crimes as to states that ratified the Rome Statute. Neither, however, supported the German proposal which would have more generally expanded the court's jurisdiction over those crimes to include nationals of states that did not commit to the court. Instead, as to non-states parties, the United Kingdom formally proposed in March 1998 that where the custodial state and territorial state are not states parties, the ICC should not be able to exercise jurisdiction without their consent.[10] The United Kingdom amended its proposal during Rome Conference negotiations to require only the consent of the territorial state, arguing that it would be illegal to require a government to comply with a ruling under a treaty that it had not joined.[11] During the negotiations in Rome, Canada was in the camp backing the United Kingdom's proposal.[12]

Not only did France not support the German proposal, but it favored an even more restrictive jurisdictional scheme than did Canada or the United Kingdom. In 1996, France proposed that the ICC should not be able to exercise jurisdiction over a matter unless all of the states with any connection to the matter consented to permitting the court to proceed. Thus, the court would need the consent of the territorial state, the custodial state, the state requesting extradition of the accused, and the state of nationality of both the accused and the victim before it could exercise jurisdiction, even if those states were parties to the ICC treaty.[13] France did not hold fast to that early proposal, though it did continue to press for a more limited consent regime as relates to crimes against humanity and war crimes. During the Rome Conference, France, like the United States, argued that as to those two crimes and absent a Security Council referral, the ICC should not be able to exercise jurisdiction absent the consent of the state of the nationality of the accused. Only three days before the conclusion of the Rome Conference, it submitted an informal proposal providing that a state could consent to the court's jurisdiction over crimes against humanity and war crimes by either a general or ad hoc declaration.[14]

Although France was not successful in convincing states to back its proposal, it did obtain a concession which ultimately appeared as Article 124 of the Rome Statute—the war crimes seven-year opt-out. France, like the United States, had voiced concerns that given its significant participation in international peacekeeping efforts, it could be subjected to unfair complaints that its soldiers were committing war crimes in violation of ICC treaty terms.[15] In those final days of the Rome Conference, the United Kingdom acted first in an effort to appease France and persuade it to join forces with the other EU states. It presented a group of interested countries with a proposal allowing states to ratify an optional protocol exempting their citizens from ICC jurisdiction over these two covered crimes for a period of 10 years.[16] Although the United Kingdom proposal was supported by the P-5, others believed it went too far. In an effort to persuade France to vote for the adoption of the Rome Statute, but also to minimize restrictions on the ICC's exercise of jurisdiction, Germany then instead proposed to allow an opt-out period for war crimes only.[17] This concession was essentially the price paid by other states for France's agreement to join the rest of Europe in voting for the creation of the ICC.[18]

The role of the Security Council

As with the issue of the court's jurisdiction, Canada, France, and the United Kingdom did not initially agree on the precise role of the Security

Council. Recall that the P-5 was generally in favor of a strong role for the Security Council in determining the ICC's docket. The United States in particular was strongly in favor of the language in the 1994 International Law Commission (ILC) Draft which essentially gave the Security Council control over whether cases could go forward before the ICC. The Singapore Compromise which formed the basis of Article 16 of the Rome Statute, however, basically reversed the relationship of the Security Council to the ICC as it had been conceived of by the 1994 ILC Draft. Now, the Security Council would only be able to defer proceedings. Although all three of Canada, France, and the United Kingdom ended up supporting the creation of a court that was more independent of the Security Council, it was Canada that most promptly indicated its support for a regime like that contemplated by Singapore's proposal. Indeed, in August 1997, it submitted a proposal building on the Singapore Compromise by suggesting that such deferral period be renewable for periods of 12 months.[19]

The United Kingdom was the next of these three countries to indicate its support for a regime like that contemplated by the Singapore Compromise. Although it had been aligned with the P-5 by its statements in the course of the December 1997 session of the Preparatory Committee, the United Kingdom was the first member of the P-5 group to indicate that it would be willing to back a proposal that would lessen the Security Council's control over the ICC's docket.[20] In March 1998, in fact, it submitted a proposal building on the Singapore Compromise and which became the basis for Article 16.[21] By that article, and in great contrast to the language spelling out the role of the Security Council in the 1994 ILC Draft, the court can proceed with a case unless all five permanent Security Council members vote for deferral.[22] Apparently, the United Kingdom did later waver somewhat on its position during Rome Statute negotiations. A report from 23 June 1998 accused the country's Labour government of backtracking on its support for the Singapore Compromise. According to that report, Britain was arguing that the Security Council should be able to retain control of any case that comes before it while it is discharging any of its responsibilities.[23] In the end, though, the United Kingdom joined the like-minded group of states in supporting what became Article 16.

With this issue, too, France may have been the most adamant of the three countries in adhering to a vision of a weaker court without too many powers to act independently. France's 1996 Draft Statute mirrored the 1994 ILC Draft in providing that the ICC could not commence a prosecution "arising from a situation which is being dealt with by the Security Council as a threat to or breach of the peace or an act of aggression under Chapter VII of the Charter, unless the Security Council otherwise decides."[24] Records from the Rome Conference proceedings reveal that France remained committed to the idea of a strong role for the Security Council in relation to the court and that it did not favor the Singapore Compromise.[25] Reports of those proceedings similarly indicate that even by 18 June 1998, France was not prepared to back the Singapore Compromise.[26] Only close to the end of the Rome Conference, on 11 July 1998, did France finally break with the remaining three members of the P-5 who argued for more Council control and agree to back what became Article 16 of the Rome Statute.[27]

The powers granted to the prosecutor

On this issue that also divided states, Canada was the most prompt of these three to side with the like-minded group of states in favoring an independent prosecutor with powers to commence investigations on his own motion. France and the United Kingdom were slower to agree to the grant of independence. Similar to the 1994 ILC Draft, France's 1996 Draft Statute did not have a provision permitting the prosecutor to commence cases on his own initiative. It instead permitted state referrals under Article 37 and Security Council referrals under Article 38.[28] It was not until sometime during the middle of the Rome Conference that France indicated its support for an independent prosecutor who could launch investigations absent a referral from the Security Council or states parties. France shared concerns similar to those voiced by the United States of a prosecutor with too much unlimited power who might then act on cases for political reasons. However, France was persuaded that a vetting procedure like that proposed by Germany and Argentina, whereby the Court would confirm the prosecutor's ability to mount investigations,[29] would provide sufficient controls on prosecutorial powers.[30]

The United Kingdom was slower than France to back the idea of an independent prosecutor. By its March 1998 proposal, the United Kingdom stated that it was still undecided on the issue of an independent prosecutor with *proprio motu* powers.[31] That undecided position turned somewhat negative on the idea by the time of Rome Conference negotiations. According to a report dated 29 June 1998, a growing number of states were comfortable with the proposal of Germany and Argentina that sought to address concerns of an overreaching prosecutor by requiring the Pre-Trial Chamber to vet cases before the prosecutor could exercise any *proprio motu* powers. The United Kingdom, nevertheless, argued that the prosecutor should not be able to proceed even upon the court's confirmation unless the territorial state where the crime was committed also consented. The country's stated reason for its position was that it would be foolish for the ICC to proceed with an investigation where it could not rely on the cooperation of the local authorities from which it would need to obtain evidence about the crimes.[32]

Commitment and compliance

Whatever their initial or evolving stances were regarding the structure of the ICC and the powers to be granted it and its prosecutor, all three of these countries ended up voting for the adoption of the Rome Statute as written. Each also promptly signed and ratified the ICC treaty. Nevertheless, the section below shows that the precise commitment timing and depth has been different for each. Each has also behaved differently in terms of evidence relating to its compliance with the terms or spirit of the Rome Statute. To explore compliance, this section looks at the state's record on implementing legislation consistent with its treaty obligations and also its reaction to the United States' request to sign a bilateral immunity agreement.

Canada: swift commitment and implementation

Consistent with its support for the court during negotiations, Canada was prompt to ratify the Rome Statute and to amend its laws to ensure compliance with the ICC treaty's provisions. Canada signed the Rome Statute on 18 December 1998 and ratified on 7 July 2000—making it the 14th state to join the court. Even before it ratified the statute, however, Canada acted to ensure that it could comply with its obligations and commitments. On 24 June 2000, Canada enacted the Crimes Against Humanity and War Crimes Act, making it the first state to adopt comprehensive implementing legislation allowing it to cooperate with the court and to exercise jurisdiction over crimes covered by the ICC treaty.[33] The Act permits Canada to exercise jurisdiction over any of these crimes committed by or against a Canadian citizen or if the accused is present in Canada after the offence was allegedly committed.[34]

The Canadian Parliament passed the Crimes Against Humanity and War Crimes Act by an overwhelming majority (226 votes for; 36 votes against).[35] The 36 negative votes all came from the conservative Canadian Alliance party which argued against the hasty passage of the

Act and emphasized sovereignty concerns. For example, at the third and final reading of the Act on 13 June 2000, Canadian Alliance member Gurrmant Grewal reminded Parliament members that his fellow party members had proposed adding a clause declaring "notwithstanding anything in this act, Canada's national sovereignty is to be protected." He also referenced another proposed amendment which would have provided that "international law is not to be permitted to supersede Canadian law."[36]

Nevertheless, the Act was passed without these amendments. Its passage was thereafter praised by then-Minister of Foreign Affairs Raymond Chan who emphasized that the Act would "strengthen the foundation for criminal prosecutions in Canada."[37] Records indicate, in fact, that the Act has strengthened the foundation for criminal prosecutions in the country. According to its Department of Justice website, Canada has used the Act as the basis to prosecute two individuals for their roles in the Rwandan genocide.[38]

The United Kingdom: swift commitment and implementation

The United Kingdom was also swift to join the court and to implement legislation permitting it to comply with treaty terms. It signed the Rome Statute on 20 November 1998 and ratified on 4 October 2001, becoming the 42nd party to join the court. That ratification, however, did not come without some debate about potential sovereignty losses because of commitment. In particular, members of the Conservative party proposed that the United Kingdom only be allowed to ratify the Rome Statute if it, like France, also invoked Article 124 and opted out of ICC jurisdiction over war crimes for seven years.[39] However, the Conservative arguments did not carry the day. In fact, one junior Foreign Office minister pointed out that British forces were trained to act appropriately in war, meaning that the country should have no reason to rely on the opt-out provision.[40]

By the International Criminal Court Act of 2001, the United Kingdom acted quickly to ensure its ability to comply with the ICC treaty and also ensure that it could prosecute any treaty violations domestically since the Act incorporated the ICC treaty offenses into domestic law.[41] It also appears that the Act is being used—to prosecute British soldiers of alleged war crimes. By way of background, various communications submitted to the ICC accused British soldiers and those from other nations of committing war crimes as defined by the Rome Statute while participating in the war in Iraq. In a 2006 letter, the ICC prosecutor advised that he had investigated the allegations (which had been advanced in some 240 communications), but in most instances had found no basis to conclude that crimes within the ICC's jurisdiction had occurred. The prosecutor did conclude there was a reasonable basis to believe that some soldiers had committed the war crime of willful killing and inhumane treatment as outlined in the Rome Statute. He declined to proceed with an ICC investigation though, citing the fewer than 20 injuries or deaths that had resulted from the soldiers' actions and the need to preserve the court's resources for crimes of sufficient gravity.[42] Moreover, the prosecutor stated that while he did not need to conduct a complementarity analysis since the allegations did not merit further ICC investigation, he had received information that national proceedings had been commenced as to the relevant incidents. Press reports do indicate that the United Kingdom has itself investigated allegations of crimes committed in Iraq and even prosecuted some of its soldiers. In 2006, in fact, Corporal Donald Payne became the first person in the British military to be convicted of committing a war crime under the United Kingdom's International Criminal Court Act. He pleaded guilty to inhumanely treating civilians in connection with military activities in Iraq.[43]

France: swift commitment, but a complicated record on implementation

France also promptly committed to the court. However, the record suggests it did not commit as deeply as did the other two countries, and its record on domestic implementation is complicated. First, as to commitment, France did sign the Rome Statute on 18 July 1998. It was also the 12th party to formally join the ICC on 9 June 2000. However, at the time of ratification, it submitted seven "interpretive declarations," notwithstanding that Article 120 of the Rome Statute prohibits states from filing reservations. The "interpretive declarations" primarily relate to Article 8's provision on war crimes. For example, in one declaration France states that it does not consider the terms of the treaty to prohibit it "from exercising its inherent right of self-defence." Another "declaration" states that France does not read the treaty to preclude it "from directing attacks against objectives considered as military objectives under international humanitarian law."[44] France's ratification of the ICC treaty came with another caveat as well: France invoked Article 124 and opted out of the court's jurisdiction over war crimes for seven years. It later withdrew its Article 124 declaration on 13 August 2008—approximately one year before the seven-year period would have passed in July 2009.[45]

Regarding implementation, with near majority support, in July 1999, Parliament amended the French Constitution to permit ratification of the ICC. The constitutional amendments, like the subsequent Bill on Cooperation with the ICC which was adopted in February 2002, eliminated certain immunities and amnesties for public officials so as to permit France to cooperate with the court on procedural matters such as the arrest and transfer of suspects.[46] Only in 2010, however, did France pass a law permitting it to exercise jurisdiction over the ICC's covered crimes.[47] Even so, some have criticized France's law for being so narrowly drawn that it would still allow criminals to escape justice within France.[48] By the Act, France may not prosecute unless the alleged perpetrator becomes a French resident. Second, the state where the crime took place must criminalize the perpetrator's alleged act or that state must be a party to the Rome Statute. Finally, the French prosecutor cannot initiate a prosecution unless no other international body or national jurisdiction requests the rendition or extradition of the alleged offender.[49] In short, the Act has been criticized because it likely does not enable France to prosecute mass atrocities committed by anyone other than a French citizen (or resident), even though the person is found in France and even for genocide, a universal jurisdiction crime.

Reaction to the United States' request to sign a bilateral immunity agreement

In terms of how these states reacted to the United States' request to sign bilateral immunity agreements, differences are again apparent. Canada and France both publicly rejected the request. Canada's Foreign Minister Bill Graham explained that decision in November 2002 by noting that the two countries already had an agreement whereby US soldiers who committed crimes on Canadian soil would be sent back to the United States for court martial. Accordingly, he stated that there was no need for any other specific agreement relating to the ICC and that Canada had no intention of signing such an agreement.[50] France refused to sign and suggested that signing such bilateral deals with the United States would be contrary to the ICC's founding statute.[51] Britain, on the other hand, indicated that it was more amenable to reaching some sort of accommodation with the Americans. Representatives from Britain's Foreign Office explained that Britain would continue to support the ICC, but that because of the United States' role in international peacekeeping, it made sense to try to provide some assurances to it that US soldiers would not be turned over to the ICC for prosecution.[52]

ICC commitment: assessing the explanatory power of the credible threat theory

Although different in some ways, the behavior of all three countries is consistent with the credible threat theory and the idea that states that can comply with treaty terms are also more likely to commit when treaty enforcement mechanisms are also strong. Canada, France, and the United Kingdom all voted for the adoption of the Rome Statute and promptly ratified it. All also have good human rights practices and strong domestic law enforcement institutions. Because their citizens are not likely to commit mass atrocities, these states should not risk great sovereignty losses by committing to the ICC. Further, should their citizens commit crimes that are covered by ICC treaty terms, these states should not have to cede any control over domestic practices to the court since they have the institutions and resources to investigate and prosecute any alleged crimes domestically. Indeed, although the ICC prosecutor concluded that the court should not pursue any of the allegations of wrongdoing in connection with the war in Iraq, the United Kingdom acted to ensure the court would not: it used its International Criminal Court Act to bring charges against some of its own soldiers.

On the other hand, the behavior of at least France and the United Kingdom again shows how even countries with good practices may view the prospect of a strong and independent court and prosecutor as a credible and costly threat to their sovereignty. Both of those countries have committed broadly to other international human rights treaties, and they did ultimately ratify the Rome Statute. However, France and the United Kingdom tended to act differently from Canada—and also from Germany—by arguing at first for provisions to weaken the court's power and independence. Of course, like the United States, both are permanent members of the Security Council and therefore have reasons to advance a continued role for that organization (and to hope to use their roles in it to protect their citizens from an ICC investigation). The fact of their P-5 membership distinguishes both from Germany and Canada and may help to explain why France and the United Kingdom might be more wary of relinquishing power to another body. After all, they were already part of a body with power to authorize solutions and punishment for mass atrocities.

However, France and the United Kingdom also raised some concerns similar to those raised by the United States about the risks to their military troops should the court and prosecutor be given too much power. France's concerns were raised during Rome Conference negotiations and were so great that it only joined the rest of Europe in backing the creation of the ICC after other states agreed to an opt-out provision for war crimes. Thereafter France committed to the court, but it continued to act in a way that reflected sovereignty concerns by ratifying with a series of "interpretive declarations" and by invoking Article 124. The evidence shows that some in Britain's parliament shared similar concerns about war crimes accusations. Those voices, however, did not win the debate, and the United Kingdom ratified without invoking Article 124. Those debates also show that the majority voices believed that ratification would not cause a costly loss of sovereignty because the expectation was that the country's soldiers would not commit war crimes. In short, the evidence shows that both France and the United Kingdom were aware of the strength of the ICC's enforcement mechanism and sought to minimize the likelihood that their citizens would ever be called before the ICC to defend against criminal charges.

All three countries have also demonstrated their commitment to the ICC and their intention to comply with treaty terms by passing laws permitting them to cooperate with the court and laws that implement the treaty's crimes into their domestic legislation. By passing these laws these states have also acknowledged the strength of the ICC's enforcement mechanism and their intention to minimize potential sovereignty losses associated with committing to the court. With domestic laws covering the treaty offenses, these states can ensure that their citizens will not be tried in The Hague. As noted above, the United Kingdom has already used its International Criminal Court Act to prosecute its soldiers, and while France only recently passed implementing legislation, Article 124 already gave it protection against war crimes prosecutions. Furthermore, although France's Act has been criticized, it does protect France from having its citizens hauled before the ICC since it allows prosecutions against French residents. Thus, the Act protects France's sovereignty. However, it does not appear to go as far as Canada's Act, for example, which has allowed Canada to prosecute citizens of other countries for mass atrocities.

The evidence also shows that the credible threat theory explains more about these states' ICC ratification behavior than do the other relevant theories. First, because all of these countries have good practices and are not transitioning democracies, neither the credible commitment theory nor other hand-tying theories are applicable. None of Canada, France, or the United Kingdom needs to send a credible signal of their intention to improve their practices, nor do they have reason to join international institutions so as to lock in some democratic reforms.

Second, as to external pressures theories, it bears noting that all three are wealthy democracies that ultimately broke with the United States—the country that likely could provide them the most benefits given that they were already well off. Indeed, the fact that Canada took a leadership position in pushing for a strong and independent court early in the process tends to show that it was not simply responding to external pressures. It is true that the United Kingdom and France took longer to break from the United States, but both did so and voted for the adoption of the Rome Statute. Both the United Kingdom and France also seemed to want to act as part of a united Europe, though the evidence does not suggest that they joined the like-minded group because of pressures as such. Both are strong, powerful countries within Europe and would not need to yield to pressures in order to receive some benefits within Europe. Both also were forceful in putting forth their own proposals and arguing for them. Indeed, France only joined Europe in voting for the adoption of the Rome Statute after it received some concessions to do so. Like all countries participating in ICC negotiations, these three had to agree to some compromises in order to make the court a reality, but this does not mean they voted for the adoption of the Rome Statute or ratified it without first considering compliance costs related to their sovereignty. Much evidence shows that the United Kingdom and France were particularly strong in pushing for provisions to shield their citizens from ever being subjected to an ICC prosecution. Canada and France also strongly stood up to the United States in refusing to sign bilateral immunity agreements.

None of this is to say that these countries joined the court without believing that commitment would also benefit them. Like Germany, Canada, France, and the United Kingdom are all powerful states that have played a role in supporting the spread of international human rights norms. To the extent that they can lead by example and encourage states with poor domestic practices to commit to an international institution that can hold those states accountable should they abuse human rights, these strong states necessarily gain. A permanent ICC obviates the need to create additional, and costly, ad hoc tribunals. Because it is permanent and because its enforcement mechanism is strong, the ICC has the potential to deter atrocities before they occur—a benefit to states like Canada, France, and the United Kingdom which may be called on to intervene to aid in stopping such atrocities.

Conclusion

This case study chapter has shown the power of the credible threat theory to explain the ICC ratification behavior of democratic countries with good human rights practices and strong domestic law enforcement institutions. Canada, France, and the United Kingdom all have policies and practices that should ensure their ability to comply with treaty terms, meaning that compliance costs associated with commitment should be minimal. All three did commit. They did so even though they are powerful countries. Indeed, by voting for the adoption of the Rome Statute, France and the United Kingdom went against the wishes of their fellow P-5 members, but the evidence also shows that even these countries with good practices and institutions did not commit to the ICC and its strong enforcement mechanism without considering sovereignty costs. During negotiations, France and the United Kingdom often evidenced their concerns with sovereignty costs by arguing for a weaker court and one more under the control of the Security Council. France even ratified while at the same time invoking Article 124. Furthermore, all three have acted to minimize sovereignty risks by implementing domestic legislation to ensure that should their citizens be accused of committing an ICC crime, the state can prosecute them domestically.

The case study that follows examines the ratification behavior of Trinidad and Tobago, a democracy with strong human rights practices, but one that is weaker on the world stage and that also has weaker domestic law enforcement institutions.

Notes

1 Between 1998 and 2008, Canada typically scored a 1 on the Political Terror Scale (see Chapter 2, note 24 for an explanation of the scale). France scored a 1 or 2 on the scale during those same years. With the exception of 2005, when it scored a 3 on the scale, the United Kingdom has also received ratings of 1 or 2. All three countries have had World Bank Rule of Law Scale scores consistently above 1.4 (see Chapter 3, note 1 for an explanation of this scale).

2 CICC, "Canadian Foreign Minister on ICC," *The International Criminal Court Monitor*, June 1998, www.iccnow.org (reporting on the comments of the Honorable Lloyd Axworthy to the ICC Preparatory Committee).

3 Lawyers Committee for Human Rights, "Establishing an International Criminal Court: Major Unresolved Issues in the Draft Statute," May 1998.

4 Draft Statute of the International Criminal Court, Working Paper Submitted by France, (UN Doc. A/AC 249/L.3, art. 34), 6 August 1996 (hereinafter *1996 France Draft Statute*).

5 Andreas Zimmerman, "Article 124: Transitional Provision," in *Commentary on the Rome Statute of the International Criminal Court: Observers' Notes, Article by Article*, ed. Otto Triffterer (Baden-Baden, Germany: Nomos Verlagsgesellschaft, 2008), 1767–68.

6 For a good historical perspective on Canada's involvement in the prosecution of war criminals, see Fannie LaFontaine, *Prosecuting Genocide, Crimes*

Against Humanity and War Crimes in Canadian Courts (Toronto, Canada: Thomson Reuters, 2012), 15–26.

7 Foreign Affairs and International Trade Canada, *Canada and the International Criminal Court*, www.international.gc.ca/court-cour/icc-canada-cpi.aspx?lang=eng&view=d.

8 Philippe Kirsch and John T. Holmes, "The Rome Conference on an International Criminal Court: The Negotiating Process," 93 *American Journal of International Law* 2, no. 4 (1999).

9 CICC, "British Allies, NGOs Furious at Broad UK Campaign to 'Neutralise' ICC," *On the Record*, 30 June 1998, www.iccnow.org.

10 *Proposal of the United Kingdom* (A/AC.249/1998/WG.3/DP.1), 1998.

11 CICC, "British Allies, NGOs Furious at Broad UK Campaign to 'Neutralise' ICC."

12 CICC, "Battle Lines Form on States' Ability to Block ICC," *On the Record*, 29 June 1998, www.iccnow.org.

13 *1996 France Draft Statute*, art. 34.

14 Zimmerman, "Article 124: Transitional Provision," 1767.

15 CICC, "French Position on War Crimes Sours French Support for Prosecutor, Reparations Provisions," *On the Record*, 11 July 1998, www.iccnow.org.

16 Zimmerman, "Article 124: Transitional Provision," 1767–68.

17 Ibid.

18 Shana Tabak, Note, "Article 124, War Crimes, and the Development of The Rome Statute," *Georgetown Journal of International Law* 40 (2009): 1069.

19 Morton Bergsmo and Jelena Pejic, "Article 16: Deferral of Investigation or Prosecution," in *Commentary on the Rome Statute of the International Criminal Court: Observers' Notes, Article by Article*, 597 (discussing proposal submitted by Canada for Article 23, 11 August 1997).

20 Ibid.

21 *Proposal of the United Kingdom* (A/AC.249/1998/WG.3/DP.1), 1998; Bergsmo and Pejic, "Article 16: Deferral of Investigation or Prosecution," 597–98.

22 Bergsmo and Pejic, "Article 16: Deferral of Investigation or Prosecution," 599.

23 CICC, "'Rebellious' Rome Conference Demands Curbs on Security Council Veto Power: Britain Accused of Backtracking on Council Referral," *On the Record*, 23 June 1998, www.iccnow.org.

24 Compare *1996 France Draft Statute*, art. 38(3), to 1994 ILC Draft, art. 23(3).

25 UN Diplomatic Conference of Plenipotentiaries on the Establishment of an International Criminal Court, Summary records of the plenary meetings and of the meetings of the Committee of the Whole (A/CONF.183/13 (Vol. II)), para. 78, 17 June 1998 (statement of Mr Vedrine for France noting the need for coordination between the court and the Security Council and offering some criticisms of the Singapore Compromise).

26 CICC, "Dutch Disbelief at American Defeatism," *On the Record*, 18 June 1998, www.iccnow.org.

27 CICC, "French Position on War Crimes Sours French Support for Prosecutor, Reparations Provisions."

28 *1996 France Draft Statute.*

29 *Proposal by Argentina and Germany*, reflected in A/AC.249/1998/WG.4/DP.35, 25 March 1998.

30 UN Diplomatic Conference of Plenipotentiaries on the Establishment of an International Criminal Court, Summary records of the plenary meetings

and of the meetings of the Committee of the Whole (A/CONF.183/13 (Vol. II)), para. 47, 19 June 1998 (statement of Mr Perrin de Brichambaut for France stating that France agreed with the compromise solution regarding the prosecutor's powers proposed by Germany and Argentina); CICC, "Support Growing for an Independent Prosecutor," *On the Record*, 23 June 1998, www.iccnow.org.

31 *Proposal of the United Kingdom* A/AC.249/1998/WG.3/DP.1, 1998.

32 CICC, "Dutch, UK Spar Over Whether States Should Veto Pre-Trial Investigations," *On the Record*, 29 June 1998, www.iccnow.org.

33 Bruce Broomhall, "Towards the Development of an Effective System of Universal Jurisdiction for Crimes Under International Law," *New England Law Review* 35, no. 2 (2001): 409.

34 Crimes Against Humanity and War Crimes Act, ch. 24, art. 8, 2000 (Can.).

35 Parliament of Canada, 36th Parliament, 2nd Session, 13 June 2000, www.parl.gc.ca/HousePublications/Publication.aspx?Language=E&Mode=1%0%20&DocId=2332235& File=0#LINK60Id.

36 Ibid.

37 Ibid.

38 Department of Justice Canada, *Successes*, www.justice.gc.ca/warcrimes-crimesdeguerre/successes-realisations-eng.asp; Canadian Centre for International Justice, *CCIJ'S Public Cases and Interventions*, www.ccij.ca/programs/cases/index.php?DOC_INST=19.

39 Michael Kallenbach, "Tory Fears for Troops Fail to Persuade Lords," *Daily Telegraph*, 9 March 2001.

40 Ibid.

41 UK Legislation, *International Criminal Court Act 2001, Introductory Text*, www.legislation.gov.uk/ukpga/2001/17/contents.

42 ICC, "OTP Response to Communications Received Concerning Iraq," 9 February 2006.

43 Alan Cowell, "British Soldier Pleads Guilty to War Crime," *The New York Times*, 20 September 2006.

44 France, "Interpretive Declarations," Ratification Status of the Rome Statute of the International Criminal Court, 9 June 2000, treaties.un.org.

45 Ratification Status of the Rome Statute of the International Criminal Court, treaties.un.org. The notes state that on 13 August 2008, France informed the Secretary-General that it had decided to withdraw its declaration under Article 124, which read: "Pursuant to article 124 of the Statute of the International Court, the French Republic declares that it does not accept the jurisdiction of the Court with respect to the category of crimes referred to in article 8 when a crime is alleged to have been committed by its nationals or on its territory."

46 Leila Nadya Sadat, "The Nuremburg Paradox," *American Journal of Comparative Law* 58, no. 1 (2010): 155.

47 Loi 2010-2930 du 9 août 2010 portant adaptation du droit pénal à l'institution de la Cour pénale internationale, art. 8, J.O., 10 August 2010, p. 14678.

48 Coalition française pour la Cour pénale internationale, "Those Accused of International Crimes Must be Tried in France at Last," 2010.

49 Maximo Langer, "The Diplomacy of Universal Jurisdiction: The Political Branches and the Transnational Prosecution of International Crimes," *American Journal of International Law* 105, no. 1 (2011): 25.

50 "Canada Refuses to Sign Pact to Exempt US Soldiers from International Court," *Agence France-Presse*, 4 November 2002.
51 "Germany, France Criticize U.S. on International Criminal Court," *Wall Street Journal*, 3 September 2002.
52 Vivienne Morgan, "Bush Under Fire Over War Crimes Court," *Press Association*, 14 October 2002.

6 Trinidad and Tobago
Compliance before norms

- **Trinidad and Tobago's role in the creation of the ICC**
- **Ratification of the ICC treaty**
- **Commitment to the international human rights regime: a focus on compliance costs**
- **Trinidad and Tobago and the ICC: assessing the explanatory power of the credible threat theory**
- **Conclusion**

This chapter explores Trinidad and Tobago's International Criminal Court (ICC) ratification decision and how the court's strong enforcement mechanism influenced that decision. Like the countries studied in prior chapters, Trinidad and Tobago is a democracy with relatively good human rights practices. Its domestic law enforcement institutions, however, are somewhat weak, meaning that it could have some difficulties if it were called upon to prosecute individuals accused of committing mass atrocities.[1] Trinidad and Tobago is also not as powerful as the countries previously studied. These distinguishing characteristics, however, provide an opportunity to examine the power of external pressures theories to explain the country's ratification behavior and to compare those theories to the explanatory power of the credible threat theory.

As mentioned, a 1989 request by Trinidad and Tobago to the United Nations (UN) reinvigorated discussions about creating a permanent international criminal court. The request submitted by then-Prime Minister Arthur N.R. Robinson proposed a court to address the growing problem of narcotics trafficking which was negatively affecting Trinidad and Tobago and other small Caribbean countries.[2] During negotiations, Trinidad and Tobago continued to push for a court with jurisdiction over narcotics trafficking offenses. It also tried to convince other states that the court should be able to impose the death penalty.[3]

In the end, however, it lost the battle on both fronts. Because the Rome Statute was adopted without the inclusion of the death penalty, and because the death penalty was extremely popular domestically, Trinidad and Tobago regretted that it "had to abstain in the vote for the adoption of the Statute" at the conclusion of the Rome Conference.[4] Yet, it promptly committed to the court, becoming the second state to ratify the treaty (after Senegal) on 6 April 1999.

Why would Trinidad and Tobago so promptly join the ICC even though the court has no jurisdiction over drug offenses and no authority to impose the death penalty? Case study analysis shows that Trinidad and Tobago is normatively aligned with the court and that it joined in part because of the pride it felt in being the impetus for such an important institution. However, the record also provides support for the credible threat theory. The country carefully guards its sovereignty and does not ratify treaties that run counter to its domestic interests or with which it has no intention of complying. At present, for example, it is only a party to the international human rights treaties with the weakest enforcement mechanisms that require self-reporting. The evidence shows that Trinidad and Tobago's ICC ratification decision was equally influenced by sovereignty costs: it committed only after it was satisfied that its leaders and citizens would not be punished for bad and noncompliant behavior.

This chapter proceeds by tracing Trinidad and Tobago's role in the creation of the ICC and its decision to ratify the Rome Statute promptly. In an effort to generate a more complete picture of Trinidad and Tobago's ratification behavior, it then examines the country's acts in connection with other international human rights treaties. Finally, the chapter assesses the explanatory power of the credible threat theory and other competing theories in light of Trinidad and Tobago's behavior up to and following ratification of the Rome Statute.

Trinidad and Tobago's role in the creation of the ICC

The proposal to create a court to combat narcotics trafficking

Then-Prime Minister Robinson's 1989 request asked the UN to consider establishing an international court to deal with the problems associated with international narcotics trafficking that were plaguing his small country and other Caribbean countries. Trinidad and Tobago lies just seven miles off the coast of Venezuela, and according to International Narcotics Control Strategy Reports (INCSR) issued by the US Department of State, it has served as a convenient transshipment point for cocaine, marijuana, and heroin.[5] Although those reports are not available for the period preceding 1996, reports issued towards the end of the 1990s shed some light on the nature of the narcotics trafficking situation in Trinidad and Tobago during the time period leading up to the ICC's creation. For example, the 1997 INCSR states that Trinidad and Tobago was increasingly used as a transit point for cocaine destined for the United States and Europe because of the relative ease with which maritime and air traffic could enter the country with illicit cargo undetected. Trinidad and Tobago simply did not have sufficient money, manpower, radar equipment, or serviceable coastguard boats to intercept and detect smugglers and then seize their illicit goods. In terms of quantities, the Report estimates that up to 2,000 kilograms of cocaine passed through Trinidad and Tobago every month.

Aside from the inability to detect and seize the contraband being transported through the country, Trinidad and Tobago has also had difficulty dealing with other crimes associated with narcotics trafficking offenses. Most significantly, the growing drug trade resulted in an increase in drug-related murders.[6] For example, Trinidad and Tobago's Attorney-General Ramesh Maharaj reported that protecting witnesses had become one of its biggest problems in going after drug cartels: in response to the country's crackdown on drug trafficking, some 14 or 15 key witnesses had been murdered in the five years preceding 1999.[7] Indeed, frustrated with the growing level of violent drug-related crimes, in 1999, despite the appeals of human rights groups, Trinidad and Tobago broke a five-year hiatus on implementing the death sentences of the prisoners held on its death row when it hanged nine members of Trinidad's notorious Dole Chadee gang.[8] Apparently the star witness in the case against Chadee and his men (for whose murder they were hanged) was found shot, hacked, and burned to death as soon as he left protective custody. The government only managed to convict the gang because the witness had previously recorded his testimony in a sworn affidavit.[9] The hangings were met with approval by the majority of the nation, with opinion polls showing Trinidadians strongly supported the death penalty as a deterrent to violent crime.[10]

Trinidad and Tobago's support for an international criminal court with jurisdiction over narcotics trafficking and with authority to impose the death penalty

Official records show that Trinidad and Tobago generally sided with the like-minded group of states in backing a strong and independent court with a limited role for the UN Security Council.[11] In terms of its specific proposals, however, it wanted a court with jurisdiction over narcotics trafficking offenses and with authority to impose the death penalty as punishment. During the Rome Conference, on 16 June 1998, Trinidad and Tobago's Attorney-General Ramesh Maharaj noted the devastating effects narcotics trafficking was having on the Caribbean region and urged states to consider it a crime of serious international concern that should be included within the ICC's jurisdiction.[12] Trinidad and Tobago made that same plea by formal proposal at the conclusion of the Rome Conference on 14 July 1998.[13] As to the death penalty, even though Trinidad and Tobago knew that the majority of states was unlikely to back a proposal to include it as an authorized penalty, it insisted on publicly debating the idea. On 2 July 1998, the country argued on behalf of 14 Caribbean states that the ICC should be allowed to impose the death penalty and emphasized that it would continue to impose the penalty domestically in any event.[14]

Ultimately, however, Trinidad and Tobago's proposals concerning both narcotics trafficking and the death penalty were rejected by the majority of states. Most governments believed that the ICC's jurisdiction should be limited to the three core crimes of genocide, crimes against humanity, and war crimes. Among other things, they argued that limiting the number of crimes over which the court had jurisdiction would simplify negotiations and lead to more broad-based support for the court.[15] Some also argued that the crime of narcotics trafficking was best handled by national courts.[16] By way of compromise, the parties agreed on a resolution to consider at a future Review Conference "the crimes of terrorism and drug crimes with a view to arriving at an acceptable definition and their inclusion in the list of crimes within the jurisdiction of the Court."[17]

Trinidad and Tobago was granted no such compromise with respect to the death penalty issue, and it was that issue that apparently created questions about whether the country would vote to adopt the Rome Statute. Although Trinidad and Tobago had noted that it would continue to apply the death penalty under its own domestic laws regardless of whether that penalty was authorized by the Rome Statute, it still faced the problem of a domestic population that generally favored capital punishment. By joining the ICC, it did not want to create the impression that it opposed a death penalty sentence for certain crimes. In fact, the death penalty remained so politically popular domestically that even as the debate about the death penalty proceeded during ICC negotiations, the government of Trinidad and Tobago was expediting procedures to execute several convicted murderers.[18] Finally, at the conclusion of the Rome Conference, Trinidad and Tobago abstained in the vote for the adoption of the statute, citing the failure of the treaty to include the death penalty as punishment among the reasons for its abstention.[19]

Ratification of the ICC treaty

Yet, Trinidad and Tobago rather promptly ratified the Rome Statute. Research does not reveal any unequivocal answer as to why it did so, but the evidence does suggest several explanations.

First, Trinidad and Tobago's commitment decision was likely influenced by its normative alignment with the court's goals and also the hope that it would have future opportunities to shape the court according to its wishes. Trinidad and Tobago's domestic human rights practices were good and consistent with a state that would support the idea of an international criminal court. The compromise position adopted at the conclusion of the Rome Conference assured Trinidad and Tobago that it could raise the issue of jurisdiction over narcotics trafficking in the future. As to the death penalty issue, in a statement issued on 21 October 1998, Trinidad and Tobago indicated that it had not given up hope that it could persuade states to revisit that issue again at a later date.[20]

Second, Trinidad and Tobago's swift ratification of the Rome Statute also likely had something to do with pride and its desire to continue to be praised for being behind the reinvigorated discussions to create the ICC. The whole of the Caribbean, in fact, was proud of the role one of its own played in creating the court. By a Declaration dated 18 March 1999, the Caribbean states pledged their commitment to ensure the integrity of the Rome Statute and their commitment to pursue ratification within the shortest possible time. The first acknowledgement in that Declaration specifically emphasized President Robinson's role in creating the court.[21] Robinson himself also seemed proud of his role. In May 1998 before the Rome Conference, he stated that he considered this process of working towards the establishment of a strong, independent, and impartial International Criminal Court "to be perhaps the most important" in which he had been or would ever be engaged in the course of his lifetime.[22] During parliamentary debates on the International Criminal Court Bill, a legislator also referenced the country's pride in the role it had played in creating a court which would be a "very powerful instrument to persecute and prosecute" those who have perpetrated international crimes of genocide, rape, and torture.[23]

Furthermore, although Trinidad and Tobago could have faced domestic opposition to joining a court that did not support the death penalty, it was able to minimize those costs. Since Trinidad and Tobago suggested that it would continue to argue to include the death penalty among the punishments that could be imposed by the ICC, it may also have made such an argument to its domestic audience. More significantly, however, Trinidad and Tobago could minimize domestic ratification costs since ratification decisions are made by the executive and do not require approval by the legislature.[24] In this case, President Robinson was the country's leader in 1999 and was likely instrumental in getting Trinidad and Tobago to commit promptly to the ICC. Indeed, a search of Trinidad and Tobago's parliament website did not reveal any Senate or House debates on the decision to commit to the court in the time period from the conclusion of the Rome Conference up until April 1999.

All of this evidence is helpful in explaining why Trinidad and Tobago promptly joined the ICC despite the fact that the court was not created exactly as it had wanted. However, the evidence also shows that Trinidad and Tobago's ratification decision is consistent with the credible threat theory. Trinidad and Tobago did not commit only because it was normatively aligned with the court or because it was proud of being a part of the court's creation. Trinidad and Tobago understood that the ICC treaty was designed with a strong enforcement mechanism to punish bad and noncompliant behavior, and it committed only after concluding that it would be able to comply with treaty terms and not risk a costly loss of sovereignty.

Statements by Trinidad and Tobago's own representatives show that the country guards its sovereignty, but that it committed to the court and continues to support it because it knows the court poses no real threat to its material interests. During debates in the Senate about the International Criminal Court Bill (which was to give effect to the country's obligations under the ICC treaty), Senator Parvatee Anmolsingh-Mahabir initially highlighted the normative significance of the ICC. In support of the Bill, he argued that Trinidad and Tobago must not be diverted in its "determination to prosecute and bring to justice those individuals who hide under the cover of a new state immunity to commit political crimes and atrocities of genocide, of crimes against humanity and war crimes." He further stated that "[w]e cannot be made to subscribe to the outdated and immoral aspects of 'victor justice.'" However, although the senator nodded his head to the normative importance of the ICC, his argument ultimately rested on the fact that commitment to the ICC does not impose sovereignty costs. He explained:

> The bill does not infringe our sovereignty. The International Criminal Court will only become involved when our courts fail to

> bring to effective justice those individuals who have committed crimes that fall under the purview of the International Criminal Court. The statute would have the effect of putting pressure on our local jurisdiction to prosecute those brutal offenders, since our failure to do so will involve automatic involvement of the International Criminal Court in our jurisdiction.[25]

The senator made clear that the costs of joining the ICC were not significant, and they were made even less significant by the fact that the country passed the International Criminal Court Bill: its courts could now prosecute any of the ICC core crimes in the unlikely event that Trinidad and Tobago's citizens ever committed such offenses.

Other evidence also supports Trinidad and Tobago's conclusion that ICC ratification would not result in a costly loss of sovereignty. Its human rights ratings are quite good and there is no evidence to suggest that the government engages in or condones excessive violence. In fact, it supported the death penalty precisely because it wanted to deter the violent crimes that were occurring as a result of the narcotics-trafficking offenses that were plaguing the country. Nor has Trinidad and Tobago ever experienced a genocidal episode or a violent civil war. Moreover, unlike the United States, for example, Trinidad and Tobago does not have the kind of international military presence that could cause it to worry that its soldiers would be accused of committing war crimes. In terms of military expenditures, Trinidad and Tobago ranks in the bottom 10 percent of states, and a review of UN Peacekeeping records for December of every year between 2000 and 2009 shows that Trinidad and Tobago has not contributed any forces to such operations.

Commitment to the international human rights regime: a focus on compliance costs

In addition, the idea that Trinidad and Tobago would only have joined the ICC after concluding that commitment would not impose significant sovereignty costs or otherwise be against its material interests is supported by examining the country's relationship with the international human rights regime more generally. That evidence shows that the country carefully guards its sovereignty and is extremely calculating and strategic in making its decisions about whether to join human rights treaties. Table 6.1 shows that Trinidad and Tobago is not party to any of the treaties with stronger enforcement mechanisms beyond self-reporting.

In fact, it is not a party to the main Convention Against Torture and Other Cruel, Inhuman or Degrading Treatment or Punishment (CAT), a treaty with which Trinidad and Tobago may have believed its domestic death penalty and corporal punishment practices would make compliance difficult. Also, although Trinidad and Tobago did join the Optional Protocol to the International Covenant on Civil and Political Rights (ICCPR) in 1980, it later denounced it on 27 March 2000. The country similarly denounced the American Convention on Human Rights (American Convention).[26] In both instances, Trinidad and Tobago denounced treaties that permitted individual complaints when events occurring after its ratification began affecting its ability to enforce its previously enacted domestic laws providing for the death penalty.

Table 6.1 Trinidad and Tobago's commitment to the six primary international human rights treaties

Treaty	*Enforcement mechanism*	*Date open*	*Ratification date*
ICCPR	Reports	1966	1978
ICESCR	Reports	1966	1978
CERD	Reports	1966	1973
CEDAW	Reports	1980	1990
CAT	Reports	1984	–
CRC	Reports	1989	1991
ICCPR Art. 41	State complaints	1966	–
CAT Art. 21	State complaints	1984	–
ICCPR Opt.	Individual complaints	1966	1980*
CERD 14	Individual complaints	1966	–
CAT 22	Individual complaints	1984	–
CEDAW Opt.	Individual complaints	1999	–
CAT Opt.	Committee visits	2003	–

Note: * Joined the Optional Protocol to the ICCPR in 1980, but denounced it in 2000.

The section below addresses these ratification and denunciation decisions.

Trinidad and Tobago's refusal to ratify the CAT

Both capital and corporal punishment are lawful penalties for certain crimes in Trinidad and Tobago, though not frequently used. Capital punishment is a legal sanction for murder,[27] and it has enjoyed substantial popular support in the country as a desired means to deter the violent acts that accompany narcotics trafficking offenses. The country also has a history of supporting the use of corporal punishment, including flogging and caning. For example, one law permits the court to order certain male offenders convicted of rape crimes to be struck or flogged with a "cat-o'-nine tails."[28] According to Amnesty International country reports, however, Trinidad and Tobago has not actually carried out an execution since the Chadee hangings in 1999.[29] According to a 2005 Amnesty International report, corporal punishment had not been imposed since 2002,[30] though news searches indicate that courts have imposed birch caning for sexual offenses and murder between 2006 and 2009.[31]

Trinidad and Tobago's preference for continuing to have both punishments on its law books may help explain the country's decision to refuse to commit to the CAT. Indeed, commitment to the CAT may impose significant sovereignty costs that the country would not wish to assume given its domestic penalty preferences. Each of the CAT, the ICCPR, and the American Convention prohibits torture, or cruel, inhuman, or degrading treatment or punishment.[32] However, the language of the CAT treaty is unique among the three in failing to specifically exempt from the definition of torture the lawful imposition of the death penalty according to previously enacted domestic law. By contrast, Article 6, paragraph 2, of the ICCPR provides that in "countries which have not abolished the death penalty, the sentence of death may be imposed only for the most serious crimes in accordance with the law in force at the time of the commission of the crime … " Article 4, paragraph 2, of the American Convention similarly provides that in "countries that have not abolished the death penalty, it may be imposed only for the most serious crimes and pursuant to a final judgment rendered by a competent court and in accordance with a law establishing such punishment, enacted prior to the commission of the crime." In addition, the CAT has stated that it considers corporal punishment to constitute torture, even when national legislation permits it.[33]

Thus, based on treaty language and Committee statements, Trinidad and Tobago could rationally decide that ratifying the Convention Against Torture could impose significant sovereignty costs because it would interfere with the country's ability to impose the death penalty and corporal punishment for certain crimes.

Commitment to, and denunciation of, the ICCPR Optional Protocol and the American Convention

Concerns about sovereignty costs related to its right to be able lawfully to impose the death penalty certainly seem to explain Trinidad and Tobago's decision to denounce the ICCPR Optional Protocol and the American Convention. True, by committing to these treaties, Trinidad and Tobago initially agreed to be subjected to stronger enforcement mechanisms beyond self-reporting, but when later events it could not have foreseen at the time of ratification threatened its domestic penalty regime, Trinidad and Tobago acted rationally and strategically in denouncing those treaties.

By way of background, Trinidad and Tobago ratified the ICCPR in 1978. In 1980, it ratified the ICCPR Optional Protocol allowing for individual complaints before the Human Rights Committee. In 1991, Trinidad and Tobago joined the American Convention, a regional treaty modeled on the ICCPR. Parties to the American Convention are automatically subject to the jurisdiction of the Inter-American Human Rights Commission (IAHRC, or Commission), which like the Human Rights Committee can make findings and issue nonbinding recommendations in response to individual complaints. Also in 1991, however, Trinidad and Tobago voluntarily recognized the jurisdiction of the Inter-American Court of Human Rights (IACtHR). Although individuals cannot directly petition the IACtHR, the Commission may refer to the court any petitions it has been unable to settle amicably. By the terms of the American Convention, the IACtHR is empowered to interpret the treaty's provisions and issue legally binding decisions against states that have recognized its jurisdiction.[34]

To understand why Trinidad and Tobago took the unusual step of later denouncing the ICCPR Optional Protocol and the American Convention, one must first understand how the country's death penalty practices were affected by its membership in these two treaties. First, like other Caribbean nations, Trinidad and Tobago's highest court of appeal was the London-based Judicial Committee of the Privy Council (Privy Council).[35] Initially, Trinidad and Tobago had no problem with that court even though it had authority to hear death sentence appeals.[36] That changed with the 1993 Privy Council decision in *Pratt v. Attorney General for Jamaica*.[37] In *Pratt*, the Council held that carrying out a capital sentence after a five-year delay not the fault of the accused would be in contravention of a constitutional provision against cruel, inhumane, and degrading punishment. Notably, delays resulting from domestic appeals processes (including to the Privy Council) and petitions to international human rights bodies would be included in calculating the five-year time period.[38] As a result of the *Pratt* ruling, Trinidad and Tobago had to commute the death sentences of 53 inmates who had been on death row for more than five years.[39]

The *Pratt* decision also tied the country's ability to carry out its domestic death penalty policies to the timeliness of the review processes capital defendants were allowed to pursue because of the country's membership in the ICCPR Optional Protocol and the American

Convention. Those review processes were not quick to conclude since the committees and court had crowded dockets and only met a few times per year.[40] The review processes became even slower after *Pratt* because more capital defendants filed appeals in order to create the five-year delay on the execution of their sentences.[41] In 1995, Trinidad and Tobago did try to convince the Privy Council to change the *Pratt* decision.[42] In 1997, it tried to get the committees and the court to decide appeals more expeditiously.[43] None of these efforts, though, was successful.[44] Thus, as a result of the Privy Council's decision, Trinidad and Tobago became effectively banned from imposing the death penalty: by invoking domestic review mechanisms and those afforded them by the country's membership in the ICCPR and American Convention, capital defendants were able to force the country to commute their sentences to life imprisonment.

Finally, in 1998, Trinidad and Tobago took the unusual step—after Jamaica—of denouncing its treaty obligations under the ICCPR Optional Protocol and the American Convention.[45] On 26 May 1998, Trinidad and Tobago denounced the ICCPR Optional Protocol and then re-acceded with a reservation to the effect that the Human Rights Committee would not be competent to consider petitions from capital defendants. In a December 1999 decision, however, the Human Rights Committee stated that it would not "accept a reservation which singles out a certain group of individuals for lesser procedural protection than that which is enjoyed by the rest of the population."[46] In response, on 27 March 2000, Trinidad and Tobago denounced the ICCPR Optional Protocol in its entirety.[47]

As to the American Convention, Trinidad and Tobago notified the Secretary-General of the Organization of American States that it was withdrawing its ratification of that treaty on 26 May 1998.[48] Again, Trinidad and Tobago made clear that its reasons for withdrawing from the treaty related to the threat being posed to its sovereign right to enforce its lawful domestic penalty regime. It noted that it would not "allow the inability of the Commission to deal with applications in respect of capital cases expeditiously to frustrate the implementation of the lawful penalty for the crime of murder in Trinidad and Tobago."[49]

In sum, the evidence suggests that Trinidad and Tobago's decisions to denounce the ICCPR Optional Protocol and the American Convention were based on rational and strategic calculations regarding the costliness of commitment. The country joined both treaties and committed to their stronger enforcement mechanisms rationally believing that neither treaty would threaten its domestic penalty regime since both treaties expressly exempted from their torture definition the lawful imposition of the death penalty according to previously enacted law. Only with the Privy Council's 1993 decision did Trinidad and Tobago become aware that its treaty obligations would interfere with its domestic death penalty practices. Additionally, it only denounced the treaties after the bodies that could consider individual death row petitions refused to conclude reviewing those petitions promptly enough so that Trinidad and Tobago could carry out its death sentences within the required five-year period. Even then, it did not fully denounce the ICCPR Optional Protocol until its reservation carving out death row petitions was rejected by the Human Rights Committee. Trinidad and Tobago only denounced its treaty obligations after events transpired to change the costliness of its commitments in a way that it could not have foreseen at the time of ratification.

Trinidad and Tobago and the ICC: assessing the explanatory power of the credible threat theory

Why did Trinidad and Tobago commit to the ICC treaty? Normative alignment with the treaty's terms and goals and national pride in being the impetus for renewed discussions to create the ICC at least partially explain the country's ratification behavior. The country has good human rights practices and its leader Arthur N.R. Robinson played a significant role in the court's creation by his letter to the UN and his active engagement thereafter in pushing for the court's creation. Trinidad and Tobago necessarily would want to take advantage of the opportunity to show the world that this small country not only supported international human rights norms, but also helped to create them.

However, the evidence also supports the explanatory power of the credible threat theory and the idea that states that are more able to comply with treaty terms are most likely to commit to treaties with stronger enforcement mechanisms. The evidence shows that ICC commitment should not impose significant sovereignty costs on Trinidad and Tobago—a fact which its own representative emphasized when supporting the passage of the International Criminal Court Bill. It has no reason to believe its citizens would commit the kinds of crimes covered by the Rome Statute. The country does have a problem with narcotics trafficking and associated crimes like murders, but those are not crimes covered by the ICC treaty. As to the death penalty and corporal punishment, neither is illegal under international law or by the terms of the ICC treaty. Even if the death penalty and corporal punishment did constitute torture, the Rome Statute makes torture a crime only in the context of war crimes or crimes against humanity.

However, Trinidad and Tobago does not participate in international wars or in UN Peacekeeping efforts, and judicially imposed punishments should not rise to the level of a crime against humanity, which requires a systematic attack against a civilian population.

Nor does the fact that Trinidad and Tobago has relatively weak domestic law enforcement institutions mean that it is unable to comply with the terms of the ICC treaty. The evidence from parliamentary debates shows that Trinidad and Tobago believes that its commitment to the ICC will not result in a loss of sovereignty since it can avoid ICC prosecutions if its citizens do not commit mass atrocities. The fact that it passed the International Criminal Court Bill in 2006 shows that Trinidad and Tobago views the ICC treaty's enforcement mechanism as a credible threat, but the passage of that law also means that the country has increased its ability to prosecute domestically any mass atrocities in the unlikely event they occur.

Examining the country's prior actions with respect to other human rights treaties further supports the power of the credible threat theory to explain Trinidad and Tobago's ICC ratification behavior. The country tends to avoid treaties with all but the weakest enforcement mechanisms. It did not even join the CAT. It denounced the ICCPR Optional Protocol and the American Convention when later events (which it could not have anticipated at the time of joining) showed that its continued commitment would significantly impinge on its domestic penalty regime. One should expect that Trinidad and Tobago learned from that experience not to take its commitments to treaties with stronger enforcement mechanisms lightly. In this case, because the terms of the ICC treaty address only mass atrocities and because the evidence suggests that Trinidad and Tobago's citizens will not commit those crimes, the country could rationally conclude that commitment would not impose significant sovereignty costs.

It is true that since joining the court, Trinidad and Tobago has acted in ways that demonstrate its commitment to the court and its goals, but these acts do not detract from the explanatory power of the credible threat theory. Trinidad and Tobago publicly refused to sign a bilateral immunity agreement with the United States, a decision which cost it US$450,000 in funding for its coastguard.[50] However, this decision did not make commitment to the ICC more costly in terms of Trinidad and Tobago's sovereign rights to conduct its internal affairs without interference from others. It entailed only a loss of aid and assistance. It was also a cost that Trinidad and Tobago could not have anticipated in 1999 when it ratified the Rome Statute. The George W. Bush Administration instituted the policy of pursuing bilateral immunity agreements, and it only started pursuing them at about the time the court became a reality in July 2002.[51] At the time it joined the ICC, Trinidad and Tobago would not have been able to calculate these additional costs of joining the court, and in any event, the costs did not impinge on its sovereignty.

Moreover, Trinidad and Tobago worked to minimize the costs associated with refusing to sign a bilateral immunity agreement, again showing its tendency to act rationally and strategically to minimize its commitment costs. By US law, military assistance would not be withdrawn for states that refused to sign a bilateral immunity agreement until July 2003, and the president had authority to waive any withdrawal of military aid if he deemed doing so in the national interest.[52] In 2003, at the same time it was refusing to sign a bilateral immunity agreement, Trinidad and Tobago was also trying to convince the United States that it and other Caribbean nations were effectively a "Third Border," which they alone could not protect and which was critical to the national interest of the United States.[53] Trinidad and Tobago was not initially successful in seeking a waiver, but by 2006 the United States cleared a block on military assistance to Trinidad and Tobago and to other countries that had not signed bilateral immunity agreements.[54] Therefore, the threat to Trinidad and Tobago's ability to receive military aid was resolved relatively quickly, such that the country's initial ratification decision remained relatively costless.

Finally, other theories advanced cannot explain Trinidad and Tobago's ICC ratification behavior. The credible commitment theory about hand-tying is not applicable because Trinidad and Tobago has good human rights practices and no recent history of government-sponsored violence. Nor is this a case where the country needs to lock in democracy. Trinidad and Tobago has been a democracy since its independence in 1962, and no evidence suggests its government has ever acted violently against its citizenry. Even though the country is weaker within the world community, external pressures did not seem to drive Trinidad and Tobago's commitment to the court. It reinvigorated the idea of an international criminal court, and it was the second state to join the court.

Conclusion

This case study has shown that Trinidad and Tobago was a leader in pushing for the ICC, that it is normatively aligned with the court, and that it joined in part because it wanted the benefit of showing the world that it could play such an important role in creating a new institution designed to end impunity for mass atrocities. However, the record also shows that Trinidad and Tobago did not place norms before compliance concerns. The evidence shows that the country is concerned with sovereignty costs and does not commit to treaties that run counter to its domestic interests and with which it has no intention of complying. Trinidad and Tobago was well aware of the strength of the ICC's enforcement mechanism, and it committed to the court knowing that its citizens would not commit mass atrocities, and after it had passed a law enabling it to prosecute any such atrocities should they occur.

The remaining case study chapters provide a contrast to this and the case study chapters before it by examining the ICC ratification behavior of countries with poor human rights practices and weak domestic law enforcement institutions.

Notes

1 Between 1998 and 2008, Trinidad and Tobago generally scored a 1 or 2 on the Political Terror Scale (see Chapter 2, note 24 for an explanation). During those same years, it scored approximately 0 on the World Bank's Rule of Law Scale (see Chapter 3, note 1).
2 *Letter from the Permanent Representative of Trinidad and Tobago to the Secretary-General* (UN GAOR, 44th Sess., Annex 44, Agenda Item 152, UN Doc. A/44/195), 21 August 1989.
3 Press Release L/2875, "Diplomatic Conference Begins Four Days of General Statements on Establishment of International Criminal Court," 16 June 1998.
4 Press Release L/2889, "UN Diplomatic Conference Concludes in Rome with Decision to Establish Permanent International Criminal Court," 20 July 1989.
5 See the INCSR Reports for Trinidad and Tobago 1997–2010, www.state.gov/j/inl/rls/nrcrpt/.
6 Serge F. Kovaleski and Douglas Farah, "Organized Crime Finds New Target in Island Nations," *South Florida Sun-Sentinel*, 22 February 1998.
7 Mark Fineman, "The Americas/A Weekly Look at People and Issues in Latin America/How to Hide Drug Witnesses/Caribbean Island Nations Aim to Beef Up Protection by Sharing Safe Havens," *Newsday*, 31 January 1999.
8 Stephen Breen, "Trinidad Begins Executing Killers," *The Scotsman*, 5 June 1999, available at 1999 WL 18798193.
9 Fineman, "The Americas/A Weekly Look at People and Issues in Latin America/How to Hide Drug Witnesses/Caribbean Island Nations Aim to Beef Up Protection by Sharing Safe Havens."
10 Tony Thompson, "No Mercy for Trinidad's Ruthless Gang Bosses: Caribbean Gallows Fever Reflects a Society Sick to Death of Violent Crime," *The Observer*, 30 May 1999, available at 1999 WL 13403710.
11 "Preparatory Committee on International Criminal Court Discusses Power to be Given Prosecutor" (Press Release L/2778), 4 April 1996; "International Criminal Court Should be Independent Body, and Not Subsidiary of

Security Council, Speakers Tell Legal Committee" (Press Release, GA/L/3044), 21 October 1997.

12 "Diplomatic Conference Begins Four Days of General Statements on Establishment of International Criminal Court" (Press Release, L/2875), 16 June 1998.

13 *Proposal Submitted by Barbados, Dominica, India, Jamaica, Sri Lanka, Trinidad and Tobago and Turkey* (A/Conf. 183/C.1/L.71), 14 July 1998.

14 CICC, "Penalties: Conference Escapes Death Penalty Noose," *On the Record*, 2 July 1998, www.iccnow.org.

15 *1995 Ad Hoc Committee Report* (UN GAOR, 52nd Sess., Supp. No. 22 and 22A, UN Doc. A/51/22 (1995)), paras. 54, 81; Preparatory Committee on the Establishment of an International Criminal Court, Summary of the Proceedings of the Preparatory Committee during the period 25 March–12 April 1996, UN Doc. A/AC.249/1, para. 63.

16 CICC, "Forget the Square Brackets, Go Back to Square One, Urges Trinidad and Tobago," *On the Record*, 16 June 1998, www.iccnow.org.

17 Herman von Hebel and Darryl Robinson, "Crimes Within the Jurisdiction of the Court," in *The International Criminal Court: The Making of the Rome Statute: Issues, Negotiations, Results*, ed. Roy S. Lee (The Hague, The Netherlands: Kluwer Law International, 1999), 87.

18 "Trinidad in a Spot over Death Penalty," *TerraViva: The Conference Daily Newspaper*, 26 June 1998, www.ips.org/icc/tv260602.htm.

19 "UN Diplomatic Conference Concludes in Rome with Decision to Establish Permanent International Criminal Court" (Press Release L/2889), 20 July 1989.

20 Trinidad and Tobago stated that although it was gratifying that the world community had adopted the Rome Statute for the creation of an international criminal court, it was disappointed that the treaty did not provide for jurisdiction over narcotics trafficking offenses or allow the imposition of the death penalty. However, it suggested both issues of concern to the Caribbean states could be revisited at a later date (A/C.6/53/SR.9), 21 October 1998.

21 Port of Spain Declaration on the International Criminal Court, 18 March 1999.

22 Statement by H.E. Arthur N.R. Robinson, the President of the Republic of Trinidad and Tobago, May 1998.

23 Trinidad and Tobago International Criminal Court Bill, Second Reading, Senate, Tuesday, 6 December 2005, 847 (statement of Senator Dr Jennifer Kernahan). Parliamentary materials are available at www.ttparliament.org/publications.php?mid=28&id=179.

24 Beth A. Simmons, *Mobilizing for Human Rights* (Cambridge: Cambridge University Press, 2009), scholar.harvard.edu/bsimmons/mobilizing-for-human-rights (listing country domestic ratification processes).

25 Trinidad and Tobago International Criminal Court Bill, Second Reading, Senate, Tuesday, 29 November 2005, 815.

26 *American Convention on Human Rights*, Nov. 22, 1969, O.A.S.T.S. No. 36, OEA/ser. L/V/II.34 doc. Rev. 2 (entered into force 18 July 1978), reprinted in Basic Documents Pertaining to Human Rights in the Inter-American System, Signatures and Current Status of Ratifications of the American Convention, www.oas.org/en/iachr/mandate/basic_documents.asp.

27 See www.fco.gov.uk/en/travel-and-living-abroad/travel-advice-by-country/country-profile/north-central-america/trinidad-tobago/.
28 See www.endcorporalpunishment.org/pages/progress/reports/trinidad.html.
29 Amnesty International, "Trinidad and Tobago: First Execution in 10 Years Threatened" (AMR/49/001/2009).
30 Amnesty International, "Amnesty International Report 2005—Trinidad and Tobago," 25 May 2005, www.unhcr.org/refworld/docid/429b27f920.html.
31 Keino Swamber, "Twelve Strokes for Sex with Girl, 12," *Trinidad & Tobago Express*, 1 June 2006, corpun.com/ttj00606.htm#19099; Keino Swamber, "25 years, 10 strokes for Cutlass Attack," *Trinidad & Tobago Express*, 30 May 2009, corpun.com/ttj00905.htm.
32 See CAT, art. 1, ICCPR, art. 7, and American Convention, art. 5.
33 *Committee Against Torture, Concluding Observations on Namibia* (UN Doc. A/52/44, paras. 227–52), 6 May 1997; *Committee Against Torture, Concluding Observations on Saudi Arabia* (UN Doc. CAT/C/CR/28/5, para. 4(b)), 12 June 2002.
34 American Convention, art. 1.
35 In April 2012, Trinidad and Tobago's prime minister announced the government's intention to table legislation to abolish appeals to the Privy Council in criminal matters and send them instead to the Caribbean Court of Justice, which was established in 2003. Richard Lord, "Out Goes Privy Council," *Trinidad & Tobago Guardian Online*, 26 April 2012, www.guardian.co.tt/news/2012-04-26-000000/out-goes-privy-council.
36 In fact, in *De Feitas v. Benny* [1976] A.C. 239 (P.C. 1975), the Privy Council had upheld the government's right to impose the death penalty for murder, holding that the imposition of the death penalty was not per se cruel and unusual punishment.
37 *Pratt v. Attorney General for Jamaica* [1994] 2 A.C. 1, 33–36 (P.C. 1993).
38 Ibid. The Privy Council stated that if the appellate procedure enables the prisoner to prolong the appellate hearings over a period of years, the fault should be attributed to the system, not to the prisoner who takes advantage of it.
39 Laurence R. Helfer, "Overlegalizing Human Rights: International Relations Theory and the Commonwealth Caribbean Backlash against Human Rights Regimes," *Columbia Law Review* 102, no. 7 (2002): 1872.
40 Ibid., 1873.
41 Ibid., 1875.
42 *Bradshaw v. Attorney General of Barbados* [1995] 1 W.L.R. 936, 941 (P.C. 1995).
43 Glenn McGrory, "Reservations of Virtue? Lessons from Trinidad and Tobago's Reservation to the First Optional Protocol," *Human Rights Quarterly* 23, no. 3 (2001): 778 and n. 41.
44 Helfer, "Overlegalizing Human Rights," 1880–81.
45 Natalia Schifferin, "Jamaica Withdraws the Right of Individual Petition Under the International Covenant on Civil and Political Rights," *American Journal of International Law* 92, no. 3 (1998): 563.
46 *Kennedy v. Trinidad and Tobago*, Communication (No. 845/1999, UN GAOR, Human Rights Committee, 55th Sess., Supp. No. 40, vol. 2, at 266, (UN Doc. A/55/40), 1999).
47 Helfer, "Overlegalizing Human Rights," 1881.

48 *Trinidad and Tobago: Notice to Denounce the American Convention on Human Rights* (26 May 1998), reprinted in Basic Documents Pertaining to Human Rights in the Inter-American System, Signatures and Current Status of Ratifications of the American Convention, OAS/ser.L/V/I.4, doc. Rev. 7, www.oas.org/en/iachr/mandate/basic_documents.asp.
49 Ibid.
50 Letta Tayler, "U.S. at Odds over World Tribunal: Bush Administration Suspends Aid to Nations that Refuse to Shield Americans from War-crimes Court," *Newsday*, 16 October 2004.
51 Human Rights Watch, "Bilateral Immunity Agreements," 3 June 2003, 2–3, www.iccnow.org/documents/HRWBIATableJune03.pdf.
52 Ibid.
53 "Trinidad's Premiere to Bring Up Caribbean Concerns on US Visit," *BBC News*, 3 August 2003.
54 Country Report, Aruba, December 2006, "The Region: Caricom Presses US to Discuss Important Issues for the Region," 8 December 2006, available at 2006 WLNR 24286918.

7 Rwanda

Credible threat, not credible commitment

- **Background: the 1994 genocide and its aftermath**
- **Rwanda and the ICTR**
- **Rwanda's participation in the international human rights regime: avoiding costly commitment**
- **Rwanda and the ICC: assessing the explanatory power of the credible threat theory**
- **Conclusion**

This case study examines Rwanda's refusal to join the International Criminal Court (ICC) and how the court's enforcement mechanism may have influenced that decision. Unlike the states previously studied, Rwanda is a non-democratic state with poor human rights practices and weak domestic law enforcement institutions.[1] In 1994, Rwanda experienced a horrendous genocide that left approximately 800,000 Tutsi men, women, and children dead at the hands of the Hutu majority. Even after the genocide, Rwanda's human rights practices remained poor. Rwanda's World Bank Rule of Law Scale ratings are low, and other anecdotal evidence indicates that Rwanda may not have the kinds of judicial institutions that would enable it to prosecute mass atrocities fairly.[2]

This case study is also the first of two that assesses the power of both the credible threat theory and the credible commitment theory to explain ICC ratification. The credible threat theory predicts that Rwanda should fear the ICC's strong enforcement mechanism and be wary of committing to the court because its domestic policies and practices suggest it will not be able to comply with treaty terms. By contrast, according to Simmons and Danner's credible commitment theory, non-democratic states with poor human rights practices and weak domestic legal institutions—like Rwanda—should embrace the ICC's stronger enforcement mechanism so as to tie their leaders' hands and credibly commit to their domestic audience to refrain from using violence to settle domestic crises. In short, the potential future gains of making a credible commitment should outweigh the sovereignty costs associated with being unable presently to comply with treaty terms.[3]

The case study evidence adduced below indicates that the credible threat theory better explains Rwanda's ICC ratification behavior than does the credible commitment theory. Rwanda's leader, President Paul Kagame, wants no constraints on his power to lead the country even if that means using force and violence. The evidence also suggests he realizes that the international community could conclude some of his actions or those of his people constitute human rights abuses or crimes deserving of punishment. However, Kagame does not want to relinquish his own power to decide what conduct is deserving of punishment to an international institution. Instead, the facts show that Rwanda carefully guards its sovereignty and is wary of joining international human rights institutions with any but the weakest enforcement mechanisms.

To help understand why Rwanda refused to commit to the ICC, this chapter begins with background on Rwanda's ethnic conflict and the 1994 genocide. The next section explores Kagame's actions in the aftermath of the 1994 genocide. The chapter follows by examining Rwanda's relationship with the ICTR—the International Criminal Tribunal for Rwanda. Although the ICTR is not identical to the ICC, Rwanda's relationship with it provides much evidence regarding Rwanda's reluctance to relinquish to the international community its sovereign right to administer justice to its citizens within its own borders. To give additional context for Rwanda's decision to refrain from joining the ICC, the chapter then examines Rwanda's relationship with the international human rights regime more generally. It concludes with a section that assesses the explanatory power of the credible threat theory and other competing theories in view of Rwanda's words and acts as they relate to the ICC.

Background: the 1994 genocide and its aftermath

The 1994 genocide

The 1994 genocide occurred under the leadership of Rwanda's long-standing Hutu dictator, President Juvenal Habyarimana, and involved crimes by Rwanda's Hutu majority against the Tutsi minority. From the time he became president in 1973, Habyarimana's policies involved discriminating against Tutsis. When those policies became increasingly violent, a group of Tutsis who had fled to neighboring Uganda formed the Rwandese Patriotic Front (RPF) to fight against Habyarimana's regime. However, Habyarimana responded by stepping up his government's repressive policies towards Tutsis: Tutsis were imprisoned or killed, all with the help of the new civilian militias known as the "*interahamwe*" who had been trained by the government army to fight against the RPF. Fighting continued during 1992 and 1993, as did a print and radio propaganda genocidal campaign aimed at eliminating Tutsis.[4]

Although President Habyarimana entered into a peace accord with the RPF in August of 1993, that peace was short-lived. Instead, the genocidal campaign continued. When President Habyarimana's plane was shot down in Kigali by missiles on 6 April 1994, killing began in earnest.[5] In only the first weeks of April 1994, and while United Nations (UN) peacekeepers who had been deployed to Rwanda's capital city to implement the 1993 peace accord stood by, thousands of Tutsis were killed. After 10 Belgian peacekeepers were murdered by Hutu troops, the UN effectively withdrew its peacekeepers, allowing a "wholesale extermination" of Tutsis to get underway.[6] The wave of killings ended in mid-July when the RPF captured the city of Kigali. By that time, and in only a few short months, approximately 800,000 Tutsis and Hutu moderates had been slaughtered.[7]

On 19 July 1994, the RPF decided to form a power-sharing government along the lines of that envisioned by the peace accords agreed to in 1993. As Rwanda's president, the RPF chose Pasteur Bizimungu, the most prominent Hutu in the RPF. Paul Kagame assumed the role of vice-president and minister of defense. By all accounts, however, Kagame was the de facto leader of the country even before he was elected president in 2000.[8]

Kagame closes the refugee camps

In the aftermath of the genocide, and much to the new regime's dismay, rather than standing by as it had during the genocide, the world community instead rushed to the aid of the "refugees" of the genocide who were living in camps near the Rwandan border. The problem was not that the world wanted to help refugees; the problem was that most of the "refugees" were actually Hutu genocidaires who had fled Rwanda once they sensed defeat.[9] The other problem was that the ex-militiamen in these camps had weapons (although they should have been disarmed), which they then used to wage killing sprees against Tutsis in nearby Rwanda.

The mere fact of the camps and the lack of control over their inhabitants caused the new regime in Rwanda to be frustrated and angry with the international community. That frustration mounted as Rwanda sought to have the camps closed and the "refugees" returned to their homeland. The new Rwandan government said the country was safe enough for everyone to go home—though some evidence suggests the government intended to arrest persons who had participated in the genocide. However, fearing they would be treated as they had treated the Tutsis, the genocidaires refused to leave, and the international organizations running the camps refused to force their repatriation.[10]

Violence in closing the Kibeho camp

Because Kagame deemed closing the camps a necessity, and because his pleas for assistance from the international community in closing them were generally met with inaction, Kagame and his soldiers took action. Kagame's forces were able to close some camps in a relatively peaceful manner, but significant violence erupted when those forces sought to close the last remaining camp, Kibeho, in 1995. The closing of Kibeho was chaotic from the beginning since some of the genocidaires were pressuring others in the camp not to cooperate with the forced repatriation. A conflict ensued with refugees hurling rocks at soldiers, to which the soldiers responded with gun fire. When refugees began running for the hills, the army opened fire into the crowd, shooting indiscriminately and lobbing grenades at them. The soldiers engaged in another round of shooting later that day when another group of refugees broke through the army's lines. In the end, the death toll reached into the thousands. Although some had died in stampedes or been killed by *interahamwe*, many had also been killed by the Rwandan army.[11] Rwanda has estimated that about 360 people were killed during the Kibeho closing. The UN and others suggest the numbers killed ranged between 2,000 and 8,000.[12]

The Kibeho tragedy (as it has been called) provides support for the idea that autocratic leaders in post-violence situations may not want to tie their hands to act in particular ways. The situation in the aftermath was complicated, and Kagame was unable to convince the world community quickly to close the refugee camps that were housing genocidaires and being used as staging grounds to plan and execute more violent attacks against the remaining Tutsi population. He therefore sent his troops to close the camps. Although some camp closings proceeded peacefully, in the case of Kibeho, violence ensued. Indeed, an

Independent International Commission of Inquiry determined that although the violence had not been one-sided, some of Kagame's RPF soldiers had summarily executed persons in the camp.[13] Kagame has nevertheless maintained that force was the only way to obtain what was necessary for Rwanda and its people. He explained: "We said, 'If you don't want to close them, then we shall close them.' And that's what happened, that tragic situation. But, the camps were no more, you see, and you could have had more trouble for the whole country by keeping the camps there."[14]

That Kagame has also generally ignored calls by the international community to prosecute the soldiers who acted violently in closing the Kibeho camp provides further evidence that Kagame does not want his hands tied. In April 1996, Amnesty International reported that the RPF had killed thousands of people in the Kibeho camp closure and asked the government to bring to justice those who had committed the killings.[15] Journalist Philip Gourevitch reports that two RPF officers who were in command at Kibeho were arrested shortly after the event and later tried. However, he suggests the verdict only showed that the new regime did not view the soldiers' actions as particularly criminal. They were convicted, but they were found guilty only of "having failed to use the military means at their disposal to protect civilians in danger."[16]

The 1996 attack on the paramilitary camp in Zaire

The difficulties with the camps did not end with Kibeho, and nor did Kagame's difficulties with the international community. According to Kagame, by 1996, Hutu genocidaires in refugee camps in Zaire were preparing to invade Rwanda so that they could reclaim their power and conclude their extermination plan. In July 1996, Kagame visited Washington, Europe, and the UN and explained that if the international community would not stop the problem that was brewing in those camps, then Kagame would have to handle the problem himself. Apparently few believed his threat, in part because Zaire (now the Democratic Republic of the Congo) was 94 times larger than Rwanda, but also because its leader, Mobutu Sese Seko, was an extremely powerful man in Africa, and attacking camps in his country would be a direct challenge to his regime.

After the international community refused to act, though, Kagame acted: he closed the camps in Zaire, he repatriated the hundreds of thousands of Hutus who were living there as refugees, and he overthrew Mobutu. Kagame created an alliance with Congolese rebel leader Laurent Kabila in order to accomplish his plan. In October 1996, Rwandan and Congolese rebel forces began attacking the camps around Goma in Zaire (the Congo). In the course of the fighting, thousands of innocent refugees, as well as Hutu genocidaires were killed. But as a result of the attacks, the camps were disbanded and about 1 million people were returned to Rwanda. Mobutu was also forced to flee his country.[17]

Again, some accused the RPF of committing crimes in connection with closing the camps in Zaire.[18] Again, Kagame's statements stress the necessity of his actions given the international community's failure to act. When asked by journalist Philip Gourevitch about his actions in the Eastern Congo, Kagame pointed out that former Rwandan military genocidaires had begun killing Tutsis again and that the genocidaires, who were armed with weapons and grenades, were refusing repatriation. He stated that the war in the Congo happened as it had in order that Rwanda would not "be rubbed off the surface of the earth."[19]

Rwanda and the ICTR

Establishment of the ICTR and Rwanda's lone dissenting voice

An examination of the events leading up to the establishment of an international tribunal to try Rwanda's genocidaires similarly demonstrates that Rwanda is a country that closely guards its sovereignty and wants to make its own determinations about how and whether justice should be meted out to its citizens based on actions occurring inside Rwanda.

Rwanda itself asked the international community to establish an international tribunal to assist it with prosecuting perpetrators of the genocide because it did not have the institutions or resources to carry out a plan for prosecutions without assistance.[20] According to a Human Rights Watch report, as a result of the wholesale slaughter of Tutsis, Rwanda was left with only 36 judges, 14 prosecutors, and 26 police inspectors (none of whom even had access to a vehicle).[21] Among its reasons for seeking an international tribunal, Rwanda argued that genocide was a crime of an international character. It also suggested that an international tribunal would have the advantage of appearing fair and neutral and would avoid any suspicion that Rwanda was trying to organize vengeful justice. Finally, Rwanda noted that involving the international community would make it easier to arrest and bring to justice those criminals who had taken refuge in foreign countries.[22]

However, when it came time to vote for establishing that international tribunal, Rwanda, as a temporary member of the Security Council (merely coincidental), stood alone in voting against it.[23] Apparently the Rwandan government had wanted an international tribunal, but it only wanted a tribunal that would be shaped according to its wishes and would take into account its customs and concerns.[24] In voting against the tribunal, Rwanda emphasized several aspects of the ICTR's institutional design that it viewed as unacceptable.

First, Rwanda objected to the ICTR's temporal jurisdictional restrictions which would only allow it to consider crimes occurring between 1 January 1994 and 31 December 1994.[25] Rwanda had proposed instead that the ICTR should be able to consider crimes committed between 1 October 1990 and 17 July 1994 so that the tribunal would also be able to prosecute persons who participated in planning the genocide in the several years leading up to it.[26] Victor Peskin takes a different view of Rwanda's temporal request, suggesting that by seeking an end date of 17 July 1994, the Rwandan government also hoped to ensure the tribunal could not consider any of the crimes the RPF committed against Hutu civilians after the conclusion of the conflict.[27] In a related vein, Peskin points out that Rwanda also objected to the lack of clear rules requiring the tribunal to use its limited resources to prosecute the most serious crimes of genocide, rather than any lesser crimes. Peskin suggests that this objection, too, was designed to ensure that the tribunal would have no legal authority to indict RPF officers who had committed non-genocidal crimes against Hutus.[28]

Second, Rwanda objected to what it perceived to be the limited institutional capacity of the tribunal. Against its wishes, the ICTR was slated to share resources—such as a prosecutor and an appeals chamber—with the ICTY (International Criminal Tribunal for the former Yugoslavia). In addition, the ICTR was created with funding only for two courtrooms. In Rwanda's opinion, without additional resources the tribunal would not be able to fulfill its mission of efficiently and effectively dispensing justice and holding the many high-level perpetrators of the genocide accountable. Rwanda's ambassador to the UN argued that these facts showed the international community had little interest in having the ICTR succeed in its mission. He stated: "My delegation considers that the establishment of so ineffective an international tribunal would only appease the conscience of the international community rather than respond to the expectations of the Rwandan people and of the victims of genocide in particular."[29]

Third, Rwanda could not abide a tribunal that would not impose the death penalty as punishment for those found guilty of genocide and crimes against humanity. Its domestic laws in effect at the time permitted a sentence of death penalty for murder, and it accordingly believed that the serious crime of genocide warranted the same potential penalty. Rwanda pointed out the failure to authorize a sentence of death at the ICTR would create an unfair disparity in punishments since the high-level suspects the ICTR was prosecuting would receive lighter sentences than the lower-level suspects it would be trying domestically. Rwanda's ambassador to the UN further emphasized that such a situation would not be "conducive to national reconciliation in Rwanda."[30] In an interview with Philip Gourevitch, President Kagame similarly stated that Rwanda could not support a tribunal that would not provide for capital punishment out of respect for Rwanda's laws. However, according to Kagame, in response to Rwanda's objections, the UN advised Rwanda to abolish the death penalty—a position that Kagame suggested was "cynical."[31]

Finally, Rwanda stated that it could not support a tribunal that was not located within its country. The Rwandan ambassador to the UN explained that the main reason Rwanda requested an international tribunal was "to teach the Rwandese people a lesson, to fight against the impunity to which it had become accustomed since 1959 and to promote national reconciliation." Therefore, he suggested that since the tribunal would have to deal with Rwandan suspects who had committed crimes in Rwanda against Rwandans, the tribunal adjudicating those crimes should sit in Rwanda. He further noted that "establishing the seat of the Tribunal on Rwandese soil would promote the harmonization of international and national jurisprudence."[32] Nevertheless, the international community refused to agree to locate the ICTR in Rwanda (and ultimately, it was located in Arusha, Tanzania). Basically, the UN worried that concerns about fairness and independence, as well as administrative efficiency, counseled against locating the tribunal in Rwanda: if the tribunal was in Kigali, the Rwandan government might be able to wield too much influence over it and thereby undermine its independence.[33]

On the other hand, although the international community did not yield to all of Rwanda's requests when it created the ICTR, the evidence shows that the Rwandan government was able to convince the Security Council to grant it some concessions. The UN finally agreed to locate the deputy prosecutor's office in Kigali. The Council also permitted the ICTR to hold trials in Rwanda if it chose to do so. In addition, the UN changed the tribunal statute to allow convicted ICTR defendants to serve their time in Rwanda. Moreover, the temporal restrictions on the ICTR's jurisdiction actually aided the

Rwandan government, as they ensured that any crimes committed by the RPF after the conclusion of the genocide would not be investigated by the tribunal.[34]

Despite these concessions, however, Rwanda remained critical of the ICTR and continued to portray the institution as one that was created only to assuage the international community's conscience with little regard for Rwanda or its many victims. The evidence at the time of negotiations and thereafter shows that Rwanda wanted an international tribunal to try perpetrators of the genocide that was carried out within its borders, but it also wanted significant control over that organization. Absent significant control, Rwanda would not vote for establishing the ICTR, cease from criticizing the institution, or fully cooperate with it.

Rwanda and the ICTR in practice: the issue of the RPF indictments

Rwanda's interest in having a tribunal that was under its control also manifested itself in how Rwanda criticized the tribunal or, at times, sought to assert its own influence over it. Rwanda voiced criticisms about, and mounted demonstrations against, many aspects of the ICTR's operations and practices, including the slow pace of indictments and prosecutions. However, the biggest conflict between Rwanda and the tribunal was triggered when then-Chief Prosecutor Carla Del Ponte announced in December 2000 that she had decided to expand her investigation to include potential atrocities committed by Tutsi RPF army officers against Hutu civilians during 1994. Although the Rwandan government initially agreed to cooperate with the ICTR's special investigation into potential RPF crimes, the scenario played out differently. Rwanda withheld its cooperation with the tribunal, and it also went on the offensive by criticizing the ICTR's slow pace in bringing and trying cases. It also managed to mobilize Tutsi survivor groups who accused the tribunal of victim and witness mistreatment. For example, Rwanda noted that the tribunal had arrested a veteran Hutu defense investigator after evidence showed that he had participated in massacring Tutsis during the genocide. It also accused a panel of ICTR judges of demeaning and unprofessional conduct for laughing during the cross-examination of a Tutsi rape victim. The prosecutor's office countered that the arrest was an isolated incident and that the judges' behavior had been misinterpreted.[35]

By April 2002, when Prosecutor Del Ponte publicly stated that RPF indictments would be forthcoming, the Rwandan government was well poised to block her efforts. Citing concerns about witness protection, during June 2002 the Rwandan government actually managed to shut down most tribunal business when it prevented Tutsi genocide survivors scheduled to testify on behalf of the ICTR prosecution from boarding a plane to Arusha. Victor Peskin reports that his interviews with tribunal officials and Western diplomats suggested that by preventing witness travel, the government was warning the ICTR that it would not be able to count on Rwanda's cooperation if it followed through on issuing RPF indictments.[36]

The Rwandan government did resume allowing witnesses to travel in July 2002, but its offensive against Del Ponte continued until she was removed from her post as the ICTR's chief prosecutor. After she met in The Hague with a Hutu rebel group to gather facts for her proposed RPF indictments, the Rwandan government publicly alleged that she was consorting with genocidaires, had lost her moral authority to prosecute genocide cases, and was unfit to serve the ICTR. Del Ponte defended her actions, arguing that she had a right to investigate all relevant criminal activities and called for punitive action to enforce Rwanda's obligation to cooperate with the tribunal even if it was investigating RPF actions. However, 2002 passed without Del Ponte handing down any RPF indictments. Nor did Del Ponte have much chance to obtain those indictments in the following year. By the summer of 2003, and after much lobbying by the Rwandan government, the UN decided to appoint a chief prosecutor for each tribunal: it dismissed Del Ponte from her role at the ICTR and retained her as the prosecutor of the ICTY only. Del Ponte has suggested that the dismissal was meant to prevent her from gathering enough evidence to issue RPF indictments.[37]

In sum, the way the events played out again show that Rwanda—under the de facto control of former RPF leader Paul Kagame—was not interested in an international tribunal it could not control. It believed that those who committed the genocide were the most deserving of punishment, and when the ICTR turned its sights on the RPF, it refused to cooperate with the institution.

Rwanda's participation in the international human rights regime: avoiding costly commitment

Rwanda's participation in the international human rights regime is consistent with the evidence adduced above which shows that Rwanda closely guards its sovereignty and prefers few restraints on its ability to manage its domestic affairs as it deems necessary—even if not in accordance with international human rights norms. Table 7.1 shows that Rwanda tends to avoid costly commitments since, with the exception of the Convention on the Elimination of All Forms of Discrimination Against Women (CEDAW) Optional Protocol, Rwanda has only participated in the main international human rights treaties with the weakest enforcement mechanisms.

A look at Rwanda's recent ratification of the Convention Against Torture and Other Cruel, Inhuman or Degrading Treatment or Punishment (CAT) treaty and the CEDAW Optional Protocol also supports a conclusion that Rwanda approaches international human rights treaties with a goal towards avoiding costly commitments. First, Rwanda only ratified the CAT in 2008, after it had abolished the death penalty—a decision that seems to have been prompted by Rwanda's desire to recapture its sovereign rights to prosecute the perpetrators of the 1994 genocide. Indeed, one main reason that states in Europe and the ICTR were refusing to transfer genocide cases to Rwanda was because Rwanda's laws allowed it to impose the death penalty.[38] On 16 March 2007, the government abolished the death penalty—but only for persons who were convicted in a case transferred to Rwanda from the ICTR. When that change proved insufficient to satisfy the ICTR, in July 2007 Rwanda entirely abolished the death penalty, though for certain offenses it substituted life imprisonment under solitary confinement.[39] However, Rwanda had to amend its laws again after the ICTR refused a transfer request because of the possibility that Rwandan courts might impose a sentence of life imprisonment under solitary confinement. A November 2008 law now provides that such penalty shall not be imposed in cases transferred to Rwanda from the ICTR.[40]

Table 7.1 Rwanda's commitment to the six primary international human rights treaties

Treaty	*Enforcement mechanism*	*Date open*	*Ratification date*
ICCPR	Reports	1966	1975
ICESCR	Reports	1966	1975
CERD	Reports	1966	1975
CEDAW	Reports	1980	1981
CAT	Reports	1984	2008
CRC	Reports	1989	1991
ICCPR Art. 41	State complaints	1966	–
CAT Art. 21	State complaints	1984	–
ICCPR Opt.	Individual complaints	1966	–
CERD 14	Individual complaints	1966	–
CAT 22	Individual complaints	1984	–
CEDAW Opt.	Individual complaints	1999	2008
CAT Opt.	Committee visits	2003	–

Although international human rights organizations still accuse Rwanda of treating its prisoners poorly and argue that imposing a sentence of life imprisonment with solitary confinement constitutes torture,[41] the facts still demonstrate that Rwanda only ratified the CAT after it had taken steps to minimize the costs of complying with the treaty. The CAT does not expressly exempt from its torture definition the lawful imposition of the death penalty. Courts in parts of the world have concluded that the death penalty is a cruel, inhuman and degrading punishment.[42] As to life imprisonment with solitary confinement, on the other hand, whether that constitutes torture may be less clear. The Human Rights Committee has stated only that "prolonged solitary confinement of the … imprisoned person *may* amount to" torture or cruel, inhuman or degrading punishment.[43] Although Rwanda's sentencing regime still may be subjected to criticism, by joining the CAT only after it had abolished the death penalty, Rwanda eliminated the death penalty as a subject of criticism by the Committee Against Torture and others.

The evidence similarly suggests that Rwanda could have rationally committed to even the CEDAW Optional Protocol's stronger individual complaint mechanism by December 2008 without risking a costly loss of sovereignty. That Convention provides that state parties condemn discrimination against women in all its forms and agree to pursue policies of eliminating discrimination against women in all fields. A review of the Committee's 2009 draft concluding observations regarding Rwanda show that the country has recently made "a number of changes in laws, policies and programmes with positive impact on the rights of women."[44] In addition, as Rwanda was likely aware by December 2008, the CEDAW Committee reviewing individual complaints is not particularly active.[45] Moreover, even if individuals did file complaints against Rwanda, the Committee is only entitled to try to persuade the country to adopt its views.

One might ask why Rwanda would join any international human rights institution given the difficult relationship it has had with the international community both before and after the genocide. Indeed, Rwanda joined the CAT and the CEDAW Optional Protocol while under the leadership of President Kagame, a person who has been vocal in expressing his frustration with and distrust of the international human rights community. While no definitive answer is possible, the facts do suggest that its commitment decisions were based on rational calculations about the costs of compliance. By abolishing the death penalty, and thereafter joining the CAT, Rwanda hoped to make a better case for being able to try genocide cases domestically—

something of a bid to regain some sovereign rights. In any event, none of the international human rights treaties listed above has an enforcement mechanism as strong as the ICC's. Only by joining the ICC treaty would Rwanda have to agree that an international body could try its citizens in The Hague. Rwanda can commit to these other treaties as "window dressing" only so as to appear to embrace international human rights norms. Such window dressing could be beneficial given that Rwanda is presently pursuing economic growth and the international investment that can be critical to that growth. As Steven Kinzer explains, President Kagame's goal is to pull Rwanda from poverty and into prosperity in relatively short order.[46]

Rwanda and the ICC: assessing the explanatory power of the credible threat theory

Based on the evidence outlined above, Rwanda's decision to refrain from joining the ICC is not surprising. That decision is also consistent with the credible threat theory because Rwanda's human rights practices and domestic law institutions are poor and could mean that the country's citizens would be punished for bad and noncompliant behavior. Kagame could rationally believe that he or others in Rwanda would commit the kinds of acts that some in the international community would suggest deserve to be punished by the ICC. Kagame does not want to be restrained in his ability to respond with force and violence should he deem it necessary in order to provide peace to Rwandans given the country's history of ethnic violence. He also does not want to relinquish Rwanda's sovereign right to decide what acts are deserving of punishment. Furthermore, Rwanda's decision to refrain from joining the ICC is consistent with its behavior in connection with other international human rights treaties. The evidence suggests that Rwanda acts in a rational and strategic manner when determining whether or not to join international human rights treaties because it avoids those with strong enforcement mechanisms and with which it cannot comply.

The power of the credible threat theory to explain Rwanda's ICC ratification behavior compares favorably to the explanatory power of Simmons and Danner's credible commitment hand-tying theory. Those scholars argue that by committing to the ICC, states with weak domestic accountability mechanisms can credibly demonstrate that they will not resort to the usual tactics that recklessly endanger civilians, such as wantonly mistreating prisoners and violently persecuting opposition groups, since should they do so, they may be prosecuted.[47]

This case study, however, shows that at least some countries with poor practices and weak domestic accountability will not necessarily want to tie their hands by committing to the ICC and risking prosecution.

The evidence shows that Kagame wants to rule his way without interference; he does not want his actions or leadership style judged or challenged by others; and he certainly does not want himself or his colleagues to be subjected to the possibility of prosecution by an international institution. Kagame already has had the experience of having his country's and his soldiers' human rights practices criticized by the world community, and his opinion about whether some practices are worthy of punishment evidently differs from the opinions of some in the world community. When Kagame was criticized for how he and his soldiers handled closing the refugee camps, he fought back by arguing that the actions were necessary given the threat to Rwanda and the inaction of the world community. Kagame was also active in blocking the ICTR's potential prosecutions of RPF soldiers. While some soldiers have been prosecuted domestically, Kagame has stated that he does not view those crimes as deserving of the same treatment or punishment as those who committed the genocide.

An examination of Rwanda's relationship with the world community in connection with the ICTR provides further evidence supportive of the credible threat theory—as opposed to the credible commitment theory. Rwanda's actions show that it wanted a tribunal that was more or less under its control, and when the tribunal was not structured in the way it preferred, it declined to vote for its creation. It continued to show that it wanted control over the ICTR even after it was created. When the tribunal did not move quickly enough, when it did not treat Rwanda's witnesses as Rwanda would have expected, and when it turned its sights on investigating RPF crimes, Rwanda and its people voiced their displeasure and even ceased cooperating with the tribunal.

Not only is Rwanda's behavior in refusing to commit to the ICC not consistent with the credible commitment theory, but its behavior is also not explained by the other external pressures theories. Even though more than half of the countries in Africa have committed to the ICC, and even though according to the Organisation for Economic Co-operation and Development (OECD), Rwanda is classified as one of the world's poorest countries, Rwanda has not bowed to any actual or implied pressure to ratify the ICC treaty so as to be perceived as a legitimate state deserving of rewards like aid and trade. Rwanda has relationships with countries in Europe and Africa, many of which have joined the court. In fact, in 2009, Rwanda further strengthened its relationship with Britain and other countries by becoming a member of the British Commonwealth.[48] In addition, for the years between 1997 and 2007, the European Union (EU) and Kenya have been Rwanda's top two exports markets.[49] Yet, Rwanda has not joined the ICC, even though the countries from which it receives much of its trading income are members.

Rwanda did sign a bilateral immunity agreement with the United States during the period in which the United States was a vocal opponent of the ICC, but pressure from the United States does not seem to explain Rwanda's ICC ratification behavior. First, the bilateral immunity agreement was reciprocal, in that the United States also promised not to surrender any Rwandan citizen to an international tribunal.[50] In fact, Rwanda's statement at the time it signed the bilateral immunity agreement provides further evidence supportive of the idea that Rwanda's refusal to join the ICC is based on rational cost concerns and fears that its citizens could be the subject of an international prosecution. President Kagame stated:

> Well, we thought first of all, we have to deal with some of these cases that require such a treatment where if the United States, for example, had a case that it's interested in, of their citizen to be tried in the United States, we respect that. And I'm sure if we had our own citizen who has committed an offense of a criminal nature, that we would have interest in, it would be interesting to us for the United States, where that is possible, for the United States to hand over such a person.[51]

Although this case study focuses only on Rwanda, it serves to illustrate the power of the credible threat theory to explain the ratification behavior of other states with poor human rights practices and a history of violence. Like President Kagame, leaders of other states with similarly complicated and violent histories (even if the details of that history vary) also may not want to tie their hands and make a credible commitment to refuse to respond with force or violence to any domestic crises. States with a history of violence may have the kinds of social cleavages that can continue to make civil violence a possibility, and the state may feel justified in responding with force simply so as to quell that violence and establish some sense of peace and security for the population as a whole. Like Kagame, leaders of these states with a history of domestic violence are more likely to be concerned about the credible threat posed by committing to an institution like the ICC with which they may not be able to comply and which they cannot control. Particularly where the state with a history of violence is governed by an autocratic leader, commitment to the ICC seems disingenuous. If the autocratic regime is not willing to impose domestic constraints on its power to act as it pleases—thereby signaling its credible commitment not to act violently—why would it join the ICC to make that credible commitment? While the autocratic regime may be able to put a stop to the domestic machinery it creates to impose accountability, it should not be confident that it would be able to stop the international machinery of the ICC.

Conclusion

This case study shows that Rwanda's actions in refusing to join the ICC are consistent with the credible threat theory. The evidence shows that Rwanda closely guards its sovereignty and is distrustful, even disdainful, of the international community. It particularly guards its sovereign rights to govern as it deems necessary, even if that means that it may have to use force to bring order, peace, and stability to the country. In addition, the evidence shows that Rwanda wants to decide on its own what actions constitute crimes deserving of punishment. Notwithstanding harsh criticism from some in the international community, the Rwandan government has refused to consider RPF crimes as deserving of the same level of punishment as those committed by the genocidaires. It has also shown that it wants to exercise control over the trials of those who committed the 1994 genocide: it abolished the death penalty so that it may receive cases transferred from the ICTR. Given this evidence, and the fact that Rwanda has poor human rights practices and domestic law enforcement institutions, Rwanda is rational in concluding that joining an institution like the ICC with its relatively strong enforcement mechanism would impose sovereignty costs that are simply too high to accept.

The chapter that follows examines the ICC ratification behavior of another state with poor human rights practices and poor domestic law enforcement institutions. Unlike Rwanda, however, Kenya joined the ICC.

Notes

1 Rwanda typically scored a 4 or a 5 on the Political Terror Scale between 1996 and 2004. Since 2004, it has improved somewhat, scoring 2 or 3 on that scale. See Chapter 2, note 24 for an explanation of the Political Terror Scale.

2 Between 1996 and 2008, Rwanda's World Bank Rule of Law Scale ratings ranged between -1.49 and -.250 (see Chapter 3, note 1 for an explanation). Although Rwanda's judicial system has apparently been improving, criticisms concerning its ability to prosecute persons fairly who allegedly committed

genocide during 1994 caused the International Criminal Tribunal for Rwanda (ICTR) to refuse to transfer cases to Rwanda for prosecution. See *Prosecutor v. Gatete*, Case No. ICRT-2000-61-R11bis (17 November 2008), para. 95. The ICTR Trial Chamber denied the ICTR prosecutor's request to transfer defendant Jean-Baptiste Gatete to Rwanda for trial, noting concerns about the defense's ability to call witnesses and the possibility that the defendant could be sentenced to life imprisonment in solitary confinement.

3 Beth A. Simmons and Allison Danner, "Credible Commitments and the International Criminal Court," *International Organization* 64, no. 2 (2010): 233–40.

4 Letter dated 1 October 1994 from the Secretary-General Addressed to the President of the Security Council (UN Doc. S/1994/1125), 4 October 1994, paras. 49–51.

5 No one claimed responsibility for the attack on Habyarimana's plane, nor has anyone been prosecuted for that offense. Some suggest Hutu extremists mounted the attack in order further to fuel the genocide. Others, including the French, argue that the RPF shot down the plane. Vanessa Thalmann, "French Justice's Endeavours to Substitute for the ICTR," *Journal of International Law* (2008).

6 Philip Gourevitch, *We Wish to Inform you that Tomorrow we will be Killed with our Families: Stories from Rwanda* (New York: Picador, 1998), 114.

7 UN Doc. S/1994/1125, para. 43.

8 Stephen Kinzer, *A Thousand Hills: Rwanda's Rebirth and the Man Who Dreamed It* (Hoboken, NJ: John Wiley & Sons, 2008), 186, 221–24.

9 Stephen Kinzer explains that the international community mistakenly believed that the people suffering in the camps were largely those who were survivors of the genocide, rather than those who had actually perpetrated the genocide. The world saw suffering, and instead of informing itself of the actual facts, rushed to provide aid to these "refugees." Kinzer, *A Thousand Hills*, 182.

10 Ibid., 167–89.

11 Gourevitch, *We Wish to Inform you*, 190–94.

12 Amnesty International, "Burundi and Rwanda Crisis Response," 24 April 1995, at 2.

13 UN Doc. S/1995/411, Report of the Independent International Commission of Inquiry into the events at Kibeho in April 1995, 23 May 1995, at para. 49.

14 Gourevitch, *We Wish to Inform you*, 207.

15 Amnesty International, "Two Years After the Genocide—Human Rights in the Balance: An Open Letter to Pasteur Bizimungu," 4 April 1996, at 5.

16 Gourevitch, *We Wish to Inform you*, 204.

17 Kinzer, *A Thousand Hills*, 197–205.

18 Report of the Mapping Exercise documenting the most serious violations of human rights and international humanitarian law committed within the territory of the Democratic Republic of the Congo between March 1993 and June 2003 (August 2010), at 78–114.

19 Gourevitch, *We Wish to Inform you*, 339.

20 Letter from the Permanent Representative of Rwanda to the President of the Security Council (UN Doc. S/1994/1115), 29 September 1994, at 4.

21 Human Rights Watch, "Rwanda: The Crisis Continues," April 1995, www.grandslacs.net/doc/2409.pdf.

22 UN SCOR, 49th Sess., 3453 mtg., UN Doc. S/PV.3453, 8 November 1994, at 14.
23 S.C. Res. 955, UN Doc. S/Res/955, 8 November 1994.
24 Victor Peskin reports that Joseph Mutaboba, Rwanda's deputy foreign minister and former ambassador to the UN told him that Rwanda wanted a tribunal, but that it never got what it had asked for. Another senior government official similarly stated that Rwanda wanted a "tribunal set up and structured as we wished." Victor Peskin, *International Justice in Rwanda and the Balkans: Virtual Trials and the Struggle for State Cooperation* (Cambridge: Cambridge University Press, 2008), 159.
25 S.C. Res. 955, UN Doc. S/Res/955, 8 November 1994, art. 7.
26 UN SCOR, 49th Sess., 3453 mtg., UN Doc. S/PV.3453, 8 November 1994, at 15.
27 Peskin, *International Justice in Rwanda and the Balkans*, 162.
28 Ibid.
29 UN SCOR, 49th Sess., 3453 mtg., UN Doc. S/PV.3453, 8 November 1994, at 15.
30 Ibid.
31 Gourevitch, *We Wish to Inform you*, 254.
32 UN SCOR, 49th Sess., 3453 mtg., UN Doc. S/PV.3453, 8 November 1994, at, 16.
33 Peskin, *International Justice in Rwanda and the Balkans*, 166.
34 Ibid., 167–68.
35 Ibid., 178–200.
36 Ibid., 209, 212–13.
37 Ibid., 219–22.
38 Amnesty International, 2008 Report, Rwanda.
39 Audrey Boctor, "The Abolition of the Death Penalty in Rwanda," *Human Rights Review* 10 (2009): 109; Jamil Ddamulira Mujuzi, "Issues Surrounding Life Imprisonment After the Abolition of the Death Penalty in Rwanda," *Human Rights Law Review* 9 (2009): 329.
40 Organic Law No. 66/2008 of 21 November 2008 Modifying and Complementing Organic Law No. 31/2007 of 25 July 2007 Relating to the Abolition of the Death Penalty.
41 Hirondelle News Agency, "Rwanda: Human Rights Watch Urges Govt to Completely Abolish Solitary Confinement Sentence," 29 January 2009, allafrica.com/stories/printable/200902180342.html.
42 Mujuzi, "Issues Surrounding Life Imprisonment After the Abolition of the Death Penalty in Rwanda," 329.
43 Human Rights Committee, General Comment No. 20, HRI/GEN/1/Rev.1 at 30 (1994) (emphasis added).
44 Committee on the Elimination of Discrimination against Women, 43rd Sess., "Draft Concluding Observations of the Committee on the Elimination of Discrimination Against Women: Rwanda," CEDAW/C/RWA/CO/6, 8 September 2009.
45 The committee overseeing CEDAW only began issuing decisions on individual complaints in about 2004. As of October 2010, individuals had submitted 27 complaints, 11 of which the Committee had concluded were inadmissible and only seven of which it had decided. Information about the Committee's activities can be obtained from www2.ohchr.org/english/law/cedaw-one.htm.

46 Kinzer, *A Thousand Hills*, 4–8.
47 Simmons and Danner, "Credible Commitments and the International Criminal Court," 233–34.
48 "Rwanda Admitted to Commonwealth," *BBC News*, 29 November 2009, news.bbc.co.ukh/2/hi/8384930.stm.
49 UN Conference on Trade and Development, "Rwanda's Development-Driven Trade Policy Framework," prepared by the UN Conference on Trade and Development and the Ministry of Trade and Industry of Rwanda, 2010.
50 "Agreement Between the Government of the United States of America and the Government of Rwanda Regarding the Surrender of Persons to International Tribunals," www.amicc.org/docs/US-Rwanda.pdf.
51 "Stakeout Media Availability with Paul Kagame, President of Rwanda, Following his Meeting with President Bush," *Federal News Service*, 4 March 2003.

8 Kenya

Hope becomes regret

- **Background: Kenya's transition from the Moi to the Kibaki presidency**
- **Kenya's participation in the international human rights regime: avoiding costly commitment**
- **Kenya's commitment to the ICC: rationality succumbs to pressure**
- **Kenya's commitment to the ICC post-ratification: mainly a record of noncompliance**
- **Kenya and the ICC: assessing the explanatory power of the credible threat theory**
- **Conclusion**

This case study, too, provides an opportunity to assess the explanatory power of the credible threat theory to explain International Criminal Court (ICC) ratification behavior and to compare it to the explanatory power of the credible commitment theory and the external pressures theories. This chapter explores Kenya's decision to ratify the Rome Statute, notwithstanding its history of poor human rights practices and weak domestic law enforcement institutions. Kenya signed the ICC treaty on 11 August 1999 under the leadership of long-time President Daniel arap Moi. Kenya, however, did not ratify the treaty until much later on 15 March 2005 under the leadership of President Mwai Kibaki.

Unlike Rwanda's failure to commit readily to the ICC, Kenya's commitment to the ICC in 2005 is not, on its face, consistent with the credible threat theory. Like Rwanda, Kenya's human rights practices are poor,[1] and it also has a history of domestic violence. According to a Human Rights Watch report, Kenya tends to experience significant ethnic violence leading up to or following elections.[2] In addition, Kenya's World Bank Rule of Law Scale ratings are low, and it, like Rwanda, appears to lack the kinds of institutions that would enable it to prosecute mass atrocities fairly and capably.[3] Therefore, had Kenya perceived the ICC treaty's relatively strong enforcement mechanism as a credible threat, it rationally should have avoided committing because of the risks associated with being unable to comply.

Indeed, this case study of Kenya well illustrates the perils of committing to a treaty with strong enforcement mechanisms without the apparent ability to comply with treaty terms. In November 2009, the ICC's prosecutor used his *proprio motu* powers for the first time and sought authorization to open an investigation into the violence that occurred after the 2007 election of President Kibaki.[4] More than 1,000 people died and some 300,000 were displaced during the course of ethnically charged violence that erupted after Kibaki was declared the winner of the presidential elections which challenger Raila Odinga and his supporters argued were rigged.[5] Despite numerous opportunities to do so, Kenya failed to establish a local tribunal to try those responsible for the post-election violence.[6] Thereafter, the ICC authorized an investigation, and on 15 December 2010, Prosecutor Moreno-Ocampo announced that he was charging six prominent Kenyans from Kibaki's and Odinga's political parties with having committed crimes against humanity.[7] Apparently, the sovereignty costs associated with complying with the ICC treaty became overwhelmingly clear to some in Kenya after the prosecutor announced his list of suspects: immediately, a member of Kenya's parliament put forth a motion to withdraw from the ICC.[8] Even though the country did not withdraw from the court, it continued its efforts to stop the ICC's processes by appealing to the African Union, the United Nations (UN) Security Council, and the ICC.[9]

The above evidence also helps to illustrate why Kenya's ICC ratification behavior is not consistent with Simmons and Danner's credible commitment theory. Under that theory, one might have expected President Moi—an authoritarian ruler—to join the ICC so as credibly to commit to end the cycle of ethnic violence that tended to accompany Kenya's elections. However, Moi only signed the ICC treaty. Kenya ratified the treaty in 2005 under President Kibaki, who assumed the presidency in 2002 following a campaign promising democratic reforms.[10] In any event, Kenya's behavior is nevertheless inconsistent with the credible commitment theory even if one characterizes it as a non-democracy after Kibaki's election. The evidence shows that Kenya has not embraced the ICC's hand-tying mechanism post-ratification. Although Kibaki himself may not have participated in the 2007 post-election violence, Kibaki was the country's disputed leader while that violence in which his security forces participated was ongoing,[11] and his government allegedly failed to hold any high-level perpetrators accountable for the violence they inflicted during the riots.[12] Moreover, after the prosecutor named the suspects he intended to try in The Hague, Kenya acted consistently with the credible threat theory—not the credible commitment theory—by seeking to avoid its commitment to the court.

This chapter begins with background examining Kenya's transition from the leadership of President Moi to that of President Kibaki. It then looks at Kenya's behavior in connection with other international human rights treaties in an effort to generate a more complete picture of what factors influence its commitment decisions. The chapter continues by tracing Kenya's participation in the creation of the ICC and its decisions to sign and later ratify the Rome Statute. The section that follows explores Kenya's compliance with ICC treaty terms, addressing in particular the 2007 post-election violence, the ICC's investigation of that violence, and the government's responses to it. The chapter concludes by exploring whether and how the credible threat theory and other competing theories explain Kenya's ICC ratification behavior.

Background: Kenya's transition from the Moi to the Kibaki presidency

For some 24 years prior to December 2002, President Daniel arap Moi, leader of the Kenyan African National Union (KANU), ruled Kenya as an autocracy. Moi has been blamed for Kenya's abject poverty because of his administration's endemic corruption and plunder of state resources. Under Moi, Kenya's human rights practices and the quality of its domestic law enforcement institutions were poor. Human Rights Watch has charged Moi's government with using police brutality against citizens and with interfering with the judiciary's operations and decisions.[13] In addition, since multi-party politics were restored in 1991, Moi's electoral wins in 1992 and 1997 were accompanied by significant ethnic-based violence. Human Rights Watch reports that some of the worst episodes of violence occurred between 1991 and 1993 when President Moi stirred up ethnic violence against the Kikuyu in the Rift Valley to consolidate his favorable votes among the Kalinjin people once they had driven out the Kikuyu. That violence resulted in some 1,500 dead and another 300,000 displaced.[14] Although high-ranking party officials evidently directly instigated the violence, Moi generally allowed impunity to reign and refused to punish the instigators.[15]

In 2002, Kibaki came to power on a platform promising sweeping constitutional and judicial reforms and pledging to put an end to the endemic corruption that had characterized Moi's administration.[16]

Nevertheless, the promised reforms were often delayed or not forthcoming. According to a 2008 Human Rights Watch report, "[d]espite a promising start—which included improvements in freedom of expression and association coupled with strong economic growth—corruption, patronage politics, state-sponsored violence, and persistent police abuses have defined the order of the day."[17] Moreover, Kibaki did not deliver a new constitution limiting presidential powers within 100 days of assuming office as promised. He presented a draft constitution in 2005, but that constitution included a non-executive prime minister who was subservient to the president. Because Kibaki would not release his stronghold on executive power, voters rejected the 2005 draft constitution.[18] Kibaki's response to that rejection further demonstrated his reluctance to deliver on his campaign promise to limit presidential power: he thereafter dismissed his entire cabinet, including all of those who supported his opponent and the country's Prime Minister, Raila Odinga (a man who had helped get Kibaki elected in 2002).[19] Kibaki only delivered a new constitution that actually limited presidential powers in August 2010.

Kenya's participation in the international human rights regime: avoiding costly commitment

Table 8.1 shows that Kenya typically avoids costly commitments and limits on its sovereign rights to mete out justice within its borders. Kenya has ratified only those treaties with the weakest enforcement mechanisms

Table 8.1 Kenya's commitment to the six primary international human rights treaties

Treaty	*Enforcement mechanism*	*Date open*	*Ratification date*
ICCPR	Reports	1966	1972
ICESCR	Reports	1966	1972
CERD	Reports	1966	2001
CEDAW	Reports	1980	1984
CAT	Reports	1984	1997
CRC	Reports	1989	1990
ICCPR Art. 41	State complaints	1966	–
CAT Art. 21	State complaints	1984	–
ICCPR Opt.	Individual complaints	1966	–
CERD 14	Individual complaints	1966	–
CAT 22	Individual complaints	1984	–
CEDAW Opt.	Individual complaints	1999	–
CAT Opt.	Committee visits	2003	–

requiring states to self-report their compliance. Because these six treaties do not have mechanisms to actually punish bad and noncompliant behavior, Kenya can commit without facing any real negative consequences.

Accordingly, when considered in this more general context of a state that avoids costly commitments, Kenya's decision to ratify the ICC seems less than rational. At the time it ratified the ICC treaty, Kenya had poor human rights practices and poor domestic law enforcement institutions. Because the ICC treaty's enforcement mechanism is strong enough to punish bad and noncompliant behavior, Kenya should not have risked committing.

Kenya's commitment to the ICC: rationality succumbs to pressure

Kenya did participate in the negotiations leading up to the adoption of the Rome Statute, and although the few records of its statements indicate that it supported the idea of a court, it was more inclined to favor fewer powers for the prosecutor. Summary records of the proceedings at the Rome Conference show that Kenya's Head of Delegation and Attorney-General Mr Wako, "reaffirmed Kenya's commitment to the establishment of an effective, impartial, credible and independent international criminal court, free from political manipulation, pursuing only the interests of justice, with due regard to the rights of the accused and the interests of the victims" and stated that his delegation would support all efforts to seek consensus on the establishment of the court.[20] He further referenced the central importance of the principle of complementarity which would allow the ICC to act only where national criminal justice systems "were not available or were ineffective."[21] However, in the case of *proprio motu* powers for the prosecutor, Kenya's Mr Kandie stated that his delegation saw no reason why the prosecutor should have such powers inasmuch as the twin triggers of state and Security Council referrals (subject to appropriate controls) should be sufficient to cover all cases that would need to go before the court.[22] Mr Mwangi of Kenya said that while his delegation was prepared to support automatic acceptance by states of jurisdiction over the core crimes upon ratification, his delegation "continued to doubt the desirability of conferring *proprio motu* powers" on the prosecutor since he might be subject to political pressures. Nevertheless, Mr Mwangi confirmed that his delegation would not stand in the way of a consensus on the issue.[23]

However, making statements during treaty negotiations, and even signing international human rights treaties, does not subject states to significant sovereignty risks for failing to comply with treaty terms. In any event, there is little reason to believe that the statements Kenya made during the Rome Statute negotiations reflected Kenya's sincere commitment to embrace an international norm aimed at ending impunity for mass atrocities. It is worth noting that Kenya's Head of Delegation during the Rome Statute negotiations, Mr Wako, has served as Kenya's Attorney-General since 1991. This means he was Kenya's top law enforcement official during the many years Kenya had poor human rights practices, a corrupt government, and institutions that allowed impunity to reign. He was Kenya's top law enforcement official during all of the violent election-related clashes that occurred in the 1990s. Moreover, he has been criticized for failing to end Kenya's cycle of impunity by blocking political reforms following the 2007 post-election violence and accused of being an obstacle in the country's fight against corruption. In fact, in October 2009, the United States banned Attorney-General Wako from traveling to the United States, citing these very same criticisms.[24] Mr Wako denies the allegations against him. But the fact that he has been the country's top law enforcement official throughout Kenya's many years of violence and impunity suggests that his words during Rome Conference negotiations about Kenya's desire for a strong and independent international criminal court may not have been sincere.

In March 2005, however, despite the fact that its human rights ratings and Rule of Law ratings remained poor, Kenya ratified the Rome Statute. Precisely why Kenya decided to commit to the treaty at that time one may never know, but its ratification decision appears mostly inconsistent with the predictions of the credible threat theory given the country's poor prospects for compliance with treaty terms. It is true that after Kibaki was elected, Kenya was classified as a democracy, rather than an autocracy. It is also true that Kibaki was elected based on a platform that promised democratic reforms, an end to corruption, and greater respect for the rule of law. Although this evidence may have suggested a potential for compliance, other evidence indicates that Kibaki may not have been truly committed to democratic reforms. For example, Kibaki only delivered a draft constitution limiting presidential powers in 2005—years after it had been promised. Yet, that 2005 constitution did not limit presidential powers. Further, as described in more detail below, some evidence suggests that Kibaki's 2007 election may have been rigged. That Kibaki was Kenya's leader at the time of the post-election violence which involved his own security forces provides additional evidence that Kibaki's stated commitment to democratic practices or improving Kenya's human rights practices was not necessarily sincere.

However, if Kenya was unable to, or did not intend to, comply with ICC treaty terms, why would it commit to a treaty with a strong enforcement mechanism that could be invoked to punish it for failing to comply? One answer is that Kenya did not view the Rome Statute's enforcement mechanism as a credible threat. This answer, though, is less than satisfying. After all, Kenya did participate in negotiations, knew that states were fighting over the nature and strength of the ICC treaty's enforcement mechanism, and was aware that states decided to create a strong and independent prosecutor and court. Also, Kenya's failure to ratify any but the main international human rights treaties with the weakest enforcement mechanisms indicates that Kenya understands the potential threat of stronger enforcement mechanisms. Finally, by the time Kenya ratified the ICC treaty, it knew the ICC had already commenced some cases—although the prosecutor had not yet commenced a case using his *proprio motu* powers. Prior to March 2005, in fact, several other situations had been referred to the ICC, including the situation in Darfur Sudan.[25]

On the other hand, external pressures and the lure of potential extra-treaty benefits may have prompted Kenya to commit to the ICC when it did despite the treaty's strong enforcement mechanism. The evidence suggests that after Kibaki became president, Kenya was subjected to considerable domestic and international lobbying designed to persuade it to commit to the Rome Statute. After all, Kibaki and his government had claimed to be democratic reformers and refusing to commit to the ICC might be viewed as contrary to such a reformist agenda. Thus, in October 2004, the Kenya National Commission on Human Rights sponsored a forum to raise awareness about the importance of the ICC and other institutions. In January 2005, the CICC chose Kenya as its target country on which to focus its ICC ratification efforts.[26] Among other things, the CICC referenced Kenya's role as a peace builder in Africa and suggested that Kenya's ratification of the ICC would send an "important to signal to other African states who have yet to ratify about Africa's growing commitment to international justice and the rule of law."[27] Furthermore, by 2005, some 26 other African countries were already ICC members, a fact which some argued reflected badly on Kenya's image.[28] After Kenya ratified the ICC treaty, it was praised for sending a strong message that it will break from its past cycle of impunity.[29]

In fact, Kenya well illustrates a point made in the Introduction. Some states with bad practices may experience certain "windows of opportunity"—such as a change in leadership or a point where external or internal calls for commitment can no longer be ignored—where the benefits of joining a treaty may seem to outweigh potential sovereignty costs. Kenya was presented with just such a "window of opportunity" in 2005 when it was pressured to join the ICC to demonstrate its commitment to democratic reforms and to show that it could be a leader in Africa. In March 2005, Kenya likely realized that it risked being unable to comply with the ICC treaty, but at that moment in time, it could have concluded the risk was slight and that the potential benefits of appearing to be a state that was genuinely committed to democratic reforms outweighed that risk. As it turns out, Kenya's decision to join the ICC was a bad one from a sovereignty standpoint since it apparently joined without sincerely committing to make the normative changes necessary to ensure that it could comply with the treaty's terms. As discussed below, the evidence does not show that Kenya committed to the ICC so as to tie its hands and embrace positive and long-term domestic change.

Kenya's commitment to the ICC post-ratification: mainly a record of noncompliance

The refusal to sign a bilateral immunity agreement

One fact which may have suggested the sincerity of Kenya's intention to comply with the ICC's terms was its refusal to bow to US pressure to sign a bilateral immunity agreement. Apparently the United States had sought Kenya's signature on an immunity agreement since 2003, threatening to suspend a military aid package of approximately US$9.8 million should Kenya refuse to sign.[30] The United States stepped up its pressure to get Kenya to sign an immunity agreement after Kenya ratified the ICC treaty in March 2005. Although Kenya purportedly initially looked favorably on the agreement, it ultimately succumbed to domestic and international groups who were beseeching Kenya not to sign. Among other things, those groups stressed Kenya's sovereignty, but also the fact that signing the agreement would contradict its obligations under the Rome Statute.[31] Kenya's decision to withstand US pressure was well received by the international community: the CICC sent a letter to President Kibaki stating that "Kenya's decision to uphold its commitment to the ICC treaty and to the concept of equality of all before the law despite the threatened loss of US aid 'exemplifies a victory of principle over brute power.'"[32]

Thus, in the early days after ratification, Kenya's refusal to sign a bilateral immunity agreement could perhaps be viewed as evidence that Kenya was normatively committed to the court and intended to abide by its obligations under the Rome Statute. That piece of evidence suggesting an intention to comply, however, is generally outweighed by evidence that tends to demonstrate a lack of normative commitment to ending impunity.[33] First, even Kenya's refusal to sign the immunity agreement eventually became irrelevant. In January 2009, the United States waived the prohibitions on aid to Kenya after concluding that supporting Kenya militarily was important to the national interests of the United States.[34] Second, as discussed in more detail below, the facts of the 2007 post-election violence and Kenya's interactions with the ICC regarding its investigation of that violence are not compatible with those of a country committed to good human rights practices or one intending to end impunity for those who commit serious international crimes. Finally, Kenya's decision to invite Sudan's President Omar Bashir to Kenya to celebrate its new constitution in August 2010 is further evidence of Kenya's noncompliance. Indeed, Kenya's actions are quite clearly at odds with the statement Kenya's Assistant Minister for Foreign Affairs Moses Wetangula made about Kenya's intended ICC compliance shortly after it refused to sign an immunity agreement with the United States. He said: "The Kenyan government has no intention of exempting anybody or any country under any circumstances [from the operation of the ICC's processes]."[35] Yet, it was Mr Wetangula himself who invited Bashir to visit Kenya knowing there was an ICC warrant for his arrest.[36]

The 2007 post-election violence and the ICC investigation

The facts surrounding Kenya's 2007 post-election violence and Kenya's interactions with the ICC as a result of that violence provide proof that Kenya has failed to comply with the ICC treaty's terms. Those facts also suggest that Kenya's commitment to the ICC did not signify any sincere long-term commitment to positive normative change. When Kenya ratified the ICC treaty, Kibaki was certainly aware of Kenya's history of election-related ethnic violence. Yet, Kibaki and his supporters allegedly rigged election results which voting tallies had suggested were favoring Kibaki's opponent, Raila Odinga.[37] Even if Kibaki did not himself rig the results, his actions after Odinga's party alleged that Kibaki had committed electoral fraud did not help to ease an already tense situation. Within only an hour after the Chair of the Electoral Commission of Kenya declared Kibaki the winner of the presidential elections—even though Odinga's party was still alleging fraud—Kibaki quickly had himself sworn into office before the people had any chance to voice their anger or concern.[38] As might be expected given the country's history, immediately after the results were announced to the public, violence erupted. Although reports suggest that some violence was spontaneous and some was orchestrated by Odinga supporters against the ethnic groups that supported Kibaki, reports also show that Kibaki's own police forces contributed to the violence, which left more than 1,000 people dead and hundreds of thousands displaced.[39]

As the extent of the violence became known, the international community intervened and established a mediation process led by former UN Secretary-General Kofi Annan. The main outcome of that process was the formation of a grand coalition government, with Kibaki as president and Odinga as prime minister. In addition, a Commission of Inquiry, chaired by Justice Philip Waki of the Kenyan Court of Appeal, was charged with investigating the post-election violence and making recommendations. On 15 October 2008, the Commission issued its report (the Waki Report), which concluded that some individuals may have committed crimes against humanity in the post-election violence. The Waki Report recommended establishing a Special Tribunal in Kenya with judges from Kenya and from the international community to investigate, prosecute, and adjudicate the identified alleged crimes. In case the Special Tribunal was not created or failed to carry out its functions, the Commission ensured that Kofi Annan had the information necessary to refer the matter to the ICC for prosecution.[40]

Kenya's actions after the issuance of the Waki Report only serve as further proof that when Kenya committed to the ICC treaty, it did not also sincerely commit to furthering treaty goals and ending impunity for mass atrocities. Rather, the record shows a government intent on stonewalling any attempt to hold its representatives accountable, whether domestically or internationally. It was only hours before the Waki Commission's deadline was set to expire—and names forwarded to the ICC—that Kibaki and Odinga finally signed a bill starting the legislative process towards establishing a Special Tribunal to try post-election violence suspects.[41] Then, when the bill to establish a Special Tribunal came to a vote, Parliament rejected it.[42] Even though Kibaki and Odinga presented and lobbied for the bill, reports indicate that Kibaki and Odinga were actually less than supportive of it.[43] In fact, one member of Parliament argued to the press that if Kibaki and Odinga had really wanted a Special Tribunal established, they could have used their leadership roles and more assertively pressed for it.[44] Finally, Kenya has otherwise done little to hold accountable those responsible for instigating the post-election violence and causing thousands of deaths and displacements. In its 31 March 2010 decision authorizing the ICC Prosecutor's request to proceed with his investigation of the post-election violence, the ICC court noted that the only domestic investigations and prosecutions were of relatively minor offenses and against persons who did not bear the greatest responsibility.[45]

Kenya's interactions with the ICC and its investigation similarly show a government that is not committed to ending impunity or complying with its treaty obligations. Kibaki and Odinga both pledged to cooperate with the ICC's investigation, but some evidence shows that Kenya frustrated some of the ICC prosecutor's efforts to gather evidence. For example, the government argued that some documents could be withheld from the ICC on grounds of national security, and some of Kenya's police commissioners and officers refused to give statements.[46] Further, Kenya has not embraced the ICC treaty's hand-tying effects and instead has tried to release itself from its commitment. When the ICC prosecutor announced he would be proceeding with an investigation against six suspects, Kenya's parliament voted overwhelmingly to withdraw from the ICC.[47] Parliament made this decision despite the fact that polls showed most ordinary Kenyans support the ICC and want it to bring perpetrators of the violence to justice.[48] Though Kenya did not withdraw from the ICC,[49] it thereafter continued to search for ways to escape the ICC processes. It lobbied the African Union, the ICC court, and the UN to stop the ICC from proceeding, arguing that Kenya should instead be permitted to establish a local tribunal to try Kenyans for the crimes committed during the post-election violence.[50] However, as one member of Parliament argued, had the government really wanted a local tribunal, it could have voted for that option a year before.[51]

Kenya invites Sudan's President Bashir to celebrate its new constitution

Kenya's decision to invite President Bashir of Sudan to attend Kenya's August 2010 celebration of the passage of its new constitution is further evidence that Kenya did not support the ICC's normative goals when it joined the court in 2005. On one hand, Kenya finally implemented a new constitution providing for a more decentralized political system that minimized presidential power and allowed for a more independent judiciary.[52] On the other hand, Kenya invited to the celebration of its new constitution a leader who is the subject of an ICC arrest warrant charging him with war crimes, crimes against humanity, and genocide based on violence in Sudan's Darfur region which left some 300,000 people dead. Not only did Kenya extend that invitation to President Bashir, but it also hosted him inside the country and allowed him to return to Sudan. As Human Rights Watch has suggested, inviting Bashir "tarnish[es] [Kenya's] celebration of its long-awaited constitution."[53] Kenya's own National Human Rights and Equality Commission stated that the "government's lack of action is a statement of impunity and sends a worrying message on the implementation of the new constitution."[54] As a member of the ICC, Kenya was required to arrest Bashir and transfer him to The Hague. It did not do so even in the face of pleas to cooperate by the ICC and the European Union (EU).[55]

Kenya has advanced various reasons for its failure to comply with its obligations under the ICC treaty, but none changes the fact of its noncompliance. Kenyan representatives have stressed that peace in Southern Sudan and Darfur may suffer if African nations are seen to be putting too much pressure on President Bashir.[56] Kenya has further noted that by refusing to arrest Bashir, it is following the recommendation of the African Union which decided not to cooperate with the UN in arresting Bashir and instead asked for a Security Council postponement of the case.[57] Prime Minister Odinga advanced a different reason for failing to take a role in ensuring that Kenya complied with its obligations under the Rome Statute: he claimed not to have been aware that Bashir was invited to the celebration of the new constitution. Members of Odinga's party state that Bashir was invited to the celebration by Foreign Minister Wetangula, a member of Kibaki's party. Indeed, Odinga is reported as saying that he has no problem with Sudan as a neighbor, but that he knows that Kenya looks "very bad in the eyes of the international community, because we invited somebody indicted by the International Criminal Court to spoil the party for us."[58] Again, actions speak louder than words. Odinga's statement suggests he knows Kenya has an obligation to comply with the Rome Statute's terms and arrest Bashir, but the evidence does not show he took any actions to ensure that compliance.

In sum, Kenya's refusal to arrest Bashir evidences a lack of any long-term normative commitment to the ICC's goals and a refusal to comply with ICC treaty terms. This is not a situation where Bashir simply appeared in Kenya unannounced. By inviting President Bashir to visit, Kenya purposely went out of its way to demonstrate its disdain for the ICC's stated goal of ensuring that perpetrators of mass atrocities are brought to justice.

Kenya and the ICC: assessing the explanatory power of the credible threat theory

The evidence indicates that Kenya joined the ICC because of external pressures and because at a particular point in time it concluded that the benefits of joining the ICC treaty may outweigh the potential sovereignty costs of joining. In March 2005, Kenya likely realized that it risked being unable to comply with the ICC treaty given that it still had poor human rights practices and weak domestic law enforcement institutions. For whatever reason, it may nevertheless have concluded that the risk its citizens would commit mass atrocities or that the ICC would thereafter prosecute them was slight. Indeed, its later conduct shows that it believed that voting to withdraw from the ICC or lobbying the African Union, the Security Council, or the ICC itself might be sufficient to halt ICC processes. Or, it may simply have concluded that the benefits associated with putting a stop to all the lobbying pressure and critiques outweighed sovereignty risks at that moment in time. Kibaki had been elected on a platform of democratic reforms, and the world community and civil society were pressuring him to demonstrate more of a commitment to such reforms. Also adding pressure was the fact that by the time Kenya ratified the Rome Statute in 2005, 26 African states had already joined the court. That these external pressures may have contributed to Kenya's decision to join the ICC seems likely inasmuch as Kenya has not shown itself to be a state that joins international human rights treaties with which it may not be able to comply unless those treaties have the very weakest enforcement mechanisms.

Nevertheless, while the credible threat theory does not explain Kenya's 2005 ratification decision, it is helpful in explaining Kenya's behavior both before and after ratification. In 2005, Kenya did commit to the ICC treaty despite its probable inability to comply with treaty terms and despite knowing that the ICC's enforcement mechanism was stronger than the mechanisms contained in the treaties it had previously joined. However, Kenya's behavior in refusing to commit to the ICC treaty for the six years after it signed the ICC treaty in 1999 (a costless decision) is consistent with the credible threat theory. During most of these years, Moi ran the country as an autocracy, and the previous constitution would have allowed him and his cabinet to join the ICC had they wanted to without further input from the legislature. Yet, consistent with Kenya's general behavior in avoiding commitment to treaties with stronger enforcement mechanisms, it did not ratify the ICC treaty. Of course, during these six years, Kenya had the poor human rights practices and weak domestic law enforcement institutions that could cause it to run afoul of treaty terms and be punished for bad and noncompliant behavior.

Kenya has also acted consistently with the expectations of the credible threat theory post-ratification, in that it has shown that it is well aware of the strength of the ICC's enforcement mechanism and seeks now to avoid its costly commitment. The country's citizens are the subject of an ICC investigation because of the 2007 post-election violence and because the country has failed to hold those responsible for the violence accountable. Kenya did not set up a Special Tribunal to try perpetrators; it did not fully cooperate with the ICC's investigation; and it has appealed to numerous bodies to help it halt the ICC processes. Indeed, the legislature's vote for withdrawal not only shows that Kenya is not interested in any long-term hand-tying commitment to end impunity, but it also shows that Kenya recognizes the costliness of committing to the ICC. Because Kenya is either unwilling or unable to comply with the terms of the Rome Statute, and because it is only too aware of the ICC's enforcement mechanism, its behavior is consistent with that predicted by the credible threat theory: Kenya is seeking to avoid its costly commitment to the court.

On the other hand, the evidence both before and after Kenya's ratification of the ICC treaty is inconsistent with the predictions of the credible commitment theory. According to that theory, autocratic leaders of countries with poor human rights practices and weak institutions of domestic accountability will commit to strong external enforcement mechanisms so as to tie their hands and credibly signal an intention to engage in better practices in the future. However, Kenya did not commit to the court when it was under Moi's autocratic leadership. Moreover, even if one characterizes Kenya as a non-democracy when Kibaki ratified the Rome Statute in 2005 (since Kibaki has been criticized for not fully delivering the promised democratic reforms), the evidence post-ratification overwhelmingly shows that the Kenyan government has not credibly commited to end a cycle of violence and impunity. Post-ratification, Kenya descended into ethnic violence, it did not punish those who instigated the violence, and the country has sought to shake off the yoke of the ICC. Other evidence, too, shows that it is not embracing the court's hand-tying mechanisms. For example, the government essentially promoted impunity by asking President Bashir to visit the celebration of its new constitution.

Along similar lines, it bears noting that Kenya's decision to ratify the ICC treaty is also not consistent with the hand-tying theory advanced by Andrew Moravcsik to explain the ratification behavior of states that are transitioning democracies. It is true that Kenya may have been a transitioning democracy during 2005, but the same evidence discussed above also shows that Kenya was not committed to locking in domestic democratic reforms.[59] Kenya ratified the Rome Statute, but did not at the same time commit to the normative changes that would have allowed it to comply with treaty terms. Instead of locking in democratic reforms post-commitment, Kibaki failed to limit his own presidential power as promised, allegedly partecipated in rigging his own election, and failed to prevent his security forces from committing criminal acts during the violence that followed his disputed presidential win.

Conclusion

Even though ICC commitment did not cause Kenya to improve its practices, there is still good news as it relates to the power of strong enforcement mechanisms to aid in realizing treaty goals. The ICC prosecutor gave Kenya an opportunity to investigate and prosecute perpetrators of the 2007 post-election violence domestically, but when it did not, the prosecutor acted. For the very first time, the prosecutor used his *proprio motu* powers to commence a case. Despite Kenya's noncompliance and its efforts to halt the ICC's processes, the ICC case is going forward against several of Kenya's leaders who are charged with inciting the violence in the aftermath of the 2007 elections.[60] The fact of the ICC's case against Kenya should also provide a warning to other states. Others that have joined the ICC knowing they may not be able or willing to comply with treaty terms will have to improve their domestic practices—or face a fate similar to Kenya's.

Notes

1 Kenya scored a 3 or 4 on the Political Terror Scale between 1996 and 2008. For an explanation of the scale, see Chapter 2, note 24.

2 Human Rights Watch, "Ballots to Bullets: Organized Political Violence and Kenya's Crisis of Governance," 17 March 2008, Vol. 20, No. 1 (A), www.unhcr.org/refworld/docid/47de7bd22.html.

3 Between 1996 and 2008, Kenya's World Bank Rule of Law Scale ratings averaged around -1.00. See Chapter 3, note 1 for an explanation of the scale. A Special Rapporteur for the United Nations has called the Kenyan criminal justice system "terrible," and has explained that the investigation, prosecution, and judicial processes in Kenya are slow and corrupt. See Philip Alston, "Human Rights Council, Report of the Special Rapporteur on Extrajudicial, Summary or Arbitrary Executions, Mission to Kenya, 26 May 2009," at para. 23, 16–17.

4 CICC, "ICC Opens Kenya Investigation," *CICC Update*, 31 March 2010; ICC Press Release, "ICC Judges Grant Prosecutor's Request to Launch Investigation in Kenya," 31 March 2010.

5 Tristan McConnel, "International Prosecutor in Kenya to Press Charges," *Globalpost*, 13 May 2010, ww.globalpost.com/dispatch/kenya/100512/international-criminal-court-nairobi.

6 Jeffrey Gettleman, "Kenya's Bill for Bloodshed Nears Payment," *The New York Times*, 16 July 2009.

7 Steve Inskeep, "ICC Case Accuses 6 Prominent Kenyans of Violence," *NPR*, 16 December 2010; Collins Mbalo, "Kenya: ICC Prosecutor Names 2008 Post Election Violence Suspects," *Global Voices Online*, 16 December 2010.

8 Michael Onyiego, "Kenya's Politicians Look to Withdraw from ICC as Suspects Named," *VOANews.com*, 16 December 2010.

9 Emeka-Mayaka Gekara, "Kenyan Security Chiefs' Bid to Suspend Ocampo Probe Fails," *Daily Nation*, 9 February 2011; Samuel Kumba, "Kenya's Bid to Defer ICC Cases Faces More Hurdles," *Daily Nation*, 9 February 2011; Oliver Mathenge, "Rough Road Ahead as Kenya Plans to Lobby UN's Big Five," *Daily Nation*, 9 February 2011; Michael Onyiego, "Kenya Seeks Another Way to Stall Hague Proceedings," *VOANews.com*, 21 March 2011.

10 In December 2001, Kibaki was elected president to replace President Moi who had ruled the country as an autocracy since 1978. Kibaki's campaign platform included promised reforms to the constitution to limit presidential power, judicial reforms, and an end to the pervasive corruption that had characterized Moi's government and which the populace blamed for Kenya's economic woes. See Andrew England, "New President of Kenya Vows to End 'Malaise': Kibaki Sworn in, Pledges to Undo Years of Corruption," *The Chicago Tribune*, 31 December 2002; "Democracy in Kenya," *The Register Guard*, 31 December 2002. Until President Kibaki's victory in 2002, Kenya typically scored a 0 on the democracy scale which ranges from 0 to 10. Although Kibaki has been roundly criticized for failing to deliver his promised reforms, or for failing to deliver some as promptly as he said he would, since Kibaki has been president, the country has scored a 7 or 8 on that scale.

11 UN High Commissioner for Human Rights, Report from OHCHR Fact-finding Mission to Kenya, 6–18 February 2008, 8–11; Amnesty International, "Kenya: Amnesty International Condemns Excessive Use of Force by Police," 18 January 2008.

12 Amnesty International, "Human Rights in Republic of Kenya 2009," www.amnesty.org/en/region/kenya/report-2009.

13 Human Rights Watch, "Kenya's Unfinished Democracy: A Human Rights Agenda for the New Government," 12 December 2002, 1–4, 7–8, www.hrw.org/legacy/reports/2002/kenya2/.

14 Human Rights Watch, "Ballots to Bullets," 18.

15 Human Rights Watch, "Ballots to Bullets," 6; Human Rights Watch, "Playing With Fire: Weapons Proliferation, Political Violence, and Human Rights in Kenya," 1–2, hrw.org/reports/2002/Kenya.

16 Kibaki actually served for many years under Moi's leadership as, among other things, vice-president and minister of finance. However, in 1991, when multi-party politics again became allowed, Kibaki resigned from government and the KANU party and founded the Democratic Party. Kibaki competed in the presidential elections of 1992 and 1997, losing both times to Moi. Kibaki, however, was the landslide winner of the 2002 elections, having been elected as the presidential candidate for the recently formed coalition party called the National Rainbow Coalition (NARC).

17 Human Rights Watch, "Ballots to Bullets," 12.

18 Ibid., 17–18.

19 Michela Wrong, *It's Our Turn to Eat: The Story of a Kenyan Whistleblower* (London: Fourth Estate, 2009), 241–45.

20 "United Nations Diplomatic Conference of Plenipotentiaries on the Establishment of an International Criminal Court: Summary Records of the Plenary Meetings and of the Meetings of the Committee of the Whole," 15 June–1 July 1998, A/Conf.183/13 (Vol. II), 16 June 1998, 77 at para. 63.
21 Ibid., 77, para. 64 (16 June 1998).
22 Ibid., 199, para. 92 (22 June 1998).
23 Ibid., 317, para. 33 (9 July 1998).
24 "Banned Kenya Official 'to Sue' US," *BBC News*, 4 November 2009, news.bbc.co.uk/2/hi/africa/8343088.htm.
25 See www.icc-cpi.int/Menus/ICC/Situations+and+Cases/Situations/.
26 CICC, "Global Coalition Calls on Kenya to Ratify International Criminal Court Treaty: As Conflicts Rage in Neighboring Countries, Kenya's Ratification Can Offer Beacon of Hope," 11 January 2005, www.iccnow.org.
27 CICC, "Kenya: Urge the Government to Ratify the Rome Statute of the International Criminal Court," 19 January 2005, www.iccnow.org.
28 Godfrey O. Ogongo, "ICC: Kenya Narrowly Avoids 'Criminal Haven' Image," *East African*, 18 April 2005, available at 2005 WLNR 6529753.
29 Kenya National Commission on Human Rights, "Ratification of International Criminal Court is an Essential Pillar for Securing the Rights of Kenya," www.knchr.org/index.php?option=com_content&task=view&id=23&Itemid=89.
30 Fred Oluoch, "Kenya: Will Kibaki Succumb to U.S. Pressure?" *New African*, August/September 2005, findarticles.com/p/articles/mi_qa5391/is_200508/ai_n21377670/.
31 Fred Oluoch, "Kenya on Collision Course with U.S. on ICC Treaty," *East African*, 25 April 2005, available at 2005 WLNR 6529705.
32 CICC Press Release, "Global Coalition Voices Support for Kenya's On-Going Resistance to U.S. ICC Immunity Agreement: Kenya's Firm Stand in Defending ICC Integrity is Welcomed by International NGOs," 20 July 2005.
33 Nor should one consider Kenya's passage of national legislation implementing the ICC treaty as evidence of its intent to comply with the Rome Statute. Although it began the process of adopting an International Crimes Act in 2005, the Act was only passed in January 2009. Therefore, it was not passed until after the 2007 post-election violence and Prosecutor Moreno-Ocampo's threats to launch an ICC investigation into that violence. Antonia Okuta, "National Legislation for Prosecution of International Crimes in Kenya," *Journal of International Criminal Justice* 7, no. 5 (2009): 1063. That timing, and Kenya's other conduct in relation to the post-election violence and the ICC investigation tend to discredit any claim that the Act was passed because Kenya is fully committed to complying with treaty terms. Kenya's International Crimes Act is available at www.kenyalaw.org/kenyalaw/klr_app?frames.php.
34 Memorandum for the Secretary of State, Presidential Determination No. 2009-14, 16 January 2009, www.whitehouse.gov/news/releases/2009/01/20090116-18.html.
35 Oluoch, "Kenya on Collision Course with U.S. on ICC Treaty."
36 Koert Lindijer, "Al-Bashir Rains on Kenya's Party," *Radio Netherlands Worldwide*, 6 September 2010, www.rnw.nl/international-justice/article/al-Bashir-rains-kenya's-party.

37 Human Rights Watch, "Ballots to Bullets," 21–23 (noting that international observer missions issued statements condemning the tallying results and casting doubt on the conclusion that Kibaki was the rightful winner of the election).

38 Ibid., 22.

39 The ICC's decision authorizing the ICC Prosecutor's Investigation into Kenya's post-election violence indicates that about 37 percent of the killings were caused by police forces. ICC Pre-Trial Chamber II, "Decision Pursuant to Article 15 of the Rome Statute on the Authorization of an Investigation into the Situation in the Republic of Kenya," 31 March 2010, para. 106 and n. 110, www.icc-cip.int/iccdocs/doc854287.pdf.

40 Okuta, "National Legislation for Prosecution of International Crimes in Kenya," 1063–65; Gettleman, "Kenya's Bill for Bloodshed Nears Payment."

41 David Mugonyi, "Secret List: Now Kibaki and Raila Sign Pact," *Daily Nation*, 17 December 2008, www.nation.co.ke/News/-/1056/503642/-/view/printVersion/-/14c3qeg/-/index.html.

42 One lawyer from the Kenyan National Commission on Human Rights offered his opinion that members of Parliament would only vote to establish a Special Tribunal if they could be sure that it would be totally ineffectual since many of the murderers responsible for the post-election violence are in government. Gettleman, "Kenya's Bill for Bloodshed Nears Payment."

43 Bernard Namunane and Macharia Gaitho, "Puzzling Alliances in Fight Against Tribunal Bill," *Daily Nation*, 12 February 2009, www.nation.co.ke/News/politics/-/1064/529716/-/view/printVersion/-/v2xbgg/-/index.html.

44 Sarah Wambui, "Anger Over MPs Vote Against ICC," *Capital News*, 25 December 2010, www.philsinfo.com/new/component/content/article/173-anger-over-mps-vote-against-icc.html.

45 ICC Pre-Trial Chamber II, "Decision Pursuant to Article 15 of the Rome Statute on the Authorization of an Investigation into the Situation in the Republic of Kenya" (31 March 2010), paras. 183–86, www.icc-cip.int/iccdocs/doc854287.pdf.

46 Michael Onyiego, "Legal Challenges Threaten to Undermine ICC Investigation in Kenya," *VOANews.com*, 4 October 2010, www.voanews.com/content/legal-challenges-threaten-to-undermine-icc-investigation-in-kenya-104287214/155957.html.

47 Wambui, "Anger Over MPs Vote Against ICC."

48 Gettleman,"Kenya's Bill for Bloodshed Nears Payment."

49 Even if Kenya did withdraw from the ICC, by treaty terms, its withdrawal would not have the effect of halting the present ICC investigation. Kevin Jon Heller, "Kenya Moves Closer to Withdrawing from the ICC," *Opinio Juris*, 12 December 2010, opiniojuris.org/2010/12/23/kenya-moves-closer-to-withdrawing-from-the-icc/ (referencing Article 127 of the Rome Statute).

50 Jijuze, "UNSC Declines Kenyan Bid on ICC Deferral," *Kenyan Daily News*, 19 March 2011, www.jijuze.com/2011/03/29/unsc-declines-kenya-deferral-bid/; Onyiego, "Kenya Seeks Another Way to Stall Hague Proceedings; Benjamin Muindi, "Minister Says Kenya a 'Laughing Stock' Over ICC Deferral," *All Africa & Daily Nation*, 25 March 2011, www.allafrica.com/stories/201103110913.html.

51 Wambui, "Anger Over MPs Vote Against ICC."

52 A copy of Kenya's 2010 constitution can be found at www.nation.co.ke/blob/view/-/913208/data/157983/-/l8do0kz/-/published+draft.pdf.
53 "Kenya, African Union Defend Bashir Visit," *CNN World*, 31 August 2010, articles.cnn.com/2010-08-31/world/kenya.bashir.visit_1_al-bashir-new-constitution-president-mwai-kibaki?_s = PM:WORLD.
54 Koert Lindijer, "Al-Bashir Rains on Kenya's Party," *Radio Netherlands Worldwide*, 6 September 2010, www.rnw.nl/international-justice/article/al-bashir-rains-kenya%E2%80%99s-party.
55 "Court Worry at Omar al-Bashir's Kenya Trip," *BBC News Africa*, 27 August 2010, www.bbc.co.uk/news/world-africa-11117662.
56 Lindijer, "Al-Bashir Rains on Kenya's Party."
57 Ibid.; Samantha Spooner and Charles Onyango-Obbo, "Kenya: Why Country Chose to Ignore Warrants by ICC and Sup With the Devil," *East African*, 6 September 2010, allafrica.com/stories/201009060847.html.
58 "Kenian PM says Bashir must stand before ICC, wants apology made to int'l community," *Sudan News*, 29 August 2010,
59 Andrew Moravcsik, "The Origins of Human Rights Regimes: Democratic Delegation in Postwar Europe," *International Organization* 54, no. 2 (2000): 225–30.
60 Nzau Musau, "Kenya: ICC Trials May Start May 2013," *AllAfrica*, 30 March 2012, allafrica.com/stories/201206130141.html.

9 Conclusion

Why did states decide to create the International Criminal Court (ICC) and design the institution with an enforcement mechanism that is so uniquely strong in the context of the international human rights regime? Will the ICC's enforcement mechanism be sufficient to hold states accountable to their commitment so that the ICC can realize its goal of ending impunity for genocide, crimes against humanity, and war crimes? What states comprise the court's membership? Are states with bad domestic human rights practices joining the court or do they view the ICC's enforcement mechanism as a credible threat and refuse to join because they do not want to be punished for bad and non-compliant behavior? If many of the states that most need to improve their domestic legal practices as relates to protecting against human rights abuses do not join the court, is there any hope that the threat of punishment by the ICC can play a role in bettering states' human rights practices and deterring individuals from committing mass atrocities?

These are the questions that were posed in the Introduction and to which this book has provided some answers. Both the statistical and case study analyses show that states tend to view the ICC's enforcement mechanism as a credible threat and are more likely to commit to the court when their calculations about their ability to comply with treaty terms show that commitment will pose little threat to their sovereignty. The results of the statistical analyses show that states with good human rights records are more likely to ratify the ICC treaty than are states with poor human rights records. This finding regarding ICC commitment is in stark contrast to other published findings for international human rights treaties with the weakest enforcement mechanisms.[1] Only very recently, Christine Wotipka and Kiyoteru Tsutsui found that states with poor human rights practices were actually more likely to ratify international human rights treaties; however, all of the treaties included in their study only require states to file reports regarding their compliance.[2]

The finding regarding state commitment to the ICC is also in stark contrast to the results of the statistical tests conducted of state commitment to other international human rights treaties. Those results show that states with poor human rights records regularly commit to international human rights treaties with the weakest enforcement mechanisms, but they are wary of committing to the treaty creating the ICC. Thus, it may be that states are committing to treaties with weak enforcement mechanisms in an effort to signal their legitimacy, without any real intention of bettering their human rights practices. At least some of those states may conclude that the costs of commitment are cheap and the consequences of noncompliance are meager or nonexistent.

On the whole, states may commit to the ICC for other reasons entirely: because they intend to comply with treaty terms and seek to realize the treaty's goals. After all, according to the terms of the Rome Statute, states can be punished for failing to comply by an independent prosecutor and court that can require the state's citizens to appear in The Hague to stand trial for any of the covered crimes. The implication is that where enforcement mechanisms are stronger, states take their commitment more seriously and consider the likely costs to their sovereignty by committing to a treaty that can actually punish bad and noncompliant behavior.

However, the results of the statistical analyses also show that states only view enforcement mechanisms as a credible threat where those mechanisms include a formal grant of power to engage in legally binding decision making accompanied by resources to coerce compliance. The results in Chapter 2 show that states did not view any of the enforcement mechanisms in Levels 1 through 4 as a credible threat. In none of those cases was a state's level of human rights practices a consistent significant and positive predictor of ratification, suggesting that states are not overly concerned with the costs of complying with treaty terms where enforcement mechanisms do not include a grant of power to engage in legally binding decision making. In the case of the ICC treaty, by contrast a state's level of human rights practices was a significant and positive predictor of ratification.

It is true that the ICC's powers may not be as great as those of domestic law enforcement institutions since it operates in the international arena and must rely on states for assistance to enforce its orders. However, its powers are as strong as those granted to the ad hoc international criminal tribunals. Indeed, the ICC has much greater powers in some ways since it is a permanent court—it does not have to wait for a vote of the United Nations (UN) Security Council to be created. The ICC's jurisdiction is also less circumscribed than the jurisdiction of the ad hoc tribunals. Each of those courts is limited to dealing with atrocities in a particular state during a particular time period. The ICC's powers are also uniquely strong when compared to the other international human rights treaties in this study. In no case do those treaties authorize an independent body the power to issue legally binding decisions or to arrest and punish those who fail to abide by treaty terms. Thus, while the ICC may have more difficulties enforcing its orders than would a domestic law enforcement institution, in the international realm the ICC's powers are on the enforceable end of the spectrum.

On the other hand, there is little evidence—either quantitative or qualitative—to support the power of the credible commitment theory or the external pressures theories to explain generally and overwhelmingly state decisions to join the ICC. For the most part, states are not committing to the Rome Statute despite their inability to comply with its terms so as to demonstrate any future promise to change their ways and commit to ending violence and impunity in the future. Nor are states as a rule committing to the ICC despite their ability to comply because of pressures and the associated extra-treaty benefits states may hope to obtain by appearing to be a legitimate state that embraces international human rights norms. The case study of Rwanda well illustrates the explanatory power of the credible threat theory as it relates to states with poor human rights practices, a recent history of domestic conflict, and weak domestic law enforcement institutions. The facts show that President Paul Kagame is aware of the ICC's strong enforcement mechanism and also that he is aware that Rwanda's government and its people may not be able to comply with treaty terms. Kagame has made clear that he believes the government may need to resort to force and violence in order to ensure that Rwanda does not experience another genocidal episode. Even though some in the international community have severely criticized Kagame for failing to hold his soldiers sufficiently accountable for acts of violence committed during the genocide and thereafter, he continues to maintain that he and Rwanda should be the judge of what justice is proper in Rwanda for acts involving its citizens. Given these facts, the country rationally engaged in cost of compliance calculations and refused to commit to the ICC.

Furthermore, although the Rwanda case study necessarily involves only one state, there is reason to believe that the credible threat theory can also help explain why other states with poor human rights records, a history of domestic violence, and poor domestic law enforcement institutions may refuse to ratify the Rome Statute. Like President Kagame, leaders of other states with similarly complicated and violent histories may be wary of committing to international institutions that can tie their hands and prevent them from responding with force or violence to domestic crises. States with a history of violence may have the kinds of social cleavages that can continue to make civil violence a possibility, and the state may feel justified in responding with force simply so as to quell that violence and establish some sense of peace and security for the population as a whole. Like Kagame, leaders of states with a history of domestic violence are likely to be concerned about the credible threat posed by committing to an institution like the ICC with which they may not be able to comply and which they cannot control. Because the costs of committing to such a treaty are high, states that cannot, or do not intend to, comply with treaty terms will more typically avoid commitment.

However, even if the evidence does suggest that states typically engage in cost of compliance calculations when determining whether or not to commit to the ICC, does this also mean that states that join the ICC on the whole also intend to comply with treaty terms? Is there evidence that those states embrace and intend to promote international human rights norms, including the Rome Statute's stated goal of ending impunity for those who commit mass atrocities? Although this study cannot provide unequivocal answers to these questions, there is some support for a conclusion that on the whole states are committing to the ICC treaty because they intend to abide by treaty terms and seek to end impunity for perpetrators of mass atrocities. First, the fact that states with better human rights practices ratify the Rome Statute more readily than do states with bad practices indicates that states are generally committing because their rational cost/benefit calculations show they can comply with treaty terms. The case study evidence shows that even states with good human rights practices make efforts to comply with ICC treaty terms after ratifying the statute. Each of Germany, Canada, France, the United Kingdom, and Trinidad and Tobago has enacted domestic legislation enabling them to prosecute mass atrocities domestically. Such legislation serves as a warning to the states' leaders and citizens that human rights abuses will not be tolerated in the future. In some cases, those laws also signal that the country will not permit impunity and will even prosecute non-citizens who commit any of the covered crimes. The enactment of the legislation alone serves to further the goal of deterring crime and ending impunity for mass atrocities. Ratification of the ICC treaty served as the impetus for enactment.

The evidence also suggests that the credible threat associated with the ICC treaty's relatively strong enforcement mechanism is generally deterring states with poor human rights practices and weak domestic law enforcement institutions from committing to the court. Does this fact mean that the ICC cannot then make a difference where it most needs to? Again, although no unequivocal answer to this question is possible, there is reason to believe the ICC can play a role in improving the behavior of these states. We know that some states with bad human rights practices and weak domestic law enforcement institutions have joined the court. For example, Kenya joined despite its poor practices, but at a moment in time when it could no longer ignore the calls of civil and international society arguing that it needed to provide some concrete evidence of its supposed intention to reform. However, the Kenya case now serves as a warning to other states that decide to join the court despite their poor practices that failing to comply with the terms of the ICC treaty can result in serious consequences for the state and its citizens. Several of Kenya's leaders are now the subject of an ICC investigation, and many in the Kenyan government do not seem happy about that fact: Kenya has tried various ways to escape from the yoke of the ICC treaty's strong enforcement mechanism so that those individuals may not be tried in The Hague. Other similarly situated states will have to improve their potential for compliance with ICC treaty terms if they want to avoid Kenya's fate.

In addition, the ICC has the potential to improve the behavior of states with poor domestic human rights practices because the court may investigate and prosecute in some circumstances even where atrocities are not committed by citizens of state parties to the court. First, the Security Council may refer some matters and it has done so—a fact that is an overall positive sign that the international community views the ICC as a legitimate institution with the powers and ability to render justice when mass atrocities are committed. Sudan is not a party to the court, but because the Security Council referred that matter to the ICC, President Omar Bashir is the subject of an ICC arrest warrant. Although he has not yet been arrested, the fact of the arrest warrant has most certainly curtailed his activities. In 2011, the Security Council also referred the Libya situation to the court. Even the United States voted for the Libya referral, which is another signal of the court's legitimacy given the strong stance the United States initially took against the ICC. While it is too early to predict the outcome of the Libya referral, it too is a positive sign in terms of the court's legitimacy and its ability to play a role in deterring mass atrocities and ending impunity for those who commit them. As one commentator noted, by virtue of the referral to the ICC, those who instruct or carry out instructions to bomb or otherwise use violence against the civilian population in Libya were warned that they could potentially be subject to international justice.[3]

Finally, the ICC also has jurisdiction in cases where the citizens of states not party to the ICC treaty commit atrocities in the territory of a state party.[4] It is this jurisdictional provision that caused the United States to seek bilateral immunity agreements from states parties refusing to transfer any US personnel to the custody of the ICC. This same jurisdictional provision is what caused the United States to insist on the provision in the Libya referral carving out from the ICC's jurisdiction any citizens of non-parties based on alleged actions stemming from actions in Libya authorized by the Security Council. Therefore, states with bad practices—and with leaders and citizens who commit mass atrocities—may have reason to fear the ICC even if those states do not become ICC parties.

It is true that the ICC is only as effective as the states parties, and some critics have noted that it has obtained custody over very few of its subjects since it began operating. Some also wonder about the eventual effectiveness of the court without the participation of the United States. While both are valid concerns, the evidence still shows that while not perfect, the court is functioning and that it is altering state behavior. It bears remembering that the court is a young institution. In its relatively short life, the court has commenced a number of cases, and issued arrest warrants for suspects—some of which, as discussed in earlier chapters, have been arrested or appeared before the court voluntarily. Although President Bashir is one notable suspect who as of 2012 had not been arrested, the evidence shows that countries that did welcome him have been criticized for doing so. As discussed in Chapter 1, President Joyce Banda of Malawi will not now allow Bashir to visit because doing so would strain ties with key donors in the international community. Indeed, the fact that the ICC has done as much as it has in the relatively short period in which it has been functioning tends to show that it can be effective—even if the United States is not a member. In any event, even though there is no indication that the United States will become a party to the court any time soon, as discussed in Chapter 3, the United States is actually helping to support the court. It abstained from the vote to refer the Darfur matter; it voted for the referral of the Libya matter; it refused to assist Kenya in its bid to defer its case before the ICC; and it has promised to assist in locating suspects.

In sum, the evidence does suggest that the ICC treaty's strong enforcement mechanism can make a difference not only in screening states at the ratification stage, but also in constraining state behavior—and thereby preventing mass atrocities and ending impunity for those who do commit mass atrocities. Of course, it is hard to measure the absence of an event, and one may never know for certain what mass atrocities have been deterred because of the creation of the ICC. In addition, from the Kenya case study, we do know that ratifying states may still commit crimes covered by the ICC treaty. Furthermore, the existence of the ICC apparently did not deter Libya from committing crimes against humanity. However, this does not mean that the ICC and its potential to actually punish bad and noncompliant behavior is not a catalyst for positive change. Again, it appears that one way or another, some of the instigators of the 2007 post-election violence in Kenya will be brought to justice. In addition, the very existence of the ICC has made it much easier than it would otherwise have been for the Security Council to send a strong message to Libya. Without the ICC, the Security Council would have had to threaten to create an ad hoc tribunal like the International Criminal Tribunal for Rwanda (ICTR) or the International Criminal Tribunal for the former Yugoslavia (ICTY). Threatening a court and actually having a court are two different things. In this case, Libya knew that the threat of investigation and prosecution was real since the ICC exists and is functioning.

The fact that states appear to be focused on compliance costs and the credible threat associated with the ICC's strong enforcement mechanism is a positive sign. After all, the point of having states commit to international human rights treaties is actually to encourage those states to promote better human rights practices. But the ICC treaty can only deal with a small portion of human rights abuses: those that amount to mass atrocities and that are committed by the highest-level offenders. If we hope to improve states' domestic human rights practices using international human rights treaties, we should structure those treaties with "hard law" enforcement provisions that are clear, precise, binding, and backed by resources to coerce compliance and punish noncompliance. Otherwise, without the threat of punishment via strong enforcement mechanisms, states may commit as window dressing only and without an actual intention to further the goals of the treaty or abide by its terms. Historically, some states have done just that according to the studies which have found that states frequently join international human rights treaties, but thereafter continue to abuse human rights.

Some may argue that ramping up the enforcement mechanisms could create a situation where only those states with good human rights practices will actually commit to human rights treaties. This potential issue is not a reason to proceed with a regime that is essentially toothless and which encourages states to commit to treaties with which they have no intention of complying. As noted above, some states with bad practices are joining the ICC. We should expect some states with bad practices may experience certain "windows of opportunity"—such as a change in leadership or a point where external or internal calls for commitment can no longer be ignored—where the benefits of joining may seem to outweigh the costs of joining a treaty with the potential to punish bad and noncompliant behavior. At least if treaties are designed with "hard law," legally binding enforcement mechanisms, states that do commit to the treaty will also be required to comply.

Second, designing international human rights treaties with strong enforcement mechanisms can still make sense even if the majority of states that will join such treaties are those with good practices. Strong enforcement mechanisms can incentivize states with good practices to make their practices even better. Because the ICC relies on a system of complementarity, even states with good practices will want to ensure that should they experience a mass atrocity, they have the domestic wherewithal to handle the matter. In the case of the ICC, states with generally good human rights practices may still have reason to fear the court because it covers war crimes. One main reason the United States refused to commit to the ICC is because it feared its citizens could be accused of committing war crimes during international conflicts. France voiced similar concerns during negotiations, and other states may also have similar fears. Those fears could prove beneficial if as a result, states change their military codes or military training practices so that their military personnel are forced to comply with the terms of the ICC treaty.

Naturally, even with the credible threat of a strong enforcement mechanism, states simply may not have the ability to improve their human rights practices and/or domestic law enforcement institutions without help. In some cases, nongovernmental organizations (NGOs) may be able to provide that support. The Coalition for the International Criminal Court (CICC) provides some resources and advice to states that need to implement the ICC treaty crimes into their domestic legislation (so that such crimes theoretically can be prosecuted domestically).[5] William Burke-White argues that the ICC should have the power and ability to engage in a policy of "proactive complementarity," whereby the court can help states with the training and resources actually to prosecute mass atrocities domestically.[6] States and other policy makers should consider assisting further in these and other ways so that states currently without the ability to comply with the

Rome Statute are able to take steps towards compliance. States may more readily commit to human rights treaties with strong enforcement mechanisms if they know they will receive assistance in their efforts to comply.

This study provides evidence that states do view strong enforcement mechanisms in international human rights treaties as a credible threat, causing them to care about their ability to comply with those treaties when making commitment decisions and thereafter. For all of the reasons discussed above, there is reason to believe that structuring international human rights treaties with stronger, "hard law" enforcement mechanisms will produce greater international cooperation precisely because states will be more likely to comply with, rather than ignore, the international agreements they make. This study has looked at the role treaty terms can play in states' *ex ante* beliefs about the institution and the role that the existence of apparently stronger enforcement mechanisms can play in screening states at the ratification stage and constraining their behavior both before and after ratification so that the state can comply with treaty terms. Among other reasons, it makes sense that at this early stage of the ICC's life, treaty terms will guide state behavior. Time and future research will provide more guidance as to whether the ICC's enforcement mechanism will be as strong in practice as it appears to be on paper.

Future research should look at whether and how the ICC's activities and behavior relative to carrying out its duties independently to prosecute mass atrocities influences state ratification, commitment, and/or compliance behavior. As information about the institution's actual activities and functioning accumulates, that actual functioning might alter states' posterior beliefs about whether ICC commitment is or is not costly. If the ICC proves over time to be ineffective at holding suspects accountable, then as in the case of other international human rights treaties, even states with bad practices may join because they will see that commitment is not costly to state sovereignty. On the other hand, if states see that the ICC is functioning and is able to obtain and prosecute suspects, states should have even more reason to view the ICC treaty's enforcement mechanism as a credible threat and behave accordingly. If future research shows that the ICC treaty's enforcement mechanism is as strong in practice as it appears to be on paper, there is even more hope that states will alter their behavior so as to comply. If states do alter their behavior accordingly, the ICC may actually realize its goal of ending impunity for those who commit the most heinous crimes of genocide, crimes against humanity, and war crimes.

Notes

1 For example, see Wade M. Cole, "Sovereignty Relinquished? Explaining Commitment to the International Human Rights Covenants, 1966–99," *American Sociological Review* 70, no. 3 (2005): 483–84 (noting the insignificance of the variable measuring the influence of human rights ratings on ratification of the International Covenant on Civil and Political Rights (ICCPR) and the International Covenant on Economic, Social and Cultural Rights (ICESCR)).
2 Christine M. Wotipka and Kiyoteru Tsutsui, "Global Human Rights and State Sovereignty: States Ratification of International Human Rights Treaties, 1965–2001," *Sociological Forum* 23, no. 4 (2008): 744–47.
3 Edith M. Lederer, "US Supports War Crimes Tribunal for First Time," *Associated Press*, 2 March 2011.
4 *Rome Statute*, art. 12 (2) (a).
5 See www.coalitionfortheicc.org/?mod=romeimplementation.
6 William W. Burke-White, "Proactive Complementarity: The International Criminal Court and National Courts in the Rome System of International Justice," *Harvard International Law Journal* 49 (2008).

Appendix A

States parties to the 14 different treaties, articles, and/or protocols (31 December 2008)

ICCPR (166 states parties)

Afghanistan, Albania, Algeria, Andorra, Angola, Argentina, Armenia, Australia, Austria, Azerbaijan, Bahamas, Bahrain, Bangladesh, Barbados, Belarus, Belgium, Belize, Benin, Bolivia, Bosnia and Herzegovina, Botswana, Brazil, Bulgaria, Burkina Faso, Burundi, Cambodia, Cameroon, Canada, Cape Verde, Central African Republic, Chad, Chile, Colombia, Congo, Costa Rica, Côte d'Ivoire, Croatia, Cyprus, Czech Republic, North Korea, Democratic Republic of Congo, Denmark, Djibouti, Dominica, Dominican Republic, Ecuador, Egypt, El Salvador, Equatorial Guinea, Eritrea, Estonia, Ethiopia, Finland, France, Gabon, Gambia, Georgia, Germany, Ghana, Greece, Grenada, Guatemala, Guinea, Guyana, Haiti, Honduras, Hungary, Iceland, India, Indonesia, Iran, Iraq, Ireland, Israel, Italy, Jamaica, Japan, Jordan, Kazakhstan, Kenya, Kuwait, Kyrgyzstan, Latvia, Lebanon, Lesotho, Liberia, Libya, Liechtenstein, Lithuania, Luxembourg, Madagascar, Malawi, Maldives, Mali, Malta, Mauritania, Mauritius, Mexico, Monaco, Mongolia, Montenegro, Morocco, Mozambique, Namibia, Nepal, Netherlands, New Zealand, Nicaragua, Niger, Nigeria, Norway, Panama, Papua New Guinea, Paraguay, Peru, Philippines, Poland, Portugal, South Korea, Moldova, Romania, Russia, Rwanda, Samoa, San Marino, Saudi Arabia, Senegal, Serbia, Seychelles, Sierra Leone, Singapore, Slovakia, Slovenia, Somalia, South Africa, Spain, Sri Lanka, St Vincent and the Grenadines, Sudan, Suriname, Swaziland, Sweden, Switzerland, Syria, Tajikistan, Thailand, Macedonia, Timor-Leste, Togo, Trinidad and Tobago, Tunisia, Turkey, Turkmenistan, Uganda, Ukraine, United Kingdom, Tanzania, United States, Uruguay, Uzbekistan, Vanuatu, Venezuela, Vietnam, Yemen, Zambia, Zimbabwe.

Article 41 (48 states parties)

Algeria, Argentina, Australia, Austria, Belarus, Belgium, Bosnia and Herzegovina, Bulgaria, Canada, Chile, Congo, Croatia, Czech Republic, Denmark, Ecuador, Finland, Gambia, Germany, Ghana, Guyana, Hungary, Iceland, Ireland, Italy, Liechtenstein, Luxembourg, Malta, Netherlands, New Zealand, Norway, Peru, Philippines, Poland, South Korea, Russia, Senegal, Slovakia, Slovenia, South Africa, Spain, Sri Lanka, Sweden, Switzerland, Tunisia, Ukraine, United Kingdom, United States, Zimbabwe.

Optional Protocol (115 states parties)

Albania, Algeria, Andorra, Angola, Argentina, Armenia, Australia, Austria, Azerbaijan, Barbados, Belarus, Belgium, Benin, Bolivia, Bosnia and Herzegovina, Bulgaria, Burkina Faso, Cameroon, Canada, Cape Verde, Central African Republic, Chad, Chile, Colombia, Congo, Costa Rica, Côte d'Ivoire, Croatia, Cyprus, Czech Republic, Democratic Republic of Congo, Denmark, Djibouti, Dominican Republic, Ecuador, El Salvador, Equatorial Guinea, Estonia, Finland, France, Gabon, Gambia, Georgia, Germany, Ghana, Greece, Guatemala, Guinea, Guyana, Honduras, Hungary, Iceland, Ireland, Italy, Jamaica, Kazakhstan, Kyrgyzstan, Latvia, Lesotho, Libya, Liechtenstein, Lithuania, Luxembourg, Macedonia, Madagascar, Malawi, Maldives, Mali, Malta, Mauritius, Mexico, Mongolia, Montenegro, Namibia, Nepal, Netherlands, New Zealand, Nicaragua, Niger, Norway, Panama, Paraguay, Peru, Philippines, Poland, Portugal, South Korea, Moldova, Romania, Russia, San Marino, Senegal, Serbia, Seychelles, Sierra Leone, Slovakia, Slovenia, Somalia, South Africa, Spain, Sri Lanka, St Vincent and the Grenadines, Suriname, Sweden, Tajikistan, Togo, Trinidad and Tobago (denounced 2000), Turkey, Turkmenistan, Uganda, Ukraine, Uruguay, Uzbekistan, Venezuela, Zambia.

ICESCR (161 states parties)

Afghanistan, Albania, Algeria, Angola, Argentina, Armenia, Australia, Austria, Azerbaijan, Bahamas, Bahrain, Bangladesh, Barbados, Belarus, Belgium, Benin, Bolivia, Bosnia, Brazil, Bulgaria, Burkina Faso, Burundi, Cambodia, Cameroon, Canada, Cape Verde, Central African Republic, Chad, Chile, China, Colombia, Costa Rica, Croatia, Cyprus, Czech Republic, Democratic Republic of Congo, Denmark, Djibouti, Dominica, Dominican Republic, Ecuador, Egypt, El

Salvador, Equatorial Guinea, Eritrea, Estonia, Ethiopia, Finland, France, Gabon, Gambia, Georgia, Germany, Ghana, Greece, Grenada, Guatemala, Guinea, Guinea-Bissau, Guyana, Honduras, Hungary, Iceland, India, Indonesia, Iran, Iraq, Ireland, Israel, Italy, Ivory Coast, Jamaica, Japan, Jordan, Kazakhstan, Kenya, Kuwait, Kyrgyzstan, Laos, Latvia, Lebanon, Lesotho, Liberia, Libya, Liechtenstein, Lithuania, Luxembourg, Macedonia, Madagascar, Malawi, Maldives, Mali, Malta, Mauritania, Mauritius, Mexico, Moldova, Monaco, Mongolia, Montenegro, Morocco, Namibia, Nepal, Netherlands, New Zealand, Nicaragua, Niger, Nigeria, North Korea, Norway, Pakistan, Panama, Papua New Guinea, Paraguay, Peru, Philippines, Poland, Portugal, Republic of Congo, Romania, Russia, Rwanda, San Marino, Senegal, Serbia, Seychelles, Sierra Leone, Slovak Republic, Slovenia, Solomon Islands, Somalia, South Korea, Spain, Sri Lanka, St Vincent and the Grenadines, Sudan, Suriname, Swaziland, Sweden, Switzerland, Syria, Tajikistan, Tanzania, Thailand, Timor-Leste, Togo, Trinidad and Tobago, Tunisia, Turkey, Turkmenistan, Uganda, Ukraine, United Kingdom, Uruguay, Uzbekistan, Venezuela, Vietnam, Yemen, Zambia, Zimbabwe.

CERD (172 states parties)

Afghanistan, Albania, Algeria, Andorra, Antigua, Argentina, Armenia, Australia, Austria, Azerbaijan, Bahamas, Bahrain, Bangladesh, Barbados, Belarus, Belgium, Belize, Benin, Bolivia, Bosnia, Botswana, Brazil, Bulgaria, Burkina Faso, Burundi, Cambodia, Cameroon, Canada, Cape Verde, Central African Republic, Chad, Chile, China, Colombia, Comoros, Costa Rica, Croatia, Cuba, Cyprus, Czech Republic, Democratic Republic of Congo, Denmark, Dominican Republic, Ecuador, Egypt, El Salvador, Equatorial Guinea, Eritrea, Estonia, Ethiopia, Fiji, Finland, France, Gabon, Gambia, Georgia, Germany, Ghana, Greece, Guatemala, Guinea, Guyana, Haiti, Honduras, Hungary, Iceland, India, Indonesia, Iran, Iraq, Ireland, Israel, Italy, Ivory Coast, Jamaica, Japan, Jordan, Kazakhstan, Kenya, Kuwait, Kyrgyzstan, Laos, Latvia, Lebanon, Lesotho, Liberia, Libya, Liechtenstein, Lithuania, Luxembourg, Macedonia, Madagascar, Malawi, Maldives, Mali, Malta, Mauritania, Mauritius, Mexico, Moldova, Monaco, Mongolia, Montenegro, Morocco, Mozambique, Namibia, Nepal, Netherlands, New Zealand, Nicaragua, Niger, Nigeria, Norway, Oman, Pakistan, Panama, Papua New Guinea, Paraguay, Peru, Philippines, Poland, Portugal, Qatar, Republic of Congo, Romania, Russia, Rwanda, San Marino, Saudi Arabia,

Senegal, Serbia, Seychelles, Sierra Leone, Slovak Republic, Slovenia, Solomon Islands, Somalia, South Africa, South Korea, Spain, Sri Lanka, St Kitts and Nevis, St Lucia, St Vincent and the Grenadines, Sudan, Suriname, Swaziland, Sweden, Switzerland, Syria, Tajikistan, Tanzania, Thailand, Timor-Leste, Togo, Tonga, Trinidad and Tobago, Tunisia, Turkey, Turkmenistan, Uganda, Ukraine, United Arab Emirates, United Kingdom, United States, Uruguay, Uzbekistan, Venezuela, Vietnam, Yemen, Zambia, Zimbabwe.

Article 14 (53 states parties)

Algeria, Andorra, Argentina, Australia, Austria, Azerbaijan, Belgium, Bolivia, Brazil, Bulgaria, Chile, Costa Rica, Cyprus, Czech Republic, Denmark, Ecuador, Finland, France, Georgia, Germany, Hungary, Iceland, Ireland, Italy, Kazakhstan, Liechtenstein, Luxembourg, Macedonia, Malta, Mexico, Monaco, Montenegro, Morocco, Netherlands, Norway, Peru, Poland, Portugal, Romania, Russia, San Marino, Senegal, Serbia, Slovak Republic, Slovenia, South Africa, South Korea, Spain, Sweden, Switzerland, Ukraine, Uruguay, Venezuela.

CEDAW (184 states parties)

Afghanistan, Albania, Algeria, Andorra, Angola, Antigua and Barbuda, Argentina, Armenia, Australia, Austria, Azerbaijan, Bahamas, Bahrain, Bangladesh, Barbados, Belarus, Belgium, Belize, Benin, Bhutan, Bolivia, Bosnia and Herzegovina, Botswana, Brazil, Brunei, Bulgaria, Burkina Faso, Burundi, Cambodia, Cameroon, Canada, Cape Verde, Central African Republic, Chad, Chile, China, Colombia, Comoros, Congo, Cook Islands, Costa Rica, Côte d'Ivoire, Croatia, Cuba, Cyprus, Czech Republic, Democratic Republic of Congo, Denmark, Djibouti, Dominica, Dominican Republic, Ecuador, Egypt, El Salvador, Equatorial Guinea, Eritrea, Estonia, Ethiopia, Fiji, Finland, France, Gabon, Gambia, Georgia, Germany, Ghana, Greece, Grenada, Guatemala, Guinea, Guinea-Bissau, Guyana, Haiti, Honduras, Hungary, Iceland, India, Indonesia, Iraq, Ireland, Israel, Italy, Jamaica, Japan, Jordan, Kazakhstan, Kenya, Kiribati, Kuwait, Kyrgyzstan, Laos, Latvia, Lebanon, Lesotho, Liberia, Libya, Liechtenstein, Lithuania, Luxembourg, Macedonia, Madagascar, Malawi, Malaysia, Maldives, Mali, Malta, Marshall Islands, Mauritania, Mauritius, Mexico, Micronesia, Moldova, Monaco, Mongolia, Montenegro, Morocco, Mozambique, Myanmar, Namibia, Nepal, Netherlands, New Zealand, Nicaragua, Niger, Nigeria, North Korea,

Norway, Oman, Pakistan, Panama, Papua New Guinea, Paraguay, Peru, Philippines, Poland, Portugal, Romania, Russia, Rwanda, Samoa, San Marino, Sao Tome and Principe, Saudi Arabia, Senegal, Serbia, Seychelles, Sierra Leone, Singapore, Slovakia, Slovenia, Solomon Islands, South Africa, Spain, Sri Lanka, St Kitts and Nevis, St Lucia, St Vincent and the Grenadines, South Korea, Suriname, Swaziland, Sweden, Switzerland, Syria, Tanzania, Tajikistan, Thailand, Timor-Leste, Togo, Trinidad and Tobago, Tunisia, Turkey, Tuvalu, Uganda, Ukraine, United Arab Emirates, United Kingdom, Uruguay, Uzbekistan, Vanuatu, Venezuela, Vietnam, Yemen, Zimbabwe.

Optional Protocol (98 states parties)

Albania, Andorra, Angola, Antigua and Barbuda, Argentina, Armenia, Australia, Austria, Azerbaijan, Bangladesh, Belarus, Belgium, Belize, Bolivia, Bosnia and Herzegovina, Botswana, Brazil, Bulgaria, Burkina Faso, Cameroon, Canada, Colombia, Cook Islands, Costa Rica, Croatia, Cyprus, Czech Republic, Denmark, Dominican Republic, Ecuador, Equatorial Guinea, Finland, France, Gabon, Georgia, Germany, Greece, Guatemala, Guinea-Bissau, Hungary, Iceland, Ireland, Kazakhstan, Kyrgyzstan, Lesotho, Libya, Liechtenstein, Lithuania, Luxembourg, Macedonia, Maldives, Mali, Mauritius, Mexico, Moldova, Mongolia, Montenegro, Mozambique, Namibia, Nepal, Netherlands, New Zealand, Niger, Nigeria, Norway, Panama, Paraguay, Peru, Philippines, Poland, Portugal, South Korea, Romania, Russia, Rwanda, San Marino, Senegal, Serbia, Slovakia, Slovenia, Solomon Islands, South Africa, Spain, Sri Lanka, St Kitts and Nevis, Sweden, Switzerland, Tanzania, Thailand, Timor-Leste, Tunisia, Turkey, Turkmenistan, Ukraine, United Kingdom, Uruguay, Vanuatu, Venezuela.

CAT (146 states parties)

Afghanistan, Albania, Algeria, Andorra, Antigua and Barbuda, Argentina, Armenia, Australia, Austria, Azerbaijan, Bahrain, Bangladesh, Belarus, Belgium, Belize, Benin, Bolivia, Bosnia and Herzegovina, Botswana, Brazil, Bulgaria, Burkina Faso, Burundi, Cambodia, Cameroon, Canada, Cape Verde, Chad, Chile, China, Colombia, Comoros, Congo, Costa Rica, Côte d'Ivoire, Croatia, Cuba, Cyprus, Czech Republic, Democratic Republic of the Congo, Denmark, Djibouti, Ecuador, Egypt, El Salvador, Equatorial Guinea, Estonia, Ethiopia, Finland, France, Gabon, Georgia, Germany, Ghana, Greece,

Guatemala, Guinea, Guyana, Honduras, Hungary, Iceland, Indonesia, Ireland, Israel, Italy, Japan, Jordan, Kazakhstan, Kenya, Kuwait, Kyrgyzstan, Latvia, Lebanon, Lesotho, Liberia, Libya, Liechtenstein, Lithuania, Luxembourg, Madagascar, Malawi, Maldives, Mali, Malta, Mauritania, Mauritius, Mexico, Monaco, Mongolia, Montenegro, Morocco, Mozambique, Namibia, Nepal, Netherlands, New Zealand, Nicaragua, Niger, Nigeria, Norway, Panama, Paraguay, Peru, Philippines, Poland, Portugal, Qatar, South Korea, Moldova, Romania, Russia, Rwanda, San Marino, Saudi Arabia, Senegal, Serbia, Seychelles, Sierra Leone, Slovakia, Slovenia, Somalia, South Africa, Spain, Sri Lanka, St Vincent and the Grenadines, Swaziland, Sweden, Switzerland, Syria, Tajikistan, Thailand, Macedonia, Timor-Leste, Togo, Tunisia, Turkey, Turkmenistan, Uganda, Ukraine, United Kingdom, United States, Uruguay, Uzbekistan, Venezuela, Yemen, Zambia.

Article 21 (60 states parties)

Algeria, Andorra, Argentina, Australia, Austria, Belgium, Bolivia, Bulgaria, Cameroon, Canada, Chile, Costa Rica, Croatia, Cyprus, Czech Republic, Denmark, Ecuador, Finland, France, Georgia, Germany, Ghana, Greece, Hungary, Iceland, Ireland, Italy, Japan, Kazakhstan, Liechtenstein, Luxembourg, Malta, Monaco, Montenegro, Netherlands, New Zealand, Norway, Paraguay, Peru, Poland, Portugal, South Korea, Russia, Senegal, Serbia, Slovakia, Slovenia, South Africa, Spain, Sweden, Switzerland, Togo, Tunisia, Turkey, Uganda, Ukraine, United Kingdom, United States, Uruguay, Venezuela.

Article 22 (64 states parties)

Algeria, Andorra, Argentina, Australia, Austria, Azerbaijan, Belgium, Bolivia, Bosnia and Herzegovina, Brazil, Bulgaria, Burundi, Cameroon, Canada, Chile, Costa Rica, Croatia, Cyprus, Czech Republic, Denmark, Ecuador, Finland, France, Georgia, Germany, Ghana, Greece, Guatemala, Hungary, Iceland, Ireland, Italy, Kazakhstan, Liechtenstein, Luxembourg, Malta, Mexico, Monaco, Montenegro, Morocco, Netherlands, New Zealand, Norway, Paraguay, Peru, Poland, Portugal, South Korea, Russia, Senegal, Serbia, Seychelles, Slovakia, Slovenia, South Africa, Spain, Sweden, Switzerland, Togo, Tunisia, Turkey, Ukraine, Uruguay, Venezuela.

Optional Protocol (41 states parties)

Albania, Argentina, Armenia, Benin, Bolivia, Bosnia and Herzegovina, Brazil, Cambodia, Chile, Costa Rica, Croatia, Czech Republic, Denmark, Estonia, France, Georgia, Germany, Guatemala, Honduras, Kazakhstan, Kyrgyzstan, Lebanon, Liberia, Maldives, Mali, Malta, Mauritius, Mexico, Moldova, New Zealand, Paraguay, Peru, Poland, Senegal, Serbia, Slovenia, Spain, Sweden, Ukraine, United Kingdom, Uruguay.

CRC (190 states parties)

Afghanistan, Albania, Algeria, Andorra, Angola, Antigua, Argentina, Armenia, Australia, Austria, Azerbaijan, Bahamas, Bahrain, Bangladesh, Barbados, Belarus, Belgium, Belize, Benin, Bhutan, Bolivia, Bosnia, Botswana, Brazil, Brunei, Bulgaria, Burkina Faso, Burundi, Cambodia, Cameroon, Canada, Cape Verde, Central African Republic, Chad, Chile, China, Colombia, Comoros, Cook Islands, Costa Rica, Croatia, Cuba, Cyprus, Czech Republic, Democratic Republic of Congo, Denmark, Djibouti, Dominica, Dominican Republic, Ecuador, Egypt, El Salvador, Equatorial Guinea, Eritrea, Estonia, Ethiopia, Fiji, Finland, France, Gabon, Gambia, Georgia, Germany, Ghana, Greece, Grenada, Guatemala, Guinea, Guinea-Bissau, Guyana, Haiti, Honduras, Hungary, Iceland, India, Indonesia, Iran, Iraq, Ireland, Israel, Italy, Ivory Coast, Jamaica, Japan, Jordan, Kazakhstan, Kenya, Kiribati, Kuwait, Kyrgyzstan, Laos, Latvia, Lebanon, Lesotho, Liberia, Libya, Liechtenstein, Lithuania, Luxembourg, Macedonia, Madagascar, Malawi, Maldives, Mali, Malta, Marshall Islands, Mauritania, Mauritius, Mexico, Micronesia, Moldova, Monaco, Mongolia, Montenegro, Morocco, Mozambique, Myanmar, Namibia, Nauru, Nepal, Netherlands, New Zealand, Nicaragua, Niger, Nigeria, North Korea, Norway, Oman, Pakistan, Palau, Panama, Papua New Guinea, Paraguay, Peru, Philippines, Poland, Portugal, Qatar, Republic of Congo, Romania, Russia, Rwanda, Samoa, San Marino, Sao Tome and Principe, Saudi Arabia, Senegal, Serbia, Seychelles, Sierra Leone, Singapore, Slovak Republic, Slovenia, Solomon Islands, South Africa, South Korea, Spain, Sri Lanka, St Kitts and Nevis, St Lucia, St Vincent and the Grenadines, Sudan, Suriname, Swaziland, Sweden, Switzerland, Syria, Tajikistan, Tanzania, Thailand, Timor-Leste, Togo, Tonga, Trinidad and Tobago, Tunisia, Turkey, Turkmenistan, Tuvalu, Uganda, Ukraine, United Arab Emirates, United Kingdom, Uruguay, Uzbekistan, Vanuatu, Venezuela, Vietnam, Yemen, Zambia, Zimbabwe.

ICC (108 states parties)

Afghanistan, Albania, Andorra, Antigua and Barbuda, Argentina, Australia, Austria, Barbados, Belgium, Belize, Benin, Bolivia, Bosnia and Herzegovina, Botswana, Brazil, Bulgaria, Burkina Faso, Burundi, Cambodia, Canada, Central African Republic, Chad, Colombia, Comoros, Congo, Cook Islands, Costa Rica, Croatia, Cyprus, Democratic Republic of Congo, Denmark, Djibouti, Dominica, Dominican Republic, Ecuador, Estonia, Fiji, Finland, France, Gabon, Gambia, Georgia, Germany, Ghana, Greece, Guinea, Guyana, Honduras, Hungary, Iceland, Ireland, Italy, Japan, Jordan, Kenya, Latvia, Lesotho, Liberia, Liechtenstein, Lithuania, Luxembourg, Macedonia, Madagascar, Malawi, Mali, Malta, Marshall Islands, Mauritius, Mexico, Mongolia, Montenegro, Namibia, Nauru, Netherlands, New Zealand, Niger, Nigeria, Norway, Panama, Paraguay, Peru, Poland, Portugal, South Korea, Romania, St Kitts and Nevis, St Vincent and the Grenadines, Samoa, San Marino, Senegal, Serbia, Sierra Leone, Slovakia, Slovenia, South Africa, Spain, Suriname, Sweden, Switzerland, Tajikistan, Tanzania, Timor-Leste, Trinidad and Tobago, Uganda, United Kingdom, Uruguay, Venezuela, Zambia.

Appendix B
Description of additional variables

- *Democracy*: The democracy indicator is a time-varying measure coded on a 0 to 10 scale, with scores based on several dimensions of democracy: 1 competitiveness of political participation; 2 openness and competitiveness of executive recruitment; and 3 constraints on the chief executive. Monty G. Marshall, Ted Robert Gurr, and Keith Jaggers, *Dataset Users' Manual, Policy IV Project: Political Regime Characteristics and Transitions, 1880–2009*, 30 April 2010, www.systemicpeace.org/inscr/p4manualv2009.pdf.
- *GDP per capita*: The GDP per capita "level of economic development" variable is from the World Bank *World Development Indicators* dataset. The measure is logged to reduce a skewed distribution. This measure indicates the level of a state's wealth and is correlated with its level of industrialization. This is a time-varying measure that is reported in constant US dollars. US Data, The World Bank, data.worldbank.org/country/united-states.
- *Difficulty of domestic treaty ratification process*: The Simmons data used to measure this concept codes state ratification processes using a four-category scale designed to capture the level of difficulty in the formal domestic ratification process. The categories are as follows: 1 treaties may be ratified by an individual chief executive or cabinet; 1.5 there is a rule or tradition of informing the legislature of signed treaties; 2 treaties may only be ratified upon consent of one legislative body; 3 treaties may only be ratified by a supermajority vote in one legislative body or by a majority vote in two separate legislative bodies. The source and detailed description of these data are available on Simmons's website. Beth A. Simmons, *Mobilizing for Human Rights: International Law in Domestic Politics* (Cambridge: Cambridge University Press, 2009), scholar.iq.harvard.edu/bsimmons/mobilizing-for-human-rights.

- *Common law state or not*: This is a dichotomous variable measuring whether or not a state follows a common law tradition. The data are from the Global Network Growth Database created by William Easterly. William Easterly, *Global Development Network Growth Database, World Bank*, 1 June 2001, econ.worldbank.org/WBSITE/EXTERNAL/EXTDEC/EXTRESEARCH/0,contentMDK:20701055~pagePK:64214825~piPK:64214943~theSitePK:469382,00.html#4.
- *Transitioning democracy or not*: This is also a dichotomous variable that measures whether or not a state is a newly transitioning democracy or based on the Polity IV democracy variable. I follow Simmons, who used 7 as the number above which she considered countries to have transitioned to "democracy" in her work testing state commitment to and compliance with various international human rights treaties. See Simmons, *Mobilizing for Human Rights*, 385. I code states as a 1 and as new democracies in a given year if they transitioned from anywhere below a 7 on the Polity IV scale to a 7 or above. If states were consistently above 7 for the post-World War II period, I consider them to be stable democracies and code them 0. If states were consistently below a 7, I consider them non-democracies and also code them 0.
- *Official development assistance*: The time-varying official development assistance (ODA) data measure the idea that states may be pressured to join international human rights treaties to obtain extra-treaty benefits like aid. The data are from the World Bank World Development Indicators dataset and are reported in constant 2007 US dollars as a share of GDP. See US Data, The World Bank, data.worldbank.org/country/united-states.

Select bibliography

Kenneth W. Abbott and Duncan Snidal, "Why States Act Through Formal International Organizations," *The Journal of Conflict Resolution* 42, no. 1 (1998): 3–32.

——"Hard and Soft Law in International Governance," *International Organization* 54, no. 3 (2000): 421–56.

Thomas Buergenthal, "The Normative and Institutional Evolution of International Human Rights," *Human Rights Quarterly* 19, no. 4 (1997): 703–23.

William W. Burke-White, "Proactive Complementarity: The International Criminal Court and National Courts in the Rome System of International Justice," *Harvard International Law Journal* 49, no. 1 (2008).

Wade M. Cole, "Sovereignty Relinquished? Explaining Commitment to the International Human Rights Covenants, 1966–99," *American Sociological Review* 70, no. 3 (2005): 472–95.

Jack Donnelly, "International Human Rights: A Regime Analysis," *International Organization* 40, no. 3 (1986): 599–642.

George W. Downs, David M. Rocke, and Peter N. Barsoom, "Is the Good News About Compliance Good News About Cooperation?" *International Organization* 50, no. 3 (1996): 379–406.

Mark S. Ellis and Richard J. Goldstone, eds., *The International Criminal Court: Challenges to Achieving Justice and Accountability in the 21st Century* (New York: International Debate Education Association, 2008).

Lee Feinstein and Tod Lindberg, *Means to an End: U.S. Interest in the International Criminal Court* (Washington, DC: Brookings Institution Press, 2009).

Jay Goodliffe and Darren G. Hawkins, "A Funny Thing Happened on the Way to Rome: Explaining International Criminal Court Negotiations," *Journal of Politics* 71, no. 3 (2009): 977–97.

Emilie M. Hafner-Burton, "Trading Human Rights: How Preferential Trade Agreements Influence Government Repression," *International Organization* 59, no. 3 (2005): 593–629.

Emilie M. Hafner-Burton and Kiyoteru Tsutsui, "Human Rights in a Globalizing World: The Paradox of Empty Promises," *American Journal of Sociology* 110, no. 5 (2005): 1373–411.

Oona A. Hathaway, "The Cost of Commitment," *Stanford Law Review* 55, no. 5 (2003): 1821–62.

Darren Hawkins, "Explaining Costly International Institutions: Persuasion and Enforceable Human Rights Norms," *International Studies Quarterly* 48, no. 4 (2004): 779–804.

Roy S. Lee, ed., *The International Criminal Court: The Making of the Rome Statute: Issues, Negotiations, Results* (The Hague, The Netherlands: Kluwer Law International, 1999).

Andrew Moravcsik, "The Origins of Human Rights Regimes: Democratic Delegation in Postwar Europe," *International Organization* 54, no. 2 (2000): 217–52.

William Schabas, *An Introduction to the International Criminal Court* (Cambridge: Cambridge University Press, 2001).

Beth A. Simmons, *Mobilizing for Human Rights: International Law in Domestic Politics* (New York: Cambridge University Press, 2009).

Beth A. Simmons and Allison Danner, "Credible Commitments and the International Criminal Court," *International Organization* 64, no. 2 (2010): 225–56.

Michael J. Struett, *The Politics of Constructing the International Criminal Court: NGOs, Discourse, and Agency* (New York: Palgrave Macmillan, 2008).

Christine Min Wotipka and Kiyoteru Tsutsui, "Global Human Rights and State Sovereignty: State Ratification of International Human Rights Treaties, 1965–2001," *Sociological Forum* 23, no. 4: 724–54.

Routledge Global Institutions Series

76 Rules, Politics, and the International Criminal Court (2013)
Committing to the court
by Yvonne M. Dutton (Indiana University)

75 Global Institutions of Religion (2013)
Ancient movers, modern shakers
by Katherine Marshall (Georgetown University)

74 Crisis of Global Sustainability (2013)
by Tapio Kanninen

73 The Group of Twenty (G20) (2013)
by Andrew F. Cooper (University of Waterloo) and Ramesh Thakur (Australian National University)

72 Peacebuilding (2013)
From concept to commission
by Rob Jenkins (Hunter College, CUNY)

71 Human Rights and Humanitarian Norms, Strategic Framing, and Intervention (2013)
Lessons for the Responsibility to Protect
by Melissa Labonte (Fordham University)

70 Feminist Strategies in International Governance (2013)
edited by Gülay Caglar (Humboldt University, Berlin), Elisabeth Prügl (the Graduate Institute of International and Development Studies, Geneva), and Susanne Zwingel (the State University of New York, Potsdam)

69 The Migration Industry and the Commercialization of International Migration (2013)
edited by Thomas Gammeltoft-Hansen (Danish Institute for International Studies) and Ninna Nyberg Sørensen (Danish Institute for International Studies)

68 Integrating Africa (2013)
Decolonization's legacies, sovereignty, and the African Union
by Martin Welz (University of Konstanz)

67 Trade, Poverty, Development (2013)
Getting beyond the WTO's Doha deadlock
edited by Rorden Wilkinson (University of Manchester) and James Scott (University of Manchester)

66 The United Nations Industrial Development Organization (UNIDO) (2012)
Industrial solutions for a sustainable future
by Stephen Browne (FUNDS Project)

65 The Millennium Development Goals and Beyond (2012)
Global development after 2015
edited by Rorden Wilkinson (University of Manchester) and David Hulme (University of Manchester)

64 International Organizations as Self-Directed Actors (2012)
A framework for analysis
edited by Joel E. Oestreich (Drexel University)

63 Maritime Piracy (2012)
by Robert Haywood (One Earth Future Foundation) and Roberta Spivak (One Earth Future Foundation)

62 United Nations High Commissioner for Refugees (UNHCR) (2nd edition, 2012)
by Gil Loescher (University of Oxford), Alexander Betts (University of Oxford), and James Milner (University of Toronto)

61 International Law, International Relations, and Global Governance (2012)
by Charlotte Ku (University of Illinois)

60 Global Health Governance (2012)
by Sophie Harman (City University, London)

59 The Council of Europe (2012)
by Martyn Bond (University of London)

58 The Security Governance of Regional Organizations (2011)
edited by Emil J. Kirchner (University of Essex) and
Roberto Domínguez (Suffolk University)

57 The United Nations Development Programme and System (2011)
by Stephen Browne (FUNDS Project)

56 The South Asian Association for Regional Cooperation (2011)
An emerging collaboration architecture
by Lawrence Sáez (University of London)

55 The UN Human Rights Council (2011)
by Bertrand G. Ramcharan (Geneva Graduate Institute of International and Development Studies)

54 Responsibility to Protect (2011)
Cultural perspectives in the Global South
edited by Rama Mani (University of Oxford) and
Thomas G. Weiss (The CUNY Graduate Center)

53 The International Trade Centre (2011)
Promoting exports for development
by Stephen Browne (FUNDS Project) and
Sam Laird (University of Nottingham)

52 The Idea of World Government (2011)
From ancient times to the twenty-first century
by James A. Yunker (Western Illinois University)

51 Humanitarianism Contested (2011)
Where angels fear to tread
by Michael Barnett (George Washington University) and
Thomas G. Weiss (The CUNY Graduate Center)

50 The Organization of American States (2011)
Global governance away from the media
by Monica Herz (Catholic University, Rio de Janeiro)

49 Non-Governmental Organizations in World Politics (2011)
The construction of global governance
by Peter Willetts (City University, London)

48 The Forum on China-Africa Cooperation (FOCAC) (2011)
by Ian Taylor (University of St. Andrews)

47 Global Think Tanks (2011)
Policy networks and governance
by James G. McGann (University of Pennsylvania)
with Richard Sabatini

46 United Nations Educational, Scientific and Cultural Organization (UNESCO) (2011)
Creating norms for a complex world
by J.P. Singh (Georgetown University)

45 The International Labour Organization (2011)
Coming in from the cold
by Steve Hughes (Newcastle University) and
Nigel Haworth (University of Auckland)

44 Global Poverty (2010)
How global governance is failing the poor
by David Hulme (University of Manchester)

43 Global Governance, Poverty, and Inequality (2010)
edited by Jennifer Clapp (University of Waterloo) and
Rorden Wilkinson (University of Manchester)

42 Multilateral Counter-Terrorism (2010)
The global politics of cooperation and contestation
by Peter Romaniuk (John Jay College of Criminal Justice, CUNY)

41 Governing Climate Change (2010)
by Peter Newell (University of East Anglia) and
Harriet A. Bulkeley (Durham University)

40 The UN Secretary-General and Secretariat (2nd edition, 2010)
by Leon Gordenker (Princeton University)

39 Preventive Human Rights Strategies (2010)
by Bertrand G. Ramcharan (Geneva Graduate Institute of International and Development Studies)

38 African Economic Institutions (2010)
by Kwame Akonor (Seton Hall University)

37 Global Institutions and the HIV/AIDS Epidemic (2010)
Responding to an international crisis
by Franklyn Lisk (University of Warwick)

36 Regional Security (2010)
The capacity of international organizations
by Rodrigo Tavares (United Nations University)

35 The Organisation for Economic Co-operation and Development (2009)
by Richard Woodward (University of Hull)

34 Transnational Organized Crime (2009)
by Frank Madsen (University of Cambridge)

33 The United Nations and Human Rights (2nd edition, 2009)
A guide for a new era
by Julie A. Mertus (American University)

32 The International Organization for Standardization (2009)
Global governance through voluntary consensus
by Craig N. Murphy (Wellesley College) and JoAnne Yates (Massachusetts Institute of Technology)

31 Shaping the Humanitarian World (2009)
by Peter Walker (Tufts University) and Daniel G. Maxwell (Tufts University)

30 Global Food and Agricultural Institutions (2009)
by John Shaw

29 Institutions of the Global South (2009)
by Jacqueline Anne Braveboy-Wagner (City College of New York, CUNY)

28 International Judicial Institutions (2009)
The architecture of international justice at home and abroad
by Richard J. Goldstone (Retired Justice of the Constitutional Court of South Africa) and Adam M. Smith (Harvard University)

27 The International Olympic Committee (2009)
The governance of the Olympic system
by Jean-Loup Chappelet (IDHEAP Swiss Graduate School of Public Administration) and Brenda Kübler-Mabbott

26 The World Health Organization (2009)
by Kelley Lee (London School of Hygiene and Tropical Medicine)

25 Internet Governance (2009)
The new frontier of global institutions
by John Mathiason (Syracuse University)

24 Institutions of the Asia-Pacific (2009)
ASEAN, APEC, and beyond
by Mark Beeson (University of Birmingham)

23 United Nations High Commissioner for Refugees (UNHCR) (2008)
The politics and practice of refugee protection into the twenty-first century
by Gil Loescher (University of Oxford), Alexander Betts (University of Oxford), and James Milner (University of Toronto)

22 Contemporary Human Rights Ideas (2008)
by Bertrand G. Ramcharan (Geneva Graduate Institute of International and Development Studies)

21 The World Bank (2008)
From reconstruction to development to equity
by Katherine Marshall (Georgetown University)

20 The European Union (2008)
by Clive Archer (Manchester Metropolitan University)

19 The African Union (2008)
Challenges of globalization, security, and governance
by Samuel M. Makinda (Murdoch University) and F. Wafula Okumu (McMaster University)

18 Commonwealth (2008)
Inter- and non-state contributions to global governance
by Timothy M. Shaw (Royal Roads University)

17 The World Trade Organization (2007)
Law, economics, and politics
by Bernard M. Hoekman (World Bank) and Petros C. Mavroidis (Columbia University)

16 A Crisis of Global Institutions? (2007)
Multilateralism and international security
by Edward Newman (University of Birmingham)

15 UN Conference on Trade and Development (2007)
by Ian Taylor (University of St. Andrews) and
Karen Smith (University of Stellenbosch)

14 The Organization for Security and Co-operation in Europe (2007)
by David J. Galbreath (University of Aberdeen)

13 The International Committee of the Red Cross (2007)
A neutral humanitarian actor
by David P. Forsythe (University of Nebraska) and
Barbara Ann Rieffer-Flanagan (Central Washington University)

12 The World Economic Forum (2007)
A multi-stakeholder approach to global governance
by Geoffrey Allen Pigman (Bennington College)

11 The Group of 7/8 (2007)
by Hugo Dobson (University of Sheffield)

10 The International Monetary Fund (2007)
Politics of conditional lending
by James Raymond Vreeland (Georgetown University)

9 The North Atlantic Treaty Organization (2007)
The enduring alliance
by Julian Lindley-French (Center for Applied Policy, University of Munich)

8 The World Intellectual Property Organization (2006)
Resurgence and the development agenda
by Chris May (University of the West of England)

7 The UN Security Council (2006)
Practice and promise
by Edward C. Luck (Columbia University)

6 Global Environmental Institutions (2006)
by Elizabeth R. DeSombre (Wellesley College)

5 **Internal Displacement (2006)**
Conceptualization and its consequences
by Thomas G. Weiss (The CUNY Graduate Center) and David A. Korn

4 **The UN General Assembly (2005)**
by M.J. Peterson (University of Massachusetts, Amherst)

3 **United Nations Global Conferences (2005)**
by Michael G. Schechter (Michigan State University)

2 **The UN Secretary-General and Secretariat (2005)**
by Leon Gordenker (Princeton University)

1 **The United Nations and Human Rights (2005)**
A guide for a new era
by Julie A. Mertus (American University)

Books currently under contract include:

The Regional Development Banks
Lending with a regional flavor
by Jonathan R. Strand (University of Nevada)

Millennium Development Goals (MDGs)
For a people-centered development agenda?
by Sakiko Fukada-Parr (The New School)

UNICEF
by Richard Jolly (University of Sussex)

The Bank for International Settlements
The politics of global financial supervision in the age of high finance
by Kevin Ozgercin (SUNY College at Old Westbury)

International Migration
by Khalid Koser (Geneva Centre for Security Policy)

Human Development
by Richard Ponzio

The International Monetary Fund (2nd edition)
Politics of conditional lending
by James Raymond Vreeland (Georgetown University)

The UN Global Compact
by Catia Gregoratti (Lund University)

Institutions for Women's Rights
by Charlotte Patton (York College, CUNY) and Carolyn Stephenson (University of Hawaii)

International Aid
by Paul Mosley (University of Sheffield)

Global Consumer Policy
by Karsten Ronit (University of Copenhagen)

The Changing Political Map of Global Governance
by Anthony Payne (University of Sheffield) and Stephen Robert Buzdugan (Manchester Metropolitan University)

Coping with Nuclear Weapons
by W. Pal Sidhu

Private Foundations and Development Partnerships
by Michael Moran (Swinburne University of Technology)

The International Politics of Human Rights
edited by Monica Serrano (Colegio de Mexico) and Thomas G. Weiss (The CUNY Graduate Center)

Twenty-First-Century Democracy Promotion in the Americas
by Jorge Heine (The Centre for International Governance Innovation) and Brigitte Weiffen (University of Konstanz)

EU Environmental Policy and Climate Change
by Henrik Selin (Boston University) and Stacy VanDeveer (University of New Hampshire)

Making Global Institutions Work
Power, accountability and change
edited by Kate Brennan

The Society for Worldwide Interbank Financial Telecommunication (SWIFT)
by Susan Scott (London School of Economics and Political Science) and Markos Zachariadis (University of Cambridge)

Global Governance and China
The dragon's learning curve
edited by Scott Kennedy (Indiana University)

The Politics of Global Economic Surveillance
by Martin S. Edwards (Seton Hall University)

Mercy and Mercenaries
Humanitarian agencies and private security companies
by Peter Hoffman

Regional Organizations in the Middle East
James Worrall (University of Leeds)

Reforming the UN Development System
The politics of incrementalism
by Silke Weinlich (Duisburg-Essen University)

Corporate Social Responsibility
by Oliver Williams (University of Notre Dame)

Post-2015 UN Development
Making change happen
Stephen Browne (FUNDS Project) and Thomas G. Weiss (The CUNY Graduate Center)

For further information regarding the series, please contact:

Craig Fowlie, Publisher, Politics & International Studies
Taylor & Francis
2 Park Square, Milton Park, Abingdon
Oxford OX14 4RN, UK
+44 (0)207 842 2057 Tel
+44 (0)207 842 2302 Fax
Craig.Fowlie@tandf.co.uk
www.routledge.com

Index

For Product Safety Concerns and Information please contact our EU representative GPSR@taylorandfrancis.com Taylor & Francis Verlag GmbH, Kaufingerstraße 24, 80331 München, Germany

Batch number: 08153772

Printed by Printforce, the Netherlands